THE SCORPION AND THE FROG: A NATURAL CONSPIRACY

THE SCORPION AND THE FROG: A NATURAL CONSPIRACY

William A. Borst Ph.D.

To order additional copies of this book, contact:
Xlibris Corporation
1-888-795-4274
www.Xlibris.com
Orders@Xlibris.com
25019

CONTENTS

This book is dedicated to all those members of the "grassy knoll club," or the "black helicopter brigade," whose relentless search for the truth has led to their public mockery, ridicule and vilification.

Acknowledgment

In all honesty, I am directly responsible for everything in this book. Since I have been reading, writing, and debating these ideas on my weekly radio show on WGNU for eighteen years, I guess I owe some consideration to my many "devil's advocates," who have ably represented the other side of the issues in the book. Indirectly, Rush Limbaugh was responsible for my relentless search in seeking the truth about conspiracies that has been hidden from the public view for centuries. His own lack of curiosity in this matter, just urged me to push the envelope even further.

On a personal note, Joanne Riassetto, whom I met at the Mindszenty Foundation in 2003, was superb in editing and proofreading the manuscript. I have admired and relished the work of syndicated columnist, Joseph Sobran for years. I have tried to fashion my own thinking and consequently my writing, after his direct and penetrating style. Any failure to approximate his articulate understanding of human events is due solely to my own inadequacies. I would also like to thank the people at Xlibris for their assistance and direction, especially Tracy Festinger and Molly Helgesen in the Art Studio

It also has been my position as primary contributing editor at the Mindszenty Foundation that has inspired me to a deeper understanding of many of the complex ideas in this book. Eleanor Schlafly velvet touch as editor and publisher helped me hone my craft to a sharp edge.

An old fable relates the tale of the scorpion and the frog, who meet on the banks of a stream. The scorpion asks the frog to carry him on his back across the stream. The frog asks: "How do I know you won't sting me?" The scorpion replies: "Because if I do, we will both die." Satisfied, the frog agrees and they enter the stream. In midstream, the frog feels a sharp, stinging sensation in his neck. As his paralysis starts to set in, he looks at the scorpion and asks: "Why?" Replies the scorpion: "it's in my nature."

PART I
The Root of Evil

1

Killer Bees

When you have excluded the impossible, whatever
remains, no matter how improbable, must be the truth.
Arthur Conan Doyle

By definition a conspiracy is a secret meeting of two or more
individuals to plan an illegal or immoral activity. In cosmological
terms, it is good versus evil. There is no question that their goal is
satanic. They want to erase all religions, all culture, and all good
from society. Part of the plan is to denounce Christianity in all its
forms because it stands alone as an obstacle to its growth and goals.
If they are successful in this goal, they win. It is not evil to them,
but just a part of their hedonistic life styles. It is the ultimate
result of moral relativism. The American people have been
brainwashed for a 100 years that there is no right and wrong.
People determine for themselves what is right and wrong. Americans
would be making a mistake if they did not view their blatant attacks
on Christianity as part of this conspiracy.

Conspiracy is not automatic. The Insiders do not control
everything to the degree that all their goals are automatically
achieved. There is great opposition to the way and the means to
affect the goal of one world, even within their ranks. This is true
because, given everything they have, the one thing they can not
get away from, is the fact that there is human nature at work.
Their fellow men have their own way of doing things and it is
against their inner drive to acquiesce in all of the proposals and

rules effected. The same aspect that led them to try for world domination is the same attribute that will prevent them from achieving the unachievable. There is also the ego of other men. Columnist Clarence Page has called the idea of a conspiracy, "the watery plaster that seals over the gaping cracks in unsound reasoning."

The idea of a conspiracy represents a consistent cord that binds all historical progression together. It is the elementary struggle between the principles elicited in the Garden of Eden and the Luciferian plot to attack, undo, and obliterate those principles. It is part of the classic struggle of good versus evil. When the Creator made man in His own image and likeness, He established the gift of free will. This led to a choice between good and evil with evil being the negation of the good. God did not cause evil but it was inherent in the idea of free choice. Earthly life than became a battle ground between good choices and bad choices. It is part and parcel of man's human nature. Each human participates in this struggle in his or her own individual way. Conspiracy is about a collective will in the pursuit of evil, that is the attempt to negate the good.

The paradox of life is the nature of evil. Evil is an elusive idea that has filtered and slithered it sway through the pages of world history, leaving death, devastation and misery in its wake. This book is about the nature of evil and the evil that hides behind the conspiracy that is the main focus of this book. The conspiracy is real. Its origins are in the darkest and deepest circle of Dante's Inferno. Conspiracy is the physical manifestation of the devil's handiwork.

Most Americans can not conceive of anyone they know as really "evil." Evil is what is in the movies or TV or books about Adolph Hitler. Our minds have become so removed from evil that it has become a thoughtless abstraction. In our own era, when we speak of "evil" we personify it with terms like Auschwitz, the gulags, 9/ 11 and Oklahoma City. Hannah Arendt, in covering the Adolph Eichmann trial in 1961, saw a deeper quality. The Nazi's cool detachment from the six million who were murdered in the "final solution" exposed the horror of what she called "the banality of evil." Eichmann and his fellow henchmen appeared quite normal on the surface. Many were good and loving fathers and believed in specific family values. It means that evil can reside in the hearts and minds of men who can lead otherwise normal lives. This is as if their sense of conscience had been suspended or compartmentalized deep within their hearts. In the Seventh Chapter of his Gospel, Saint Mark lists the evils that often lurk in the human heart. He wrote nothing about outside forces corrupting the heart, only evils such as greed, lust, anger, impurity, and the like.

The problem of evil is, even for the Christian, insoluble. As Professor James Hitchcock has written in his article, "Confronting Evil," we do not "know why God permits evil." But we do know that God does not and can not create evil. It militates against his very nature. Since God cannot create evil, Christianity has defined evil as "the absence of being," in the words of St. Thomas Aquinas. The essence of evil is to make something into nothing that is to destroy that which is good. Death is evil because it is the loss of life. Adultery is evil because it is the loss of trust and love. Illness is evil because it is the negation of health and so on.

St. Augustine wrestled with the problem of evil for many years, until he finally decided in his "Confessions" that evil did not have an existence of itself but was the negation or the absence of good. Poverty was the negation of self-sufficiency, murder was the negation of life, and impurity was the defilement of chastity and so forth. Our metaphysical understanding of the word "good" would be impossible without an opposite concept of "evil."

Evil often attempts this with the intention of remaking human nature. The French Revolution and all subsequent attempts to repeal man's human nature or what Frederic Bastiat called in his pamphlet, "The Law," that fatal "tendency of mankind have failed and failed dismally." Over 170 million have already died in the twentieth century proving the failure of reinventing human nature.

In exploring the idea more fully, there can be a strong relativistic strain. One man's evil is another man's virtue. The terrorists who destroyed the World Trade Center did not think America was good. In their frame of reference Americans were the "evildoers." To the Nazi, the Jews were defilers of their racial and ethnic purity. Their annihilation was viewed as a national good that would improve the race and return Germany to the mythological days of Nordic superiority.

Alan Dershowitz has denigrated opponents of a woman's right to unlimited access to abortion as evil and deserving of contempt. To him, people who are concerned about the destruction of the unborn in utero are an obstacle to the establishment and maintenance of the enlightened view of secular humanism, which to him is an absolute good. To Dershowitz and people like him, the absolute good revolves around the autocratic ability to choose whatever one wants to do as opposed to the traditionalists who still recognize an external moral force such as the 10 Commandments. This exposes a national, if not global dichotomy of semantics that makes it difficult to understand the realities of events. This clearly demonstrates that the two sides contradict one another, each with their own interpretation of the good. It has an Orwellian nation that George Orwell so deftly outlined in his classic novel "1984," Good is evil! Peace is War! His fears and warnings have come to fruition as we engage the 21st century on its own terms.

The movie, "The Devil's Advocate," based on the book by Andy Neiderman, made this point vividly. Starring Al Pacino and Keanu Reeves, this movie explored the darkest realms of evil and man's susceptibility to the lures of power, money, and the flesh. In what has to rank with any of the great Shakespearean soliloquies on the screen, Al Pacino, the veteran of the "Godfather Trilogy," gave the performance of his life. His deep, dark, penetrating eyes personified the devil as he criticized his divine adversary as the greatest sadist of all time. He gave us all these great instincts and then said we could not use them.

As John Milton, the devil had his law firm. I thought this was fitting since it seems that too many lawyers have conspired with the devil to undercut the traditional social norms of American society. Milton mocks the legal profession and lawyers in general when he says:

> "It (the law) puts us into everything. It is the ultimate backstage pass. It is the new priesthood! There are now more students in law school than there are lawyers walking the earth. We're coming out. Guns a blazing! Acquittal, after acquittal, until the stench of it reaches so far into the heavens. It chokes the whole lot of them. This is revolution, baby!"

Milton called himself the "last humanist." He cared about mankind. The 20th century? "That was mine." Given his boast, it is not surprising over 170 million civilians were killed by their governments. Of God Pacino, Milton has nothing but a Luciferian disgust because He

> "Wants you to be yourself. Guilt is like a sack of $%#@ bag of bricks. All you have to do is set it down . . . Who are you carrying all those bricks for? God? Is that it? Well I tell you a little inside information about God. God likes to watch! He's a prankster. He gives man instinct. He gives you these extraordinary gifts and then what does He do? For his own amusement, his own cosmic gag relief, He sets the rules in opposition. Look but don't touch! Touch but don't taste! Taste but don't swallow! And when you are jumping from one foot to the next, what does He do? He is laughing his sick . . . He's a sadist . . . . An absentee landlord! Worship that!"

Evil has been transmitted throughout history as in a cosmic relay race with each abstraction handing off to the abstraction of the next generation. Ideas, such as Evil, have a nuclear life. They may change their superficial appearance. Their rhetoric may travel down different avenues. Essentially the underlying principles are the same. This idea has been transferred under the new clothing dress of the early Gnostics, the Knights Templar, the Rosicrucians, the Illuminati, back to the Masons, the Communists, the Socialists, Fascists, liberals, progressives, modernists, and secular humanists. Whatever name it has chosen to hide its nature, it has remained essentially the same way of thinking.

Conspiracy theories are rarely accepted in sophisticated circles. To believe one of the myriads of conspiracy theories proposed today is to be swiftly relegated to the section reserved for the lunatic fringe. Our educated class, perhaps having fallen victim to two hundred years of enlightened and evolutionary ideas, are dangerously prone to believe that events happened by accident more than by the grand design of a hidden power or group. To combat such theories they have created an anti-intellectual milieu, which quickly demonizes any view that presupposes the existence of sinister human forces. It is difficult for them to believe that an individual or an oligarchy of individuals actually have and exert power over their fellow Americans, their fellow human beings. Most people, especially liberals, want to think the best of others, even those with money and power. Life is too accidental—nobody has exact and complete control over events. We are all "Children of the Enlightenment" to employ Connor Cruise O'Brien's idea. We like to think what evil there is just is, does not reside in the human heart, that is, anybody's heart. To admit such would imply that there might be some evil lurking in our own hearts. But evil does exist and sometimes it exists in our hearts because there really is such a thing as Original Sin.

People with life and death power over the masses can and do commit evil. It is not irrational to believe that there can be conspiracies since the world has been filled with groups intent on controlling and maintaining a predominant influence in a given community, state, nation, and even region. When a world leader is implicated in the conspiracy, it is difficult, if not even impossible for the average person to fathom that someone like a Roosevelt or a Churchill would deliberately permit or encourage the destruction of his own people.

The will to power existed centuries before Friedrich Nietzsche. Alexander the Great was a good man, yet he wanted to rule the known world. The Caesars, the Czars, kings, Kaisers, queens, the crusaders and even presidents have attempted to unite and control the world under one roof—whether it be in the name of the Lord, the Holy Cross, the emperor, the nation, the flag, or the United Nations. The Roman legions, through Hitler's vision of a New World Order, based on "Blut und Land," the Japanese call for a "Sphere of Co-Prosperity," the Mafia, the Yukiza, the Black Hand and other groups who wanted to subvert the freedom and intent of peoples throughout world history. History shows that it is a human impulse to want to control things and events and at the root of this is the need to have the individual's will effected whether the benighted like it or not.

The late writer Gary Allen made the point in his best selling book, "None Dare call it A Conspiracy," that if we were dealing with incompetents in government, "one would think that they would sometimes blunder in favor of the government." It is nearly a truism that virtually all of the mistakes made since the Roosevelt Administration have negatively impacted the nation's foreign policy situation. Allen called the idea of a conspiracy, "the great whodunit!"

Surely no one but the really hardcore leftists can deny that Communism was an overt and also a clandestine conspiracy. To do so would be to deny years of historical record and tons of printed and recorded evidence. Communism was at its very soul, a conspiracy to overthrow the West in one of the most epic of conflicts in world history. Ironically, the idea of a conspiracy was present after World War II. Chief prosecutor, Justice of the Supreme Court Robert Jackson developed four charges against the Nazi leadership that rested on the idea of a conspiracy to wage aggressive war. Ten members of this Nazi elite died on the gallows at Nuremberg in 1947.

How does this relate to a conspiracy? At its very core, the conspiracy has been the attempt to subvert and eventually overthrow the reigning cultural philosophy. For just under two thousand years, the religious philosophy of the Judeo-Christian

God with its attendant moral strictures, and limitations has shaped much of history. It has only been in the last two hundred plus years that the enlightened philosophy of the French Revolution has achieved a moral and religious parity with traditional behaviors. This is the war; this is the conspiracy, which is about ideas, powers, goals, money, and even sex.

The great conspiracy is not at all a secret but has been promulgated and predicted and promoted in the major media, books, TV and radio shows and the public statements of many of its proponents. The term also implies a ruling authority or control. This sounds like something out of a sci-fi film. Admittedly there are recognizable groups in this struggle, such as the Council of Foreign Relations, the Bilderbergers and the Club of Rome, millions of others flock to the acceptance of the basic liberal ideology out of conviction, attraction, seduction and just our fallen nature. Vice and evil often disguises itself so those things appear very attractive to the victim. It is the same with the intellectual and moral attraction of the conspiracy. "Be like gods!" "I did it my way!" "Do your own thing!" All these statements represent the same liberal impulse to be like God, to attain an immortal stance while still living on this earth. It is in our nature to fall for such vein and empty promises of earthly immortality. English writer and Fabian Socialist H. G. Wells wrote a rather boring novel that refers in true oxymoronic terms to an "Open Conspiracy."

Conspiracy theories are a direct response to the evil fostered by the liberal philosophy. People couched in the traditional thinking of this country know that people lie, steal, connive, and even kill. When something serious happens to the culture, their first instinct is to attribute it to a thoughtful, deliberate process, not some accident beyond the scope of human endeavor. Too often people looking for conspiracy think or expect to see a secret organization, along the lines of the Mafia or maybe Communist cells of the fifties. What has happened is more along the lines, as Dr. Dennis Cuddy suggests in his booklet, "The Road to Socialism," more of an "Open Conspiracy," like Fabian Socialist H. G. Wells wrote in

1928. It involves a type of international networking among likeminded business, political and social leaders.

Historian David Davis says Americans are "curiously obsessed" with conspiracies. Conspiracies are indelibly intertwined with the study of History. Intellectual Bernard Bailyn says that the fear of conspiracy against constitutional authority was built into the very structure of politics." While originally this obsession mirrored Europe's, as the United States withdrew from Europe's influence, its idea of a conspiracy changed to such notions as Slave Power, Black Power and the Federal Reserve. The notorious Stamp Act of 1765 was viewed as a British conspiracy to take direct control of the colonial government. History proved they were right.

Conspiracies have dominated the course of human events since we have recorded them. Dark, vile plots have surfaced to undermine crown, papacy and throne throughout the known world. It would be ignorant to hold that men have not plotted for political power, financial gain, or even personal edification. Intellectuals can not accept any of these because they are unsophisticated, might make them change their notion of man's basically good human nature.

The truth recognizes a dialectic that goes back to the beginning of time. In strict Hegelian fashion, every idea has with it opposing ideas that will often, just by its very nature do battle with the original idea. The pendulum theory of history is akin to this dialectic in that it stresses the opposing forces often evidenced in historic events. History's constant pull and tug never stops forming a perpetual motion of conflicting ideas that rises and falls with each new generation. The same is true with the idea of a conspiracy.

The late Jesuit scholar Malachi Martin, in writing about the New World Order, said that "world government was impractical and that it was impossible to micromanage the world from one spot." To him the New World Order that has been enacted since the end of World War II has been "the globalization of cash." It is one of cash and power, an outgrowth of the Imperialism of the 19th and twentieth century. These leaders, nameless powers that be realized that it is much easier to control the world through its cash. This is the New Imperialism.

James Billington, the current librarian of Congress and a member of the Council on Foreign Relations, wrote a seminal work, entitled "The Fire in the Minds of Men: The Origins of the Revolutionary Faith." Billington documents the impact of occult secret societies, that is, the Bavarian Illuminati in particular on the French Revolution and subsequent revolutionary upheaval around the world. His book implies that this revolutionary fire is still alive and may be responsible for some of the upheavals and turmoil befalling today's society. This fire could be the inherent weakness in our own social institutions, abetted by groups that would relish seeing the country is destroyed from within. Bishop Fulton J. Sheen used to argue that of all the major civilizations in recorded history, all but a few collapsed due to internal causes.

In his book, "America's 30 Years War," Balint Vazsonyi wrote that it was not "a conspiracy in the sense of a small band of people meeting in a dark cell, writing out a blueprint. It was not a process of subversion, although the Soviet Union expanded vast sums on subversion. It was not even international communism acting in concert. It was all of these—and much more." He firmly believed, "it was the first opportunity to strike at the heart of the English-speaking world. Everyone with an ax to grind got into the act and America's youth was whipped into a near-continuous state of hysteria by a judicious blend of drugs, sex, and propaganda."

Vazsonyi believes that a conspiracy is that very notion that this evil spirit of opposition to the decent and true things of life has had many different names during its historical life. "It has been Bolshevism in Russia, Fascism in Italy, National Socialism in Germany, Democratic Socialism in Sweden and the Long March in China. As this Idea kept circling the globe," since the 19th century, it has always found the United States, standing in its way. He defines the idea as "a compendium of Continental European, really Franco-Germanic theories . . ." Under a variety of labels, this Idea is "unconcerned with human nature and empirical evidence . . . ." This idea has been successfully installed in America's schools, as well as in most of the information and entertainment media. Academia, Hollywood, the news media, the NEA, and the environmentalist movement are far more effective than any political party. And as high school textbooks, college courses, TV newscasts, or national newspapers attest, their purpose is in transforming each and every American. This search of "social justice," is the current Americanized version of the Franco-Germanic line unlike communism, social justice sounds wonderfully warm, humane and even lofty. It is pure demagoguery without a basic foundation in reality.

Only two choices are possible. There is either an accidental view of history or a conspiratorial view. Facts do not lie. Either they believe that Americans have lost control of their government, their economy, and their future, or they deny everything that has happened as a distortion of reality. The accidental view of history is that history happens more by accident than intelligent design. If one believes in God, there is a divine providence for everyone, that is, everything happens for a reason. The conspiratorial view of history holds that historical events occur by design for reasons that are not generally made known to the people.

The conspiracy issue is analogous to the bitter debate between creationists and evolutionists. Neither side has conclusive scientific proof as to the truth of their relative beliefs. Religious people and scientists both make an act of faith in their respective theories. The rationale for the former is belief in a God and Creator whose divine power rationally created the universe including mankind in His image. Evolutionists deny any sort of plan. They argue that life just happened, begun by some accidental "Big Bang." I see this as the rational versus the accidental or thought and planning versus coincidence and chaos.

Not only does the idea of a conspiracy appeal to those with a sense of logic but also a sense of religious faith. Religious believers place great faith in God's plan, His divine providence, where everything happens for a reason, even the bad things in a person's life. These people have been conditioned to look for the plan, the innate human logic in events that on the surface have no rhyme or reason. Conspiracy advocates are opposed to ethical relativism because they know that it is an absolute life and death struggle for the soul of America at work here. They believe in absolute evil or evil as an absolute principle. Relativists have us believing that is was more evil for Hitler to have killed six million Jews than it was for Stalin to have murdered 20 million kulaks

Not all acts of violence are conspiracies but for the believer there is pre-ordained purpose as to why that happened. If on investigation, it is proven that the killer had intent to kill for a reason of terror than there might be reason to suspect a conspiracy. Or if the victim or victims were involved in other events as witnesses, then there might be a more man-made secular providence at work. Take the case of the assassination of John Kennedy in Dallas. Books have been written about the high incidence of death that befell many witnesses to the Dallas scenario as it was acted out. From cab drivers, landladies and Jack Ruby strippers the list grew within a few years of the 1963 killing. Was it just the odds, or a case of mathematical happenstance? An aura of death surrounded the administrations of President Bill Clinton from his time as Arkansas governor. So great was the number that it coined a term of "Arkanicides." This aura followed him to his presidency with the very suspicious "suicide" of Vince Foster, followed by the even more bizarre "accidental" death of Commerce Secretary, Ron Brown? Were these just mathematical probabilities, akin to drawing two royal straight flushes in a matter of a few years? We may never know but for anyone who is used to dealing with crime and misfortune, these frequencies point to something beyond a secular providence.

In his April 1998 newsletter, Joseph Sobran opines that there is "no mastermind or secret conspiracy behind all this." He believes "the so-called conspiracies evolve out of the natural result of godless man following his nature." There are several conspiracies at work, all working for similar self-servicing purposes. It was as if several different groups set out for the same destination but arrived at their destinations from several different directions. Some are for abortion rights. Others are environmentalists or against the death penalty. Their roadmap to the future was not a coordinated effort to have them all reach the goal simultaneously. They respond to the issues of the fight with a knee-jerk regularity that is easily predictable. Sobran says that they "represent a hive of insects, which form an observable design without knowing it." All they do is just obey their inward instincts. It is a "conspiracy of the mind," or better still, an "unconscious conspiracy." It is as if all liberals were worker bees in a "hive," and naturally went about their business of undermining the culture and thwarting America's economic progress. Like the scorpion in the fable, it is in the bees' nature to work for the destruction of its opposite number, even to the death.

The "hive idea" began with G. K. Chesterton. In his book on bees "What's Wrong with the World," Maurice Maeterlinck, in the chapter entitled, "The Empire of the Insect," investigates the "Soul of the Hive." He admired their "collective spirituality," that is their communal morality. Not unlike the modern left, his bees lived for the "Soul of the Hive." This colonial patriotism of the hive is their only religion. Chesterton concluded that the Eastern armies were like insects in their blind, busy destructiveness, in their black nihilism of personal outlook, in their hateful indifference to individual life and love. In resisting this horrible theory of "the Soul of the Hive," Christians stand not for themselves, but for all humanity for the essential and distinctive human idea that one good and happy man is an end in himself, and that the soul is worth saving.

This is not difficult to understand if one realizes that progressivism or liberalism has infected the Western culture for well over two hundred years. If the elite schools teach the same liberal approach to history, government, economics, and philosophy, it is no small wonder that millions of their graduates share the same basic approach to the issues of the day. They have drunk at the same well of liberalism and have become intoxicated by its captivating beliefs and promises of an utopian paradise. The same could probably be said of conservatives, to the extent that many read the same publications and listen to the same conservative radio stations. Yet their exposure is often dulled by the superabundance of liberal influences that have permeated the culture.

Eugene Lyon wrote a book entitled, "The Red Decade." In it he wrote of Communist attraction for the thinking elite of American society, the educated, the writers, media teachers, government bureaucrats, all seemed enamoured of liberalism's hive and its moral venom. The "Red Decade" was a conspiracy says Sobran. But in effect, it is not at all separated from the hive that follows. The conspiracy set in motion the ideas and the beliefs, the abstractions that became part and parcel to the ordinary lives of the millions who supped at its table. To be a worker bee means to sacrifice one's individuality for the solidarity of the hive and its promises of world brotherhood. The hive achieves perfect secrecy by "being perfectly public," yet the secrets of the hive are often concealed from the worker-bees themselves. The bees concentrate on the nectar but are unaware of the venom that lays dormant and can sting the stability of the world. The liberal venom becomes their second nature. No liberal has to think about what to protest, say, or write. He knows by instinct what side he is on in most instances.

His idea of the hive is praiseworthy. While the cultural Marxists in Italy and Germany were fomenting their plans for "the long march through culture," American Progressives were directing their efforts around the subversion of the United States Constitution. They would accomplish this by controlling the interpretation of the Constitution, thus reforming their early desire for a new Constitution. In effect, as Sobran reminds us, "it would choose evolution over revolution." It would do this by public opinion, a national peer pressure that would denigrate anyone who dared to speak up in opposition. It was necessary because the Constitution was the supreme law of the land, which contained the nation's basic tenets of faith and law. The hive scored its biggest coup in 1973 when it usurped the powers of fifty states with its Roe v. Wade decision that created abortion on demand across the board.

Sobran tells us that that the hive had many Communist roots. There was the American Civil Liberties Union of Roger Baldwin, an avowed Socialist, and W. E.B. Dubois of the National Association for the Advancement of Colored People. Dubois was an avowed Communist. Feminist leaders, such as Betty Friedan, Bella Abzug, and Susan Brownmiller started out as Communists. Feminism is not so much anti-male as it is anti-Christian. Sobran also reminds us that the hive's three general targets are private property, the family, and religion. The first is attacked under the guise of civil rights and affirmative rights, environmentalism, gun control etc. while the family suffers from the moral pollutants of sexual freedom, choice and gay rights, including homosexual marriage, children's rights. Religion is targeted by the canard of separation of church and state, secular humanism, dogmatic Darwinism and demands for female and homosexual clergy. He says that the Queen Bee died when the Soviet Union collapsed under its own weight. The Clintons gave the hive new life and energy.

Sobran is wrong about the hive in saying that there is no directions given to it. He says it is more a pattern, than a conspiracy, with its own internal logic, yearning for a socialist political order. Like the busy killer bees in the hive, evil liberalism and its nomenclatural descendants have effected through the centuries has not been officially under the direction of any one unified group. It has occurred because it is the basic, inherent nature of what it means to be Illuminati, a Freemason, a Communist, a Socialist, a Liberal, or a radical Feminist. They comprise a brotherhood of evil, dominated by partisan reaction to the traditions of Western civilization in a cultural clash of cosmic proportions. I believe the fable of the scorpion and the frog is a better metaphor in establishing the natural relationship between innocence and evil. Throughout history, the scorpion has always been a symbol of evil.

George Will identifies the notion of right-wing conspiracy as the one savory ingredient, missing from the Clinton's gothic tale. He contends that Hillary Clinton accusations have breathed new fire into this paranoid style that has been such a player in American history. It has an interesting pedigree, sharing allegiance with Joseph McCarthy and J. Edgar Hoover's warning about a conspiracy so immense that it was everywhere. Anticipating Oliver Stone's movie on this idea, Hillary Clinton supplies the man on the grassy knoll and he is no other than Jerry Falwell. It would have been interesting if Hofstadter had lived long enough to comment of Senator's Clinton's "paranoia" implicit in her "vast right-wing conspiracy theory," which she charged in the midst of her husband's impeachment trial.

Senator Joseph McCarthy worried about the conspiracy that was eating away at the very soul of the American people. He saw that all of these machinations were the work of a giant conspiracy. Raised the all-important question: How can we account for our present situation unless we believe that men high in Government are conspiring to deliver us to disaster? He thought that "This must be the product of a great conspiracy, a conspiracy on a scale so immense as to dwarf any previous such venture in the history of man. A conspiracy of infamy so black that when it is finally exposed, its principles shall be forever deserving of the maledictions of all honest men."

The cultural semantics are like the exact opposite of Hofstadter's paranoid mind. It could be called the popular mind. People who foment and create the cultural semantic mind can often use the paranoid mind device as a defense mechanism. The popular mind is really a state of ignorant bliss in which the people who control the money, the power and the media and the elementary means of communication create a false sense of reality that is akin to Plato's oft mention cave and its overused shadows. It is this illusion of which most people are aware. This is sort of like Will Rogers, the prescient comic cowboy, and social commentator who often quipped that "all I know, is what I read in the newspapers." The popular mind or the "conventional wisdom," has its own saints, like the late Princess Di, the Hollywood Glitterati and the poplar icons who flock to all the great parties and are seen at all the trendy night spots. What these shapers of the popular mind say and do often sets the new standard of acceptable behavior. It is the way of thinking that constantly reminds us of the health risks and evils of smoking. It also that tells us a woman's choice is sacrosanct, exercise is a must for everyone, we must save the rain forests, or we will die. It stresses the fear that there are too many people in the world and everyone must practice safe sex so that Aids, the bubonic plague of the nineties does not bring the end of the world. It is as if the left has it own brand of apocalyptic dread. It is the prevailing attitude that conditions us like the evolutionary animals we really are, mere Pavlovian dogs, trapped in a giant Skinner box.

It is this mind that refuses to discuss, intellectually analyze various examples of machination, of deceit. In Rush Limbaugh's March 1998 "The Limbaugh Letter," in discussing the web of deceit he blanches at the very thought of using the word conspiracy, yet his whole theme is about intrigue, dishonesty and deceit—all the major elements in a full fledged conspiracy. Limbaugh has fallen victim again to the historical urgencies of the popular attraction. He needs popularity to maintain his basis and is deathly afraid of stepping outside the popular milieu even with the stark truth staring him in the face.

Howard Kurtz's book "Spin Cycle" is an exhaustive study on the machinations and the web of deceit that has existed in the Clinton White House since his first inauguration in 1993. They have given the public a steady diet of lies, canards, distractions, and falsehoods, while all the time trying to level the expectations of acceptable presidential behavior and moral standard. Everyone lies. They all sleep around. They all commit adultery. Everybody gropes intern at work. This is not a random response to legitimate political questioning but a detailed plan to destroy the public outrage and maintain their political power at all costs to national security and viability. If this is not broad proof of the use of plots, deceptions, and other means to discredit critics, misinform the public and create a false image for the public consumption, then nothing is.

It is that mentality that is easily led to accept the public lies about things, whether it is Monica Lewinsky or the lone gunman theory of presidential assassination. Anyone who deviates from the acceptable public viewpoint is immediately branded as a wacko, a right-wing conspiracy nut and so forth. Any official, who attempts to fight the public mind of cultural semantics, is either bought off, demonized in McCarthyesque rhetoric or simply has an accident. This is political baseball of the hardest kind. In effect the claim that one is a conspiracist has the same deadly silent effect on critics of the government, as does the terms racist, anti-Semite and homophobe do. Over the past forty years the United States has become a nation of frogs, enjoying the "big sleep" of unending fun, games, murder mysteries and materialistic greed. All of these have been tools or weapons in this battle against the forces of evil.

No discussion of conspiracy would be complete without a treatment of the John Birch Society. In a muted defense of the John Birchers, probably considered by the conventional wisdom to be the prototypical wackos of all conspiracists, columnist Joseph Sobran summed up the true nature of the Conspiracy in his July 1997 newsletter in an article entitled "What the Birchers Can Teach Us." Sobran stated his belief that "Conspiracies are real," and "conspiratorial behavior is inseparable from politics, since politics is largely the pursuit of power by sneaky people." However he discounts large conspiracies because they are so hard to hide. Sobran would much rather talk of the tendency of political action. He believes if one were to substitute tendency for conspiracy, these theories would have certain cogency to them. It is by its very nature that power tends to corrupt and power itself has that self-fulfilling attraction to grow and consolidate under the seductive guise of empty promises. This has been the history of the United States since its inception. Abraham Lincoln did not intend to centralize government, as part of some worldwide conspiracy. It just worked out that way through the exigencies of historical context. It is the political instinct of any leader to consolidate his power for the good of his agenda.

As Sobran further elaborated, "today's globalists and internationalists, forever pursuing international treaties and alliance, may think they are promoting peace and prosperity but what they are really doing is promoting a tyrannical potential in their 'New World Order.'" Prompted by the inner drive of the liberal tendency, they may mean well but the consequences of this sinister philosophy has endangered us all. In his inestimable persuasive logic, Sobran concludes that the very people who are quick to ridicule "conspiracy theories" are also the people whose conduct invites them.

I think it is even more than tendency. I think there is a kindred spirit among conspirators that dated back to the fall of man. It is more than an attitude but a deep attraction for the evil that has been called the "disease of me." With apologies to Adam Smith, I believe that just as there is a "divine hand" guiding us through a free economy, there is a "demon hand" that moves millions of like-minded people to support and promote the Masons, the Council of Foreign Relations, the Communist Party, the Socialists, or the Liberals. It is this demonic, unseen hand that is the driving force of history that conservatives and other religious people must combat. It is this unholy hand that is responsible for the spilled blood of the world with millions of victims.

Sobran thinks that the wildest conspiracy of all is that there is one gigantic almighty conspiracy that "sees every sparrow fall." To him conspiracy is not monolithic. This was the same charge that was leveled against the anti-Communist right of the fifties. Actually he believes in a more polycentric approach, in that there are countless conspiracies, often overlapping, intersecting or competing. Many are quite informal, as in C. S. Lewis's "inner ring."

In the "National Review," August 28, 1995, Tom Bethel disagreed. He thinks the idea of a conspiracy is foolhardy. Conspiracy theories do sometimes detect a pattern of events that is real enough but when they assign the term conspiracy to this observed pattern that their adherents often arrive at the wrong conclusion. He believes that to explain an existing pattern, as a conspiracy will inevitably lead to the charge of paranoia or extremism by the general public. It is this very real fear that has silenced the loquacious Limbaugh on the idea of conspiracy. Bethel believes that the goal of world government is considered ridiculous by some of the very people who dream of it. To reduce this idea of a conspiracy to an absurdity, Bethel cited the World Federalist Movement (WFM) whose president is comedian and actor Sir Peter Ustinov.

This is all well and good but what power or influence does this fringe, unrepresentative group have? How much money and power do they generate? Do they represent all one-world power sources? Bethel's vain attempt to debunk all conspiracy theories by the calculated use of the WFM is as preposterous as is his contention that if the left calls you crazy names, it must mean your ideas are crazy.

Bethel also believes that in order to keep the conspiracy going, elderly Illuminati must have met at some point with inchoate Communists, to turn over the keys to the mystery. His arrant attempt at sarcasm betrayed an unschooled naivete that pulled his argument way off its mark. The Illuminati were the custodians of an idea that was as old as evil itself. The demise of the Illuminati had little or no bearing on the transference of their ideas. I compare this transference to the Coke bottle that was the "omphalos" in the movie, "The Gods Must be Angry." It was a humorous story about how a plane inadvertently dropped a Coke bottle in the Kalahari Desert. The strange and exotic soda bottle endured great adventures as it was passed, often accidentally, to many different owners. The bottle seems to have a life of its own as it left chaos, pain, and happiness in its wake. The idea of a conspiracy is like that elusive coke bottle.

One of the strange but not improbable terms of the "conspiracy" is the use of black helicopters. When an opponent of the idea of a conspiracy wants to defame or denigrate someone's belief, he usually refers to black helicopters. There was reference to this "hallucination," in the 1997 Mel Gibson movie, "Conspiracy Theory." In the film, Gibson's character, black-clad commandos who seek him out on the streets of New York assault Jerry Fletcher. As far fetched as the movie made it seem there is real black helicopter base in North Carolina, where these craft regularly fly over the treetops at dusk. The base stands on 1600 boggy acres surrounded by Albermarle Sound where Black Beard the Pirate once ruled. It is an area ruled by mystery. The base also has buses with blackout windows that careen by, ferrying mysterious passengers. Trucks haul in old limos and tack away bullet-riddled blackened hulks for scrap. There are also the thundering of early morning bombs that assimilate terrorist activity that resound for miles around. Jim Keith is the author of a "Black Helicopters Over America." He book lists several hundred "black helicopter" sightings.

The government would have us believe that these are just the ranting of the lunatic fringe. The intrusive arm of government is at work in every aspect of our culture. No area of concern is more at risk than the education of the nation's children—the future leaders of the country. In his column in the "New York Times," William Safire stated that "political control of thought debilitates a country." He felt that "scientist, artists and financiers need an unimpeded flow of information. Only free thinkers, instantly informed can compete on the high seas of highest tech." This is not happening in a country that plans to devalue college education and with it the liberal arts that would provide so many of the leaders Safire said are necessary. Educators have freely modified the standard curriculum so that the lack of academic proficiency of the students of the 21st century will make them fit more readily into the programmed society that has been planned for them.

Another movie, "The Twenty Dollar Bill," traced the relations and events that were triggered by an issue of U. S. currency. In these movies inanimate objects appeared to influence the many dozens and even hundreds of people who crossed their paths as they went about their daily lives. It does not require a great leap of faith or suspension of belief, to realize that an idea can remain dormant or inconspicuous for years, maybe even centuries, before it is resuscitated. Some ideas have a nuclear life, in that, they never seem to die. They may fall out of favor or be lost for a long time, but eventually they come back and influence new generations of people. The beliefs of the Illuminati and the French Revolution are like that. Free Masonry kept Illuminism alive, though in somewhat of a dormant state. The revolutionary idea was eventually passed on to the League of Just Men, which had Karl Marx as a member. This directly led to the Communist League, Progressivism, New Deal Democracy, and Liberalism.

Conspiracies abound everywhere. The black community abounds in them, whether it is the CIA unleashing crack cocaine in their neighborhoods through the mysterious death of Ron Brown. Hollywood director, Oliver Stone upset the powers that be with his movie, JFK (1991?) He contends that Paranoids have the facts. One of the more bizarre theories was broadcast o a radio show, not too long ago. "The Catholics killed Lincoln." Even though Booth had been an Episcopalian, many of the conspirators, including John and Mary Surratt and a number of leaders of the Confederacy were Roman Catholics. Pope Pius IX was an open sympathizer with the South and many Irish immigrants also fought for the Confederacy. The "headquarters" for the popish plot was Georgetown College, now a university, and the seedbed of liberal intellectual activism, a far cry from this nascent charge.

Soviet Premier Stalin thought all criticism against him amounted to a conspiracy. Some conspiracists lean toward an occult conspiracy myth that veers into the magical, permitting one ancient tradition to pile promiscuously onto another—Egyptian, Iranian and Indian mystery religions, the cabala, Gnosticism, astrology and alchemy, tales of Druids—forming a wooly indiscriminate whole.

Republican pundit and erstwhile candidate, Pat Buchanan says that real power in America belongs to the "Manhattan Money Power." In his controversial book, "The New World Order" religious leader, Pat Robertson seconds this idea of a money power. He says that they prefer the simplicity of dictatorship to the messiness of democracy. He even states that European bankers murdered President Abraham Lincoln murder because Lincoln would have used interest free currency that would have taken away their control of the money supply. It is his talk of these international bankers that has opened Robertson to a flurry of criticism from the left.

The idea of a conspiracy is intimately connected with the concept of the New World Order. Over the centuries there have been a number of works that have described ideal worlds, such as Plato's Republic and St. Thomas More's Utopia. The first proposal for a world order or world government appeared about seven centuries ago. Norman lawyer Pierre Dubois in 1306 was the first, followed by King George Podebrad of Bohemia in 1460 and French scholar Emeric Cruce in 1623. In Cruce's New Cyneas, he suggested a permanent congress of nations that would anticipate world disorders and solve them before they got out of hand. In the 17th century, Emeric Cruce opposed King Louis XIV's plan to make France the dominant power in Europe. Cruce proposed a novel thought in 1623 when he wrote what a pleasure it would be to see men going freely from one place to another without thought of country. This was the origin of the idea of the "world citizen," first echoed by firebrand, Thomas Paine when he said:

> "I am a citizen of the world and my religion is to do good, which has become a centerpiece in liberal thought, necessitating some form of world government that would eliminate the independence of nations and enforce global harmony."

Fear of or skepticism of the Great Conspiracy of the New World Order is just another sign that the American population has lost sight of history. History, especially that of Western Civilization, is replete with intrigues, plots, cabals, collusion, and connivance. Why then can we not believe there is a group intent on using the emerging technologies of cyberspace and international communications to control and dominate the world for its own benefit? It is not as preposterous as it may seem. This is not science fiction but the continuation of an impulse that has existed since the first men grouped themselves into the first family and tribe. To deny that these things did and do happen is to run the risk of seeing life through the eyes of a Pollyanna.

Many opponents of this belief cry that the term international banker is an anti-Semitic a code word, thus opening up Robertson to a fusillade of angry charges of bigotry. Many will hide behind this term to conceal their own favoritism for the Conspiracy. Granted the Rothschild name is prominent in any of these theories, Robertson did not mention Jews. Many others, who are not Jewish, are as involved as any of the Rothschild in this nefarious attempt to socialize the American way of living. It is the left that has used this anti-intellectual attack to defame the reputations of many on the right who are attempting to expose the hidden agenda many of these people have for the American people.

I am aware that ideas such as this usually elicit the conditioned response in most people that he's a religious fanatic or he is some kind of right-wing wacko. I am more than ready and willing to endure the slings and arrows of this socially ingrained reflex because what I say, I believe to be true. Educated critics often resort to playing the paranoia card. This is a tribute to Richard Hofstadter's highly touted essay, the "Paranoid Style in American Politics," first delivered in Oxford in November of 1963. For years it has reigned as a companion to his classic study, "Anti-Intellectualism in America," which was nothing more than a liberal knee-jerk to McCarthyism. Hofstadter says that the distinguishing thing about the paranoid style is not that it its exponents see conspiracies or plots here and there in history, but they regard a vast or gigantic conspiracy as the motive force in historical events. History is conspiracy.

Victims of this historical paranoia would say "history is a conspiracy, set in motion by demonic forces of almost transcendent power, and what is felt to be needed to defeat it is not the usual method of political give-and-take, but an all-out crusade." Hofstadter also adds that the paranoid spokesman sees the fate of the conspiracy in apocalyptic terms that "traffics in the birth and death of whole worlds, whole political orders, whole systems of human values." He sees himself in apocalyptic terms, always "manning the barriers of civilization." He has a sense of dread that fears the end is near. This sense that the end is near in the paranoid style "runs dangerously near to hopeless pessimism." This could be why so many of America's youth seem susceptible to conspiracies of all kinds.

Hofstadter does not deny there are conspiracies in history. He admits that all political behavior requires strategy, many strategic acts depend for their effect upon a period of secrecy and anything that is secret may be defined as may be described . . . as conspiratorial. Hofstadter continues with his belief that the distinguishing thing about the paranoid style is not that its exponents see conspiracies or plots here and there in history, "but they regard it as a 'vast' or 'gigantic' conspiracy as the motive force in historical events." He says conspiracists fall victim the belief that "historical causation is cut and dried, a black and white answer" for the eternal question of "Why?" What Hofstadter fails to note is that ideas do have consequences and they can often serve as the incendiary spark that causes the whole building of state to be consumed. In the case of the French Revolution, a strong case can be made that the triple conspiracy provided the ideas, the intellectual underpinnings that inspired the French people to throw off the vestiges of a five hundred years of civilization.

I am not presumptuous enough to say that the late professor could have me in mind when he wrote those words. I will admit to having a heightened state of awareness on what evils have permeated the society I live in today. Richard Nixon's Secretary of State, Henry Kissinger prophetically stated "Just because I am paranoid, it doesn't mean that people are not plotting against me."

Hofstadter warned of a higher paranoid scholarship, the mirror world of conspiracism, with its amateur autodidactic that lack institutional affiliation and suffer exclusion from the established institutions. He relegates these people as having uncommonly angry minds. Hofstadter, like most intellectuals of his day, detested Senator Joseph McCarthy of Wisconsin. They seem obsessed with the era. The late Richard Rovere founded his entire career on anti-McCarthyism with an obvious vengeance. McCarthy was the greatest anti-Communist of his day and much of the opposition to the idea of conspiracy has been a result of the vicious attacks and assaults he underwent. There is a small parallel between what McCarthy endured to what special prosecutor Kenneth Starr had to bear during his prosecution of President Clinton in the late nineties. Personal demonization has been a handy tool of the left for many years.

Daniel Pipes is a strong advocate of this theory. In his book, "Conspiracy: How The Paranoid Style Flourishes and Where it Comes From" he paints the Jews as victims of history's mad obsession with conspiracies. In turn, the author suffers from his own paranoia about the Jews in history. Pipes is obsessed with the role allotted to Jews in this world conspiracy. He regards in general terms that conspiracy theorists are all tainted with anti-Semitism, that is the most "virulent of Jew-hatred for it turns Jews into everyone's enemies. He calls opponents of secret societies as a non-Jewish equivalent of anti-Semitism. He says that conspiracy theories often overlap with one another, forming a giant web enclosing centuries and continents. Each is believed to pass its ideas on to the next group like in a relay race.

Pipes believes that "The hidden hand" blames murders on conspiracy theories that inspire murderous instincts, a hatred that leads to violence against certain groups in its most debased form becomes the vital accomplice of genocide. Pipes blames conspiracy ideas for the Nazis killing six million Jews and Stalin murdering 20 million kulaks. They were depersonalized and made enemies of the state. Is this is not the type of rhetoric employed by believers in these theories? Is not Pipes a victim of his own criticism?

Pipes says his book, like Hofstadter's, is the study of anti-intellectualism. He says, "Recreational conspiracism titillates sophistication, much as does recreational sex. Artist explore conspiracist fantasies in a spirit akin to sexual ones." He erroneously contends there is no logic to conspiracies. Conspiracism is a "fully formed body of ideas," passed on by books written legacy. Barruel assumes that ideas have consequences.

Noam Chomsky blames the United States Government for virtually every ill under the sun, including environmental pollution, militarism, poverty, spiritual alienation, and the drug scourge. Behind the government stands the corporate giants, especially the arms merchants. The right distributes home videos. They have Oliver Stone and theatrical movies. Gore Vidal produces best sellers. Pipes contrasts Nazism with Communism, putting Louis Farrakhan on the right of the political spectrum. To Pipes, anyone who disagrees with him is on the right. Farrakhan says it was the evil black scientist, Mr. Yacub who created the evil white man in a test tube.

The left presents conspiracy as truth, such as Afrocentrism, which is widely accepted on the college campuses and high school classrooms. Some elementary classes have made it the core of their curriculum. While the political right deals with vast historical, all-encompassing theories, the left is subtler. It has adopted conspiracy late.

This way of thinking, this evil plan of order has been educing millions with its promise of Christlike personal divinity at a rapid pace since the French Revolution. Its millions of disciples, lobbyists, and ambassadors of Satan have been more active than its religious counterparts. They have created an unholy alliance of like-minded groups that have been loosely connected by their common goal, their common bond, a unity of purpose that without any superimposing power. The central direction for this nefarious of all plans, comes directly from the fires of Hell and is only carried out through the devil's loyal followers on earth. Their main task has been the overthrow of the influence and impact of the Judeo-Christian religion and its mark on mankind. That has been their eternal goal and they made great strides within the 20th century.

Someone once said, "God can not alter the past, only historians can!" Since most historians were not privy to the smoke filled rooms, they often don't know what really happened. One-reason things are often revised. History is written through a glass darkly. If this were paranoia then its antithesis has to be an intellectual comatose state that characterizes the condition of millions of Americans these last forty years. Hofstadter is right about one thing: "seeing conspiracies can be a way of life." If one is obsessed with learning the truth, this is not a bad choice.

2

Conspiracies Against God

"The history of secret societies is the history of conspiracies." Jonathan Vankin & John Whalen in "The 50 Greatest Conspiracies of All Time"

For thousands of years, secret societies and occult groups have served as guardians of ancient esoteric wisdom and have exercised a strong and often crucial influence on the destiny of nations. Self-seeking individuals have often perverted the true ideals and esoteric principles of these societies. The Nazis, the founding fathers, the British security forces, and even the Vatican, according to some, have played a part in this perversion. Those who follow the occult today are heirs to an ancient tradition of esoteric knowledge, which are thousands of years old.

In his book, "New World Order: The Ancient Plan of Secret Societies" William T. Still wrote "secret societies have had a major, yet little known impact on world events throughout history." They are the history of civilization itself. The early Church had a great deal of trouble with mystery cults and pagan influences. At this time a new cult arose in the Middle East which attempted to blend the best features of the decaying paganism and Christian beliefs. This was Gnosticism and it stands as one of the most important anti-Christian influences in the world today. Gnostics believed that direct contact could be made with God through secret knowledge or the "gnosis" and the intervention of the priest class was not necessary. They claimed that they alone had preserved the true teachings of Jesus Christ that had been perverted by the early Councils.

The Gnostics took their inspiration from a host of sources, which included Zoroastrianism, the hermetic tradition, Middle Eastern fertility cults, and Esoteric Christianity. They derived their central teaching from Zoroaster who lived circa 1800 BC. He was a priest of the Indo-Iranian religion, which was involved, with the worship of the basic forces of water and fire. He had broken away from his established religion to teach his own philosophy based on the universe as a cosmic struggle between the opposing forces of light and darkness. This was an eternal conflict. An enlightened person had to choose between one or the other.

Gnosticism was actually a form of paganism. The Gnostics employed the language and the imagery of Christianity but maintained the essential pagan spirit. The God of the Gnostics is often described as the "alien God," "the unknown God," "the nonexistent God," or the "absolutely transcendent God." God is not the creator of the world and has nothing to do with the world's continued existence.

They also taught that even when man is enlightened by personal revelation, he could not really say anything positive about God. This scenario eliminated the need for this God. God was irrelevant and it was the ego of man that is left to assume godlike powers. While baptism liberated, it was the special internal knowledge that counted most in Gnostic thinking. Salvation was accomplished, not by the power of God, nor by faith, but by the assimilation of esoteric knowledge. Christ was not a redeemer but more like a messenger from God with this special knowledge. But it was not meant for everyone but just for the select few.

The Gnostics learned that they had to reconcile both the good and evil forces of their nature. To them evil was just a shadow image of the good. Both had to exist in an imperfect world. Gnosticism was then a hybrid faith that was tied to the heretical texts that circulated after the death of Jesus. They taught that Christ had brothers and sisters, was married, and was an ordinary man until overcome with "the Christ." Since they denied the

Resurrection, they could only explain Christ's death on the cross, by alluding to His early departure.

Others believed that Christ survived by substituting a goat in his place. Whatever the case, most Gnostics rejected the "theology of the Cross." They believed it was wrong to worship an instrument of torture and death. Others believed that the god of the Old Testament, Jehovah, was Satan and that the Supreme Creator of the universe had sent the Christ to incarnate the body of Christ to save humanity. Since the Romans and the Jews acted as agents of Satan, conspiring to have Jesus murdered, to honor the cross was to worship a symbol of satanic evil. Islam teaches a brand of perverted, watered-down Christianity that distorts the Christian message.

In his book, "Conspiracy: A Biblical View" Gary North wrote about the Gnostic heresy and its relevance for people living today. The ancient Gnostics believed that man had to be liberated from the world of matter and elevated through secret initiation and certain ascetic techniques, into the realm of the spirit. Certain groups of New Age humanists hold a very similar view, which also has an occultic ring of to it. North saw this as an alliance between the occultists and the secular humanists.

There were many Gnostic forerunners of the secret societies that evolved into our own time. The first notable forerunner was the Manicheans, who were founded by Mani who was born in 300 AD. Their religion had strict rules, including celibacy for women and men priests, a vegetarian diet, and abstinence from alcohol or drugs. Manchaenism spread all over East Asia.

Mani's heresy seemed to be a contributing factor to the rise of the Cathars. The Cathars were eleventh and twelfth century dualists. Their name comes from the Greek "Cathari," or "pre ones." The Cathars formed communities in Northern Italy, the Alpine region, and Southern France. They preached the duality of the universe, which was divided into opposing forces of light and darkness. It was an eternal struggle between God and Satan, both of whom were locked, in an eternal struggle for the souls of humankind in a cosmic chess game.

The Cathars rejected both the Cross and Redemption. Men were saved by leading moral lives. They rejected the Catholic Church as the guardians of Christ's truth. Social work and what would be called "social justice" today served as their inspiration. They worked with the poor and built hospitals. No doubt many would be happy working with Jimmy Carter and Habitat for Humanity. They taught that men and women were created equal. There was an inner circle within their priesthood.

The Catholic Church condemned and eventually destroyed them, charging them with heresy, incest; cannibalism, homosexuality, and celebrating the Black Mass of devil worship. The church launched a Crusade against the Cathars in 1209, killing thousands. The leading knight stated emphatically "Kill them all. God will know his own!" Their final defeat came in 1244 at Montsegur in the foothills of the Pyrenees Mountains when 200 of their priest were massacred.

Their secret treasure was reputed to have been moved just before their death. Occultic speculation believes that it was the Holy Grail, that is, the cup used by Jesus at the Last Supper. In his book, "The Occult Conspiracy," Michael Howard pointed out that it was their sacred writings that were removed which detailed their ancient founding from pagan teachings. This seems more likely!

Another group worthy of note was the Albigensians, a spin-off of the Cathars. They were neo-Manichean in character. Their doctrine taught that the devil was not only the creator of matter but also a rival god. The Christian God is the creator of spirit-being only. The human soul was created good, but rebelled and was expelled from heaven. The devil at once imprisoned it in matter and return to its original heavenly state. It was to teach men this truth that Christ came to earth. Christ was not God but an angelic spirit whose body had only a corporal appearance. The sacraments and other Catholic rituals are vain and sacrilegious.

One of the most interesting of all secret societies was the Knights Templar. They were one of the many spiritual descendants of the Gnostics. Many Christian pilgrims traveled to the Holy Land during the Crusades and were often in grave danger. At Easter in 1118, a group of three hundred traveled from Jerusalem to Jordan. They were attacked and massacred by the Saracens. The King of Jerusalem, Baldwin II, suggested to one of his knights, the Frenchman Sir Hugh de Payens, who had fought in the Holy Land the prior three years, that he form an order of chivalric knights to protect these travelers and pilgrims. Since the order was founded within Baldwin's palace, which was the original Temple of Solomon, he called these knights, the "Tepli Militia" or "Soldiers of the Temple." Their name was later changed to the grander "Knights of the Temple of Solomon." They participated in several crusades. They dedicated their lives to the defense of the mysteries of the Catholic Church.

Many other knights joined them and religious chivalry gathered around this nucleus. The crusades led to the "monk-knight" or "the Order of the Poor Knights of the Temple of Solomon." They had already decided that they would be warrior monks, an oxymoron that no one seemed to notice. To order their society, they adopted the monastic regimen of St. Bernard of Clairvaux, the founder of the Cistercian monks. The Templars took oaths of poverty, chastity, and obedience. They consecrated their lives and their swords to the defense of the mysteries of the Christian faith. One of the purposes of the Society was to convert and render useful knights who were leading evil lives. The Order had its own clergy exempt from diocesan rule. Its meetings were held in secret. They had their own burial grounds, did not have to pay the ordinary tithe, and could have their own chaplains. They were led by a grand master. They wore white mantles with a Red Cross for unmarried knights and a black or brown mantle with a Red Cross for the others. Its history is closely intertwined with that of the Christian crusades. Thanks to his patronage, the Rosicrucians won the support of popes and noblemen, gaining universal acclaim in Catholic Europe. This invariably led to the other Christian military orders, such as the Knights Hospitallers of St. Johns and the Teutonic Knights.

The Knights were also an economic institution. They became a great trading corporation between the east and the west. Over the years the Knights were able to amass great temporal and financial power. It stretched out to Spain and the Holy Land, made inroads in England and Scotland. In the thirteenth century they became the international bankers of Europe and were appointed treasurers to the Royal Family and the Vatican. By century's end, they controlled forty percent of the frontiers of Europe. They owned merchant and war-shipping. Part of their extraordinary power had come from Pope Alexander III who issued a special Papal Bull in 1162. Became corrupted from within.

By the twelfth century, the Knights had degenerated into ruthless loan sharks who used shady and violent tactics to extort money from the people of Medieval Europe. The Knights Templar eventually got into banking, which provided them with vast wealth and power. It was alleged that great orgies took place, with homosexual overtones that eventually led to its downfall, including the trampling of the cross. Critics said they worshiped at the foot of the god Baphomet, who was an occult idol, sometimes represented by a wooden phallus and other times by a disembodied jeweled skull. It was also alleged that their worship included the Devil in the shape of a black cat. Other tales spoke of their roasting children and smearing their bodies in the burned fat.

After Acre, the last Christian foothold in the Holy Land fell in 1291, the Vatican expelled them. In 1306 King Philip IV of France expelled the Jews from France on the grounds that they "dishonored Christian customs and behavior . . ." He then went after the Knights. Historians believe it was the king's avarice that led to their persecution. He was deeply in debt to the Knights. They had financed his wars and underwritten the election of a French puppet in the Vatican. The election of Pope Clement V, who was devoted top the interests of Philip, fell right in step, by denouncing the Order, hoping confiscate the Knights valuable land.

In 1307, on a Friday, the thirteenth of October, the Inquisition arrested Jacques De Molay and 123 of his fellow knights. The day has been regarded with superstition ever since. Philip accused them of blasphemy, homosexuality, and other foul deeds. Many admitted under the pains of torture that they had denied Christ, that he was not God and nothing more than a false prophet. They also admitted that they spat upon the cross, especially on Good Friday. It was also alleged that they took sacred oaths and did not believe in any of the sacraments. Some admitted under torture that the brother who officiated at the reception of a new member kissed the naked body of the latter, often in a very unbecoming manner. It was also reported that each different province had its own idol, a head with three faces, or even a skull. They believed that these idols had the power to make them rich.

Fifty-four Templars who refused to submit were carried to the windmill of St. Antoine in the Paris suburbs and burnt at the stake. This process ended with the Order being disbanded. Even in Italy the justice was as severe. The pope was offended by the leniency showed them in England, Germany, and Spain. The publication of these charges and forced admissions created a great furor within the country. It was at this point in their history that the Knights Templar disappeared from public view, only to resurface centuries later as a clandestine organization working underground promoting occult traditions and subversive politics.

In 1314, seven years after his arrest, De Molay was offered the opportunity to recant his beliefs. He refused, and as they were burning him at the stake, he soundly cursed both the Pope Clement V and the King Philip IV, who both oddly enough died before the end of the year. This has just added to the mystery and stark glamour of a Christian order that was condemned for Satanism.

The Gnostic connections of the Templars have become part of the accepted historical record. In some Italian chapters they worshiped cats, which some said were demons that promised them worldly riches. Some of the survivors remained together and may have even formed secret societies. Some of the Templars found refuge under the Freemason King of Scotland, Sir Robert the Bruce, who had betrayed William "Braveheart" Wallace.

The occultic ideas of the Knights had gone underground during the years of the Inquisition. In his book, "De Occulta Philosophai," published in 1530, Henry Cornelius Agrippa, a German occultist and magician, wrote about the Templars in connection with the

Gnostics and the worship of the pagan fertility god Priapus, "whose symbol was a huge erect penis and also the Greek goat-footed god Pan." He also identified the order with the survival of paganism, suggesting that he had some special inside information on the traditional pagan ideas. Some claimed that Agrippa was a member of a secret society himself, which claimed decent from the Templars.

The idea of the Templars being heretics is not farfetched. Over the years, they had lost sight of their early history. Their intimate connection with the Middle East during the Crusades had watered down their Christian beliefs. They followed many of the rites of the Gnostic Ophites of Islam. Baphomet was merely a corruption of Mohomet. The Templars had been more tolerant of paganism. It is often said that after the death of deMolay, the Templar survivors started a conspiracy, designed to destroy the papacy and several kingdoms of Europe, which they blamed for his execution. There is also the belief that their traditions, thinking and occult philosophy was handed down for generations through such societies as the Illuminati and the Freemasons, who in turn brought about the French Revolution and the downfall of the French throne.

The Templars were also thought to have received some of the secrets of the Cathars before the Vatican exterminated them in the thirteenth century. The survival of the Templar tradition was according to Masonic Christians masterminded by de Molay while he was in prison. On the night before his execution, he had a confidant go to the special crypt in Paris, where the bodies of past Grand Masters were buried. He took various symbolic sacred objects, including the crown of the King of Jerusalem, a seven-branched candlestick from Solomon's steeple and statues from the church which were alleged to have marked the burial place of Jesus. There was also a great deal of money hidden in the twin pillars at the front of the tomb. The hollow pillars also held manuscripts of the teachings of the Templars.

Another important secret society is the group was the Rosicrucians. Their early history is somewhat murky. In his book, "Foucault's Pendulum," Italian author, Umberto Eco says the Rosicrucians were founded by a group of renegade Knights Templar, who had survived the extermination of their society in the fourteenth century. Others have traced their ancestry back to the Alumbrados, Hebrew Cabalists and the hermetic magicians and alchemists. According to some sources, their roots extend back to the Pharaoh Thothmes III in the fifteenth century. The following century, they were known as "the Invisibles." Their society was a quasi-theological amalgamation of chosen individuals who fancied alchemy and occult symbolism, such as the rosy cross, swastika, and pyramid. The Rosicrucians strove for a hidden half-mystical, half-scientific wisdom, acquired through their esoteric study and intense contemplation. Their ultimate aim was the re-establishment of the ancient Mysteries. The earliest writings about this society, the Brotherhood or the Order of the Rosy Cross, began circulating in about 1605. Their teachings were mainly derived from those of apocryphal German mystic, Christian Rosencruetz. He was a student of the Cabala and the Arabian occult.

Their order has been difficult to fathom. They prided themselves on their elusiveness and the inability of their opponents to fathom even their basic existence. One of their axioms read, "Hide in the open!" They did this by creating as many false orders as possible to confuse their enemies, identified in an early manifesto merely, as "the Technomancers." Their first public notice occurred around 1614 when books, entitled "Fama Fratenitatis," "Confessio Fratenitatis Rosseae Crucis," and "The Alchemical Marriage of Christian Rosecross," appeared from unknown sources in major European centers of learning. These books proclaimed the society's existence and its possession of all advanced scientific and mystical knowledge.

Their central tenet hinges on the idea that the divine lies somewhere in all humans. This can be directly traced back to the Gnostics. Rosicrucian philosophy influenced a number of seventeenth century thinkers, among them Francis Bacon and members of the Royal Society, such as Isaac Newton. Other prominent Rosicrucians have included architect Sir Christopher Wren, Dante, and Benjamin Franklin.

The Rosicrucians were linked with Freemasonry at an early date. Since their symbol of the Rosy Cross is used in the symbolism of the Order of the Garter, they have been linked to this secret society. It is also true that many famous men who were either Rosicrucians or Masons have been knighted into the Order of the Garter. Dr. John Dee, an alleged Grand Master of the Order, was a confidant of Queen Elizabeth I. He was involved in many of the political intrigues of her reign. He was a prolific product of his times, who could easily have been called a "Renaissance Man," for his varied and extensive interests. Dee was a renowned mathematician, navigator, cartographer, magician, and natural scientist who went all over Europe studying occultic doctrines from the leading mystics. He was also well versed in the pre-Christian teachings of Hermes Trismegistus, Zoroaster, and the Gnostics. He even owned a copy of the "Corpus Hermeticum" and had made a deep study of the pagan Mysteries and mythologies of ancient Egypt.

Politically, Dee was a forerunner of Cecil Rhodes. He had dreams of an imperial England and wanted his country to assume its rightful position in the world as a maritime power. He and his followers helped foment the Protestant Reformation, not because they wanted real reform, but because they knew that a religious revolt would weaken the power of the Catholic Church, an obstacle to their visions of power. Some things never change. The Rosicrucians, as well as the Masons, were liberal in their beliefs but they favored the Royalists in many cases because so many of them were members of the upper class in England. This was an intellectual dichotomy that did not seem to bother them.

Then there is an intimate connection between the Rosicrucians and the Freemasons. They share Gnostic roots. According to Dr. James W. Wardner's book, "Unholy Alliances," Freemasonry is similar to Manchaenism. It is a derivative of Gnosticism, which is the full realization by the Initiate of his divine nature and openness with the Supreme Being. Wardner also sees these roots at work in the New Age. "Gnosticism is back again and deluding millions." The New Age teaches the modern heresy: "Your search for these inner teachings will take you to both the historic and esoteric literature of the mystery schools. For centuries these secrets have been preserved and passed down. Manly Hall has described

Masonry as a "fraternity within a fraternity." The visible society is strictly for cover and fraternization. The invisible society is a secret society, an august fraternity that devotes itself to the service of a "sacred secret." The average Mason is unaware of the special nature of his secret society. The invisible society is protected by an oath of secrecy. While it is not a real religion, it offers a secular substitute for organized religion.

Freemasonry began as an occult movement of the seventeenth century. It emerged in England as the British form of revived Gnosticism analogous to the Rosicrucian movement in Germany. It dates its modern origin to 1717, during the reign of Charles II. While tracing its roots back to the architectural and construction guilds of the middle Ages, modern Freemasonry is rooted in a post-Reformation revival of Gnostic thought and occult practice. Their mythical history serves well to protect it during the religiously intolerant atmosphere in Great Britain at the time of its founding.

Gnosticism is the doctrine of salvation by knowledge and the acknowledgement of the secret mysteries of the Universe and of magic formula indicative of that knowledge. This knowledge reflects upon man's refusal to accept the order of things with man being subject to his Creator. W. L. Wilmshurst in "The Masonic Initiation" admitted "Freemasonry is the revival of the ancient Gnosis, the notorious heresy which was a synthesis of the pagan theosophies, against which the early fathers of the Church waged such a bitter struggle." The gnosis has as its principle dogma, Pantheism, through which man gains the knowledge of the identity of his being with the divine being. Masonic author Oswald Wirth believed that man "by giving free reign to his noblest aspirations, is on the path to achieving his own divinity.

It is hard to pinpoint the origins of Freemasonry. Masonry goes back 5000 years to the secret societies of the ancient Egyptian priests. They employ the same signs, symbols, grips, and postures. Early Masonic historians regard Hiram Abiff as a symbolic representative of Osiris, the Egyptian god of death and rebirth. Occult tradition believes that Hiram was secretly a member of an ancient society, the so-called "Dionysian Artificers," who appeared around 1000 BC. They believed that the temples had to be erected through sacred geometry, which reflected the divine plan of God. By the use of symmetry, measurement, and proportion, the Artificers constructed holy buildings to represent the human body as a symbol of the universe. Their theory of architecture was based on the hermetic philosophy and the pantheistic pagan belief in the unity of the universe and God.

John Robinson has called the Freemasons the most successful secret society in the history of the world in his 1989 book "Born in Blood: The Lost Secrets of Freemasonry." Manly Hall, a high ranking Mason once wrote, "join those who are really the living powers behind the thrones of modern national and international affairs." They believe they are the guardians of the ancient secrets of life collected and practiced by history's greatest philosophers and adepts, known as the Mysteries. These Mysteries are occultic secrets based on ritual magic that aid its practitioners in learning how to gain and use power and wealth, how they can control the fate of men and nations and maybe achieve a measure of immortality.

The Freemasons, the Rosicrucians, and the Cabalists have kept these secret teachings alive for centuries. They are all a part of Luciferianism and have been dormant until the last century. They behave behind closed doors because their occultic meanings would not stand the light of public scrutiny. Their devilish scheme is simply the glorification of man at the expense of the glorification of God. The New Age has removed the conscious existence of judgment, heaven, and hell from public and personal awareness. Since moral relativism teaches that there is neither good nor evil, neither right nor wrong, how can there be any judgment.

Freemasonry is an organization based on "the Fatherhood of God and the brotherhood of man." Writer George Johnson has called their teachings, "morality veiled in allegory and illustrated by symbols." It is probably the largest secret society in history with currently nearly five million members scattered all over the globe. Masons claim that they are not a secret society, but a "society with secrets." Most Masons never advance to the inner circle of the 33rd degree and so are largely unexposed to the more esoteric secrets of advanced Freemasonry.

There is irony in the fact that Masonry is often labeled a political or religious conspiracy, its members are prohibited from discussing either during their lodge meetings. Masonry like other secret societies advocates a religion, sometimes referred to as "Illuminism." William Still says this is a polite term for "Luciferianism" but it differs significantly from Satanism "The Masonic religion should be, by all of us initiates of the high degrees, maintained in the purity of Luciferian doctrine." The Luciferian religion teaches that man can become god in that he can evolve through initiatory steps into a god state himself. They believe that man can attain more wisdom and spiritual advancement by studying their secret knowledge than he can from any traditional religion. By being freed of any creed or sect, the Mason can be the "Master of all faiths." They do not believe in a creed or a doctrine but a universal expression of Divine Wisdom. It is a very sacred and secret faith that has existed for all. As Manly Hall has written in his "Lost Keys," Freemasonry "is the perfect wisdom of God revealing Himself through the secret hierarchy of illuminated minds. The big difference between Satanism and Luciferism is that the former admits it is bad and while the latter thinks it is good. Masons have darker goals but one must penetrate their humanistic facade. They have an inner and outer doctrine like an onion.

Freemasonry is simply Theosophy. It is the perpetuation of the worship of the old pagan gods of ancient Egypt, Greece, and India or the contention is that God revealed himself ages ago, long before the Christian era, to the whole world. They believed that the "myths and legends of every race, including Christianity, are only local variations of the same revelation." They believe they are in a New Age and look forward to this transformation using the insights and wisdom of the ancient mystics. Masonry believes that when "we talk to God, we are talking to ourselves. It is all about the God within.' They hold firmly that the supreme human purpose is the perfection of man. Man is a superior being, because he contains within himself the faculties and powers by which he can perceive his true place in a divine order of things.

According to Masonic sources, the most important Masonic mystery is an ancient plan passed down for millennial by oral tradition for the establishment of a world government or plans for a universal democracy, a "New Atlantis." In the 16th century this plan was under the guardianship of the British Empire. Today the elite of the secret societies are still taught that bringing forth a new cooperative commonwealth of mankind or a new "Atlantis League" is the natural form of government and the highest calling one can dedicate himself to. This enlightened world will be free of religion. Many of the elite associate religion with persecution, inquisition, torture, and death.

Masons are as interested in symbolism and imagination as are the Catholics. Their basic beliefs show that they display all the elements of a religion and as such rival that of the Gospel of Christ. They have temples, altars, prayers, a moral code, worship, vestments, feast days, and the promise of reward or punishment, initiation and burial rites. The "Eye of Osiris" is the main symbol, found on the back of our dollar bill. The sun is the symbol that represents the Mason personally. They place great emphasis on numerical symbolism. The number "seven" is especially an important number. The pyramid on our currency is a symbol firmly fixed in the legend of Atlantis. In Atlantis stood a great university where most of the arts and sciences originated. The structure that housed the university was an immense pyramid with many galleries and corridors and observatory for the stars sitting on its immense apex.

Freemasonry has within it the core of the secret heart of the occultic mysteries, wrapped up in numbers, metaphors, and symbols. The essential features of Freemasonry are called landmarks. Masonic authority has the power to establish their number, which vary from 15 to 60. These landmarks include the ability to recognize one another by special handshakes, the three-degree system, including the royal arc, the Hiramic legends of the third degree, the right of ever Mason to visit every lodge in the world. Masons profess a belief in God and the immortality of the soul, the equality of all Masons in the lodge, the necessity of secrecy, and the symbolic way of teaching. A Masonic lodge will initiate members of all religions in a universal brotherhood.

Their promise of "hidden wisdom" was one of their great attractions. The Grand Lodge of London served as a political and social gathering for middle class liberals who sought to improve society through free speech, elections, and secularism. Their meetings resounded with tolerance, respect for all humans and altruism. They sound strikingly like a meeting of the Council of Foreign Relations today.

They believe that the fall of man, necessity of baptism, the sacraments, the church, the Incarnation and Resurrection are unfit subjects for discussion within their walls. It is indeed a religious organization. The Masonic initiate is told to seek the light. He is told that if he if he adheres to Masonic principles he will reach the haven of the celestial lodge. It is not a Christian institution. Masonic law is clear that the mention of the name of Jesus Christ within the lodge or the use of His name in prayer is forbidden as offensive to non-Christian brethren. It is also akin to the Mafia, the Chinese tong and the Mau Mau in its use of oaths, calling God down to witness a truth. The penalties for breach of their oath, like the breach of the Mafia vow of silence, omerta, is very severe. The adept believes that "under no less penalty that that of having my body severed in two, my bowels taken from then and burned to ashes, the ashes scattered before the four winds of heaven."

Masons also believe masonry was a restatement of the religion of mankind. They suggest that there are two religions, namely the one for the educated and the enlightened and the other for the masses of people. The masters have kept the religious teachings intact throughout the centuries. Hiram was a builder mentioned in 1 Kings 7:13-45. He was employed by King Solomon to help build the Temple of Jerusalem. He disappeared after this from the pages of history. The Masons have added to his biography, saying that in working on the Temple, he became aware of the Word of God. They added that he was murdered by his artisan colleagues, because he would not reveal to them what he had learned in the secret part of the temple. His death became symbolic for new members who die and are reborn into the craft. This should like their version of Jesus' death and resurrection. They have three basic realities they believe: there is an omnipresent, eternal boundless and immutable principle that is ineffable, beyond any limiting description of human language, the end point of metaphysical speculation, the rootless root and the uncaused cause. Natural law is a representation of the permanency of the absolute.

In the Middle Ages, the influence of the Masonic Guilds was still very important. Rumors connected them with the Templar Order. It was said that during the Crusades the Knights Templar rescued a small group of Syriac Christians, who claimed to be descendent from the Essene sect, from the Saracens. These Christians were initiated in the innermost circle of the Order and were taught all their occult mysteries. They later left the Holy Land and traveled all over Europe taking their ideas as far away as England and Scotland. During the Middle Ages, opposition to the Holy Roman Catholic Church was forced underground to avoid the Inquisition and its attendant horrors. This was one of the few groups that could move freely throughout Europe and were the guilds of stone masons, who maintained meeting halls or lodges in every major city.

The rites and passages through Masonry are long and involved. Basically there are two kinds of Masons, according to the York rite and the Scottish rite. The latter was established in the United Sates in 1801. There are 32 degrees with the 33rd reserved as an honorary accomplishment. Membership in the Ancient Order of the Nobles of the Mystic Shrine, the fun organization is open to 32nd-degree Masons or Knights Templar.

Some lodges began to admit honorary members to bolster their sagging membership. The first known non-working was John Boswell, who was admitted to the Edinburgh, Scotland Lodge in 1600. These non-working Masons were initiated into the secrets, grips, passwords, and symbols. Eventually the non-operative outnumbered the regular masons. The lodges became symbols of morality, which used the older symbols to inculcate particular ethical and moral lessons. These guilds employed secret symbols, the so-called masons' marks found in these old churches. They also developed secret passwords and a special handshake so they could recognize each other. It is believed that Masons received a special knowledge or a "gnosis" that was incorporated into this sacred cant.

English Freemasonry has from early Hanoverian times enjoyed the favors of the royal family and the established church. George VI, the father of Queen Elizabeth II, was an active Mason and his brother, the former King Edward VIII was a past provincial Grand Master. The Grand Lodge of Scotland, from which many American chapters have received their charters, was formed in 1736. Robert Burns, the poet was one of their most famous members.

Freemasonry crossed the English Channel, establishing its first lodge in Dunkirk in 1721. Many of these tended toward atheism and they often dallied in the occult. They honored Voltaire as one of their brothers. Some historians say that their role in the French revolution has been exaggerated. Savalette de Lage founded one of the most politically active of the Masonic lodges of the eighteenth century. It was a secret society called the "Friends of Truth." The political philosophy of the group mapped out the ground plan for the social revolution that was to energize the French Revolution.

Lodges were created all through Europe during the next fifty years. In Italy, the first lodges were established in Naples in 1764. Frederick the Great of Germany, who was a Freemason and a student of the occult, founded two Masonic lodges in 1767. The Order of the Architects of Africa, which was devoted to the Manicheanism and the Knights of the light, practiced the magical arts. One of the many titles used by the Masonic secret societies founded by Frederick was that of the Illuminati. The revolutionary Garabaldi formed a grand orient in Palermo in 1860. And in 1872 at Mazzini's funeral, Masonic symbols dominated the street decorations. In Russia, Emperor Peter III served as grand master. Leo Tolstoy discusses it in his classic War and Peace. Freemasonry has even spread to Africa, usually in European colonies. Surprisingly the Nazis, Italian Fascists, and Soviet Communists all outlawed Freemasonry are at one time or another.

Masons have been an integral part of American life since the American Revolution. The first lodges came to the American colonies in the 1730's from England's 1717 union of four major lodges into the Grand Lodge of London. Daniel Coxe became Provincial Grand Master of New York in 1730. Benjamin Franklin joined in 1731 and later served as Grand Master of the Philadelphia Lodge. That year he was elected provincial Grand Master of the Masons in Pennsylvania. In 1734, he published an edition of the Book of Constitutions in 1734. George Washington was initiated in 1752. Other patriots included Paul Revere, John Paul Jones, Alexander Hamilton, and Patrick Henry. While many of the signers of the Declaration of Independence were Masons as well as many of Washington' generals, they were unaware of Freemasonry's master plan.

Much has been made of Washington's membership in the Freemasons. The truth is at one point he was offered the leadership of American Freemasonry and turned it down. In 1798, during the controversy over French Minister, the notorious, Citizen Genet," Washington severely criticized the affiliate of the Masons, the Jacobin clubs and the Illuminati as diabolical. He later read Professor John Robinson's book, "Proofs of a Conspiracy." He thought American Freemasonry was much more honorable than that of England.

One of the great controversies in nineteenth-century history revolved around Masonry. The Anti-Masonic Party formed as a result of the mysterious disappearance of William Morgan. It generated a great deal of anti-Mason feelings unleashing with it more ideas of conspiracy. The fact that many of these anti-Masons also hated President Andrew Jackson, who was also a Mason, just intensified the situation. This was the same passionate dislike of aristocratic institutions like the National Bank but Jackson opposed that also.

In 1826 Morgan had divulged the Order's secrets. In his book, "Illustrations of Masonry By One of the Fraternity Who Has Devoted Thirty Years to the Subject," Morgan, who might be called "the Salmond Rusdie" of his day, exposed all their secrets, including emblems, grips and signs. His thin 110-page book effectively sealed his death warrant.

Morgan was a former Mason living in Western New York State. He knew the secret nature of the society. He believed it represented an affront to representative Republican government. It was held to be a fraternity of the privileged class. Hofstadter was taken back by the extreme dislike for Freemasonry. He was not content to say that Masonry was a bad idea but such anti-Masons as David Bernard, in his book "Light on Masonry" described the group as an "engine of Satan, dark unfruitful, selfish, demoralizing, blasphemous murderous, anti-republican and anti-Christian." He put an apocalyptic cast to hating the Masons.

Robert Remini in his book "The Revolutionary Age of Andrew Jackson" says the Masonic Order had arranged for his abduction and probable murder. He just disappeared less than a month after his book came out. This caused a reaction to the lodges. His book talked foretold his punishment, as this is a torture to your flesh, so may it ever is to your mind and conscience if you ever should attempt to reveal the secrets of Masonry unlawfully. He ran a third party candidate in the election of 1832. The National Bank was the big issue. They garnered eight percent at the poles. The disappearance of William Morgan led to the birth of American single-issue politics. The Strauss family built Masonic pillars into Macy's in New York.

The Catholic Church has had a long and controversial history with the Freemasons. In 1737, King Louis XV prohibited Roman Catholics from joining any Masonic group. In the papal bull, promulgated in "Eminenti," on April 28, 1738, Pope Clement XII condemned Masonry as incompatible with Catholic belief. He went further, describing the quasi religion as "Satan's synagogue." Clement condemned its secrecy as an unlawful practice that could subvert and overthrow nations and governments, thus hurting the shaky stability of Europe. He condemned and prohibited secret societies, assemblies, reunions, or any other gathering of the Masons. "We condemn and forbid them by this, our present constitution, which is to be considered valid forever." This condemnation was precipitated by the public declaration of the Grand Master of the French lodges, the Duc d'Anton who preached the revolutionary ideals of liberty, universal brotherhood, love, and equality.

No fewer than eight popes have condemned the Freemasons on over four hundred occasions. The last to do so was Pope Leo XIII, whose encyclical letter, Annum Ingressi, on March 18, 1902, reaffirmed their historic denunciation. The penalty for disobeying this papal edict was excommunication that is, a complete cutting off from the Church saving graces. The Jesuits blamed them for the suppression of their order in the 1780s, an odd occurrence since they had been accused of coming under their influence. Maybe that was a deliberate guise and they had been conquered by infiltration. Official opposition of the Catholic Church to Freemasonry dates back to the papal bulls in 1738 and 1751. The true history of the Freemasons is a thoroughly tangled and suspicious story, filled with intrigue relating to the Masonic secrecy charges of Satanism was made about Freemasonry. The last half of the nineteenth century witnessed a proliferation of secret societies modeled after the Freemasons. They included such diverse groups as the Knights of the Pythias, the Independent Order of Odd Fellows and the Sons of Temperance. In 1894 Catholics were forbidden to join these oath-taking organizations but the penalties were less severe than for the Masons.

Pope Leo XIII attacked the secret society again in 1884 and said: "Freemasons, like the Manatees of old, strive as far as possible to conceal themselves and to admit not witnesses but their own members." He provided the definitive condemnation of Freemasonry came with his encyclical "Humanum Genus." He vehemently warned that the Freemason's major aim was "to persecute Christianity untamed hatred and they will never rest until they see cast to the ground all religious institutions established by the Pope." Leo warned that the Masons had already infiltrated the Church itself. "Far too many of our compatriots, driven by hope of their personal advantage or by perverse ambition, have given their name or support to the sect." He also warned that media, including the theater and fine arts, as well as the schools and universities, conspire "to pervert minds and corrupt hearts."

Their ultimate purpose, he continued, is the "utter overthrow of that whole religious and political order of the world which Christian teaching has produced and the substitution of a new state of things in accordance with their ideas of which the foundations and laws shall be drawn from Naturalism." He added that the Masons taught, "The great error of the day," the belief that "regard for religion shall be held as an indifferent manner, and that all religions are alike." He said that this plan was "deliberate," and other groups, such as the Communists and Socialists were also involved. He vowed to "tear away the mask from Freemasonry," and let it be seen and judged for what it really was and not what it pretended to be. Christianity and Freemasonry are essentially incompatible. In 1917 the Church declared that anyone who was a Mason was excommunicated from the Church. The Roman Catholic Church sensed that the Masons were eager to destroy the Church and so the Pope condemned the Freemasons in 1938. Catholics were prohibited from joining the secret order under pain of excommunication and possible eternal damnation.

Paul Fisher, in his book "Behind Closed Doors," states that it was the courts that excised the Christian religion from America's schools. Since then the Masons have been able to install their own brand of religion or secular humanism into the schools. To Fisher, their religion is "a revolutionary world-wide movement, organized to advance Kabalistic Gnosticism." Their goal is "to undermine and, if possible, to destroy Christianity." They plan to do this by infusing "Masonic philosophy into key government structures," so as to subvert any government, which does not conform to Masonic principles. Dr, James D. Carter has called the Lodge "the missionary of the new order." It was a liberal order, with the Masons serving as "high priests." Humanists believe that any child who believes in God is mentally ill.

According to the "Sunday Visitor Catholic Almanac," the principles of Freemasonry are said to "embody a naturalistic religion, active participation in that is incompatible with Christian faith and practice." The church rejects membership in Freemasonry for Catholics because "it is a kind of religion unto itself that includes temples, altars, worship services, vestments, feast days, a hierarchy and promises of eternal reward and punishment." Were a Catholic to join, it would be like belonging to two distinctly different religions. Much later Pius XII condemned Freemasonry on the grounds of its naturalism, oaths, religious indifferentism, and its possible threat to Church and state. Pope John Paul II resisted the Church's opposition to Catholic membership in 1983 because "their principles have always been regarded as irreconcilable with the church's doctrine." They also promoted the human ideal of Utopia on earth, and expressed it in symbolic form. While many Masons are nominally Christian, their constant use of pagan symbols, rituals etc. indicate that they still remain pagan at heart. The Pope could see the full religious and geopolitical implications of Freemasonry. Its Lodges included not only the new and deeply influential intellectuals of the day but also the most powerful political leaders of the day. This spelled trouble for the Church. Occult expert, Edith Starr Miller, has called Gnosticism "the Mother of Freemasonry."

The fun-loving Shriners, founded in 1871 in New York City, have no official standing with Freemasonry, but enjoy a great following among U.S. Masons. The Order of the Eastern Star is a quasi-Masonic society that initiates women as well as men. Boys between the ages of fourteen and twenty-one, who are relatives of a Mason, can join the Order of de Molay, who was the last leader of the Knights Templar, suppressed at the Council of Vienna, in 1311. This group was founded in Kansas City in 1919. It serves as a novitiate for the Masons.

Masonry has its many defenders. One of the leading proponents of American Freemasonry was Albert Pike. (1809-1891) He was the undisputed leader of Masonry in America for many years. He once called the papacy "a deadly, treacherous enemy." In a letter he wrote near the end of 1886, Pike wrote, "The Papacy has been for a thousand years the torturer and curse of Humanity," the most shameless imposture, in pretense to spiritual power of all ages. Many Protestant denominations have also denounced Freemasonry.

Pike was an evil man. He believed that Lucifer was God. In a letter to fellow Illuminist, Giuseppe Mazzini, on August 15, 1871, he wrote: "we shall unleash the Nihilists and Atheists, and we shall provoke a formidable social cataclysm which in all its horror will show clearly to the nations the effects of absolute atheists, origin of savagery and of the most bloody turmoil." He believed the reaction of the world majority in destroying these revolutionaries and iconoclasts will cause them to be disillusioned with Christianity and then more susceptible to receiving the "true light, through the universal manifestation to the pure doctrine of Lucifer, brought finally out in the public view." Both Christianity and Atheism will be destroyed.

Pike says that it must deceive its members in the first three or the Blue Degrees. They are the outer courts of the portico of the Temple. It is well enough that most Masons believe that the essence of the faith is contained in those initial three degrees. They must swear blood oaths that they never will reveal these secrets under pain of a barbaric death. Jesus said in John 18:20 "I have said nothing secretly." Women would make their husbands quit if they knew about the bloody oaths. The secrecy makes them feel special as if they were part of an elite group.

Carl Claudy in his book, "Introduction to Freemasonry," published in 1931 called Pike "a mystic, a symbolist, a teacher of the hidden truths of Freemasonry." He quoted Pike as saying "We worship God, but it is the God that one adores without superstition." To him this was Lucifer who did not require his followers to cast a supplicant knee before him. According to Pike's duality, Lucifer is the good god and the Christian God is the real evil God. Pike's teachings are reminiscent of those of Adam Weishaupt. They both emphasized a new religion where wisdom and reason becomes god. Paul Fisher, in his book, "Behind the Lodge Door," predicted that "Masonry will eventually rule the world."

In his 2002 book, "The Freemasons," Jasper Ridley articulates on the persecution Masons have suffered through the centuries, stresses the importance of Masonry for both of these epic events. He blames the dictatorial policies of the Vatican for opposing the progress that Masonry has stood for. He emphasizes the importance of advancing the revolutionary spirit embodied in the French

Revolution without much mention of the major atrocities that sent so many Catholics to the guillotine. He uses this same omission in writing about the oppression of the Franco government in the Spanish Civil War, without mentioning the thousands of priests and nuns who were murdered by the Communists. His approach is reminiscent of the liberal avoidance and omission of the atrocities of the Russian Revolution and its ensuing seventy years of dictatorial rule, replete with mass murder. Ridley stresses their tolerance for all religions to the extent that the value of religion is dismissed into a black hole of indifferentism. This not only lessens dogmatic fidelity to a particular religion but also waters down religious faith into meaningless platitudes about the dignity of man. God is left to fend for Himself on the periphery of the public marketplace.

It is odd that in the American colonies the papal condemnation of Freemasonry was not promulgated by Bishop John Carroll, whose brother were an active Mason and a practicing Catholic. James Hobbs, the Irish-American architect who designed the White House was another example of a practicing Catholic who was a Mason. The Masons have six million members worldwide, with most of them centered in United States and England.

Fourteen American presidents have been Masons, including Andrew Jackson, Andrew Johnson, James A. Garfield, William Taft, both Roosevelts, Harry S Truman and Gerald Ford. This does not include Lyndon Johnson, who started in the Masons but never advanced. Other prominent Americans, who were Masons, include, Henry Clay, John Jacob Astor, Mark Twain, Andrew Mellon, Will Rogers, Henry Ford, Charles Lindbergh, J. Edgar Hoover and General Douglas McArthur.

Paul Fisher notes the Unitarian influence within the Masonic lodge. They focus on competence more than morals. Ralph Waldo Emerson was a Transcendentalist, which had strong strains of Unitarianism in it. They stress a liberalism that causes us to put our faith in the exertions of our own minds instead of the dogmas of the church. Fisher learned a lot about Masonry from "New Age Magazine." From reading their magazine, he concluded that international Freemasonry has been historically a revolutionary movement to advance what he terms, "Kabalistic Gnosticism," which has as its aim the undermining and the destruction of Christianity. They do this by infusing government institutions with Masonic principles. Fisher concludes that most Masons are unaware of the diabolical plans of their elite. Fisher says that John Robison, a highly regarded professor of philosophy and a member of the Royal Society of Edinburg wrote of Continental Masonry that it "was a strange mixture of mysticism, theosophy, cabalistic whim, real science, fanaticism and freethinking, both in religion and politics."

TIME Magazine's May 25, 1998 article by David Van Biema profiled the Freemasons today. It claims to be the oldest fraternal society. It does mention some of the stranger elements, including the threats of bodily mutilation if any Mason were to reveal its deep secrets, secret handshakes. To them God is "the Grand Architect." The ranks seem to be steadily declining in America, as evidenced by the title of the article "Endangered Conspirators." It started as a gentleman's club in seventeenth century England. By 1717 it became the engine of the European Enlightenment. Masonry quickly became a humanistic religion, mixing very little religious fervor with a good deal of personal ritual. This enraged clergymen and engaged conspiracy theorists.

Christianity presents the exact opposite image. Its central images include the Cross, the babe in the manger, and eternal judgment. Masonry is more interested in a secularization, an utopian idea of man's best hopes being actualized here on earth, not some" a pie in the sky when we die" vision of eternal life. Unfortunately, building man's habitat here on earth was implicit in Vatican II's ideal attempt to join with all peoples for a better world. It is apparent that the virus of secular humanism is wiping away the whole vocabulary of religious faith. It is transforming Catholicism from a religion that must adhere to the truth or die in a culture that must change with the world or be left behind, suffering from a darkening of the intellect. It is always demonic when dark forces are at work.

Any discussion of secret societies would be incomplete without, at least a cursory exploration of Adolph Hitler and his Nazi philosophy. The Nuremberg prosecutors were never allowed to delve into the occult nature of the Nazi philosophy. The multi-nation tribunal ruled it inadmissible because it feared the psychological and spiritual implications in the Western nations. Some thought the Nazi philosophy could be used to mount a defense for their human atrocities. Others realized that the United States and its allies were not free from the same blame they heaped on the Nazis.

The Nazis saw themselves as leading far more than a political movement. Their philosophy had strong metaphysical underpinnings. They regarded themselves as leading a quasi-religious movement for total control of the culture. It was born out of a secret society, which had some of the same goals and motivations as the Illuminati and the Masons. They were determined to change human nature, to create a "new man" These words were descendent from Philosophes of the French Revolution.

According to conspiracy scholar Jim Marrs, Nazis was the creation of secret societies, with the occult philosophy and western businessmen, including international bankers. Hitler served as a balance to the rise of Soviet Communism. More possibly, it created such unrest and dissolution in the world that the bankers could profit more greatly.

Marrs also says that there is "abundant evidence" that World War II was brought about by the agents and members of secret societies connected with the Illuminati and the Freemasons in both Germany and Great Britain. It was in the "good war" that the older mystic societies, "seeking freedom from both church and state merged with the modern secret societies concerned primarily with wealth, power and control." The "secret" of all secret societies is that the Biblical account of the "the fall" is false and Lucifer is really God.

3

Voltaire's Bastards

"I shall never cease to repeat that the Revolution has
come from masonry and that writers and the Illuminati
made it." Aloys Hoffman

A college friend once stated that "all originality was nothing
more than undetected plagiarism." Some ideas maintain a nuclear
life. The ideas promoted by cultural communists, Antonio Gramsci,
and the Frankfurt School fit this mold. One such "original thinker"
was Adam Weishaupt, who is best known to conspiracy theorists.
It is unfortunate that so many of these enthusiasts have been isolated
from mainstream society for their suspicions.

Born on February 6, 1748 in Bayern (Bavaria) Germany,
Weishaupt's parents were Orthodox Jews who converted to the
Catholic Church. After the death of his father, he was sent to be
educated by the Jesuits. Young Weishaupt rebelled against their
discipline but did teach at the Bavarian University of Ingolstadt,
where he was the institution's first lay professor of Canon Law.
From the slim historical record of his personal life, it is clear that
he was what E. Michael Jones, has called a "degenerate modern"
whose incestuous relationship with his sister-in-law rivaled those
of Freud, and Jung. She became pregnant and Weishaupt tried to
induce an abortion through the use of powerful "chemical weapons
of fetal destruction." The abortion failed and his son was born on
January 30, 1784.

Fortunately for historians, Weishaupt did leave papers and letters that helped explain his thinking. Weishaupt built up a large personal library. He read many ancient manuscripts and became obsessed with the Great Pyramid of Giza. He was convinced that it was a prehistoric temple of initiation. He was an eclectic thinker who drew his inspiration from a myriad of ancient and esoteric sources, which included the Greek mystic Pythagoras and the ancient pagan religions. Weishaupt became an active supporter of the Protestant Reformation and was involved with many heated discussions with Catholic clergymen. He adopted the teachings of Jean Jacques Rousseau and the anti-Christian tenets of the Manicheans.

In 1770 he made the acquaintance of Danish merchant, named Franz Kolmer, who had lived in Alexandria and had made several trips to Giza. Author Nesta Webster called him "the most mysterious of all the mystery men." He had studied the esoteric knowledge of Persia and Egypt while living in the Middle East. He was a Gnostic who prided himself on his devotion to Manicheanism. Jim Marrs points out in his book "Rule by Secrecy" that Weishaupt showed his devotion to this secret knowledge when he got the Illuminati to switch to the Persian calendar.

Weishaupt christened his philosophy "Illuminism," a combination of occultic practices and demonic principles that were capable of twisting the minds and attracting candidates for their nefarious purposes. Illuminism was the public manifestation of a centuries-old struggle between organized religion and humanism based on ancient esoteric knowledge both mystical and secular. Such knowledge required great secrecy because of the persistent effort of both the church and the monarchies to silence them. The essence of Illuminati dogma is an unfettered liberty in moral matters, and socialization in political matters, so as to break the ties that bind the individual to the state.

The first record of the Illuminati dates back to early Christian history, a group of second-century Gnostics who claimed to have received a special divine knowledge that was ritually conferred on the elite and resulted in its recipient's salvation. This sect was also purported to have had ties with the Knights Templar who had brought "enlightened ideas" to Europe from the Holy Land centuries before Weishaupt. Some of the Rosicrucians called themselves "Illuminati." The sixteenth century Spanish groups, the Alumbrados, claimed to have received illumination directly from the Holy Spirit, independent of the Catholic Church. Because of their special "gnosis," many felt that they were exempt from any prohibition and so indulged their passions without restraint.

The Illuminati or "chosen ones" were the "new men," a superior order that looked down on all others as their inferiors. They believed that they had a pure and spiritual nature that transcended the normal confines of good and evil. In Gnostic terminology, it is the idea that gold sunk in filth does not lose its beauty but preserves its own nature. The filth is to penetrate the gold's surface, as evil is unable to penetrate the Illuminati's souls. Even if they were immersed in material deeds, nothing could not hurt them, nor could they lose their spiritual essence. This superior moral attitude is more properly called "antinomian libertinism." This medieval attitude does provide some prescient insight into the sordid behavior of former President Bill Clinton.

There is a spiritual connection between the Illuminati and Freemasonry through the sun and Isis cults of ancient Egypt. Like Masonry, Illumination had several degrees of illumination. The higher up the candidate advanced, the more enlightenment he received until finally he entered the secret realm of the "deep occult." In "Conspiracy," an 1969 article written for "Teenset Magazine," Sandra Glass traced the Illuminati to the dreaded Ishmaelian sect of Islam, also known as the Order of the Assassins, founded in 1090 by Hassan Sabah. This group combined the use of the drug hashish with murder as their primary path to "illumination."

Glass' article also states that Weishaupt was known to have studied the teachings of the leader of the infamous Hassan Sabah. Weishaupt was reputed to have induced his enlightenment from smoking homegrown marijuana. It is not surprising that the Illuminati adopted as their slogan, the phrase "Ewige Blumenkraft," which translates to "Eternal Flower Power," a harbinger of the 1960s when so many of his primordial Marxist ideas took root on the American culture. If they used drugs it was to enhance their intellects and travel to another dimension where the word of God could be more audible or even visible.

According to Gerald Winrod's pamphlet on Weishaupt, "A Human Devil," French Socialist Louis Blanc was quoted as calling him "one of the profoundest conspirators who ever lived." His would be the "mother of all conspiracies." Weishaupt was not fond of rules or laws at all. He wanted to abolish patriotism, nationalism, religion, the family and establish a universal brotherhood. He envisioned a dictatorship with him and his illuminati as the ruling elite. They tried to hide themselves as a philanthropic organization, not unlike the foundations in today's parlance. Weishaupt was as much the founding father of revolutionary communism as was Karl Marx.

Next to Abbe Barruel in his mammoth book, "A History of the Jacobins," Nesta Webster's books "World Revolution," and "Secret Societies and Subversive Movements," have the most extensive summaries of Weishaupt's Weltanschauung. He was a master of human psychology and motivation. Weishaupt was a master of human psychology and motivation. He effectively employed the Machiavellian tenet that "the ends justify the means," in establishing a weblike structure of agents with access to cardinals, princes, and kings all over Europe, spreading his principles through the culture. Behold our secret. Remember that the end justifies the means, and that the wise ought to take all the means to do good, which the wicked take to do evil." He also urged his followers not to shrink from violence if it served the ultimate cause. "Sin is only that which is hurtful, and if the profit is greater than the damage, it becomes a virtue."

The "Illuminati" vowed to overthrow the monarchy, the church, civil government, and private property. Dismayed by the deplorable state of humanity, they vowed to transform the human race. Weishaupt took care to enlist in his ranks as many young men of wealth and position as possible. Their most enthusiastic recruits have come from the universities. Given the state of public and private education today, it is not difficult to see their prophecy come to nefarious fruition. It can not be denied that modern Illuminati have transformed the modern universities into hotbeds of left-wing propaganda.

Weishaupt's goal was ultimately world revolution. His purpose was to convert his followers into blind instruments of his supreme will. He modeled his system after the Jesuits, adopting their system of infiltration and working through the culture, and the maxim that the ends justify the means. He induced mysticism into the workings of the brotherhood so that an air of mystery might pervade all his actions. He also adopted many of the classes and grades of the Freemasons and held out high hopes of communication of deep occult secrets in the higher ranks. Weishaupt hoped to liberate men from the state's authoritarianism and the church's domination so that they may regain their primordial freedom and equality. His main object was to establish a new religion and politically to establish a democratic republic that would effect the overthrow of many of Europe's reigning governments.

The Illuminati, like in France was based on enlightened reason, one that was liberated from the twin domination of the church and the state. While he copied the Jesuits, he really did not understand their movement and made nothing more than a caricature of their concept of authority and obedience. He wanted a veritable "revolution of the mind." Weishaupt was not interested in conquering territories nor imposing his temporal authority. His was a more sinister revolution, a revolution of the soul and mind that would lead its disciples away from God and allegiance to the Church. Like Hillary Rodham at Wellsley, Weishaupt reasoned that people had to undergo an internal change in their very human nature to effect his world revolution.

For the next five years, Weishaupt formulated his plan by which all occult systems could be coalesced into one and led by a single powerful one. On May 1st 1776, Weishaupt announced the foundation of "the Perfectibilists," the secret society's original name. This date is still celebrated in the Communist world, purportedly because of the abortive May 1, 1905 Russian Revolution. As his code name Weishaupt chose "Spartacus," after a Roman slave who led a slave revolt against the Roman government in 73 BC

Marxists have long claimed Spartacus as their own because his was a genuine attempt to remove the chains of Roman oppression. There is no indication that the Roman Spartacus had any ideological predisposition. His revolt had more in common with that of Scottish freedom fighter, William Wallace than any Marxist revolt. This did not stop left-leaning actor, Kirk Douglas and his production company from hiring the blacklisted Dalton Trumbo to write Stanley Kubrick's 1959 movie, "Spartacus."

Weishaupt attempted to create a cellular structure, not unlike what the communist decadents would attempt to establish universally under its Commintern in the early 20th century. Each cell was engaged in a physical and a psychological form of warfare that transcended the more visible conquests of the great conquers of history, such as Alexander the Greta, Genghis Khan, and Napoleon. Weishaupt established a weblike structure of agents with access to cardinals, princes, and kings all over Europe, spreading his principles. He believed that once the world was free of Christianity, the people would demand political freedom and everyone would want the right to enjoy life without moral straitjacket imposed upon it by the Churches, especially on sexual matters. Weishaupt wanted to restore human beings to the state of perfection that existed before the fall. He felt that the Church had been corrupted irretrievably and had turned its back on its early teachings in favor of maintaining political and economic domination over the peasants.

Religion was a special enemy for Weishaupt. As Sardinian Marxist Antonio Gramsci would later do, Weishaupt tried to neutralize the religious faith of his victims. "We must preach the warmest concern for humanity," and in doing so "make people indifferent to all other relations." He said, "We must preach the warmest concern for humanity," and in doing so make them indifferent to religion and its other worldly designs.

Weishaupt believed that the evil in the world came from institutions, such as the church and not from any flaw in man's human nature. The problem of evil would be finally solved when at last reason becomes the religion of men, then will the problem be solved. Weishaupt "believed that man's reason should set the moral tone for society, not the Bible. This fits in perfectly with the Philosophes. Reason will serve as the "only code of man." It would be the "the sun of reason which will dispel the clouds of superstition and prejudice." When reason became the religion of man, the world's problems will have their solutions. Conspiracy historian Ralph Epperson sees all this as the cause for today's social ills. As he wrote "the rational, illuminated mind sees that the society, the environment, and not the criminal is at fault for the actions of the individual."

Weishaupt's goal to was to deliver the "whole human race from all religion." He planned to infiltrate all of western society with his "initiates," who would undermine the basic civilization of the community. His "initiates," would infiltrate and undermine the basic functioning of its community. The Illuminati's efforts were directed so that each individual was placed where his talents would do the most good for the Order. The Illuminati knew its people— their strengths, weaknesses and utilized them to the best advantage of the master plan of world conquest.

Weishaupt adroitly devised a patently hierarchical organization. He was a rationalist who believed in the ideals of the Enlightenment but wanted to establish them through subterfuge. He wanted to build a just society on the twisted rubble of the existing corrupt society and in the process, modernize Germany through the discipline of a secret society, which had about three thousand members. Weishaupt concluded that mass uprisings were virtually useless.

Though only five people attended the first meeting of the Illuminati, it soon attracted many prominent members of Bavarian society who shared Weishaupt's egalitarian and socialist political ideas. Illuminati lodges spread all over Germany and later Weishaupt planned to infiltrate the Masonic lodges so as to establish a foothold on all of Europe. He felt that the future of the culture resided in its educational institutions. That's where one important battlefield was. "We must acquire the direction of education . . . of church management . . . of the professional chair and of the pulpit." Weishaupt knew that the secret to control was the dissemination of information. He wanted to preach the warmest concern for humanity, and "make people indifferent to all other relations." The case can be made that this ranks as the origin of modern secular humanism and religious indifferentism. The latter tells society that, it doesn't really matter what you believe, as long as you believe in something, whether it is "Indian mysticism, earth gods, angels or the Biblical Christ. They are all the same." Weishaupt's strategy was a forerunner of both secular humanism and religious indifferentism. In his pamphlet "Adam Weishaupt, A Human Devil," Gerald Winrod wrote, "Secret societies, sometimes founded on high precepts, are frequently prostituted by men of evil genius . . ."

It is Weishaupt's views on Christianity that are the most complex. The influence of Christianity on his thinking is unmistakable. He believed that once the world was free of Christianity, the people would demand political freedom and everyone would want the right to enjoy life without the moral straitjackets imposed upon it by the Churches, especially on sexual matters. He believed that the Church had been corrupted irretrievably and had lost its early teachings in favor of maintaining political and economic domination over the peasants. He says that with illumination, through human reason, nothing is "comparable to the discovery of what we are, our nature, our obligations, what happiness we are capable of, and what the means of attaining it." In comparison, "the most brilliant sciences are but amusements for the idle and the luxurious."

Weishaupt contended that Jesus had established no new religion. He had only set religion and reason in their ancient rights. To Weishaupt "Freemasonry is concealed Christianity." He suggested that his followers throw away the name "Christian," and substitute reason. It was the "cheats and tricks" of priest who have perverted true Christianity. Weishaupt rewrote the Gospels and the Christian creed to the extent that Jesus was not recognizable within his rational screed. It was Gnosticism at its core. Weishaupt believed that the secrets of Christianity must be received as the secret documents of Freemasonry. It is apparent that deep within the dark recesses of Weishaupt's fevered soul, one could recognize the strands of pure Luciferianism, an Orwellian inversion of standard notions of good and evil. At its highest level, members of the Illuminati were Satanists. They believed that Satan was the "good god," waiting to liberate mankind from the oppressions of the past. They saw their salvation with Lucifer, the new "god of light" that would allow them to become like gods. They equated the repression of the Catholic Church with the Judeo-Christian God.

Weishaupt wanted to root out all religious ideas and superstitions and replace them with a religion of reason. "When Reason becomes the religion of men, then will the problem be solved." This presaged the revolutionary ideas of Antonio Gramsci who rerouted dialectical materialism as a "long march through the culture," in the early twentieth century.

Both men and women were to be initiated into the Illuminati where sexual equality was the rule. Weishaupt sowed the seeds, not only of cultural Marxism, but also modern feminism when he wrote "there is no way of influencing men so powerfully as by means of the women. These should therefore be our chief study." Weishaupt believed that the Illuminati "should insinuate ourselves into their good opinion, give them hints of standing up for themselves." This is the same tactic employed by Herbert Marcuse and Betty Friedan. Weishaupt knew the innate power that women have been wielding over men for millennia. His thinking presaged the theme of Friedan's "Feminine Mystique." He adds that it would be "of immense relief to their enslaved minds to be freed from any one bond of restraint, and it will fire them the more . . . to work for us with zeal."

Weishaupt developed into a brilliant strategist who taught his followers that the way to completely transform society and culture was to acquire the direction of education, of church management of the universities and the pulpit. "We must bring our opinions into fashion by every art." Weishaupt also proposed that his adepts should try to influence "the military academies . . . the printing houses, booksellers shops, chapters and in short in all offices which have any effect in forming, or in managing, or even directing the mind of man." Weishaupt wanted to establish reading societies and subscription libraries. If Weishaupt's members could influence all the means of mass and personal communication, even the legal system, then he could "we may turn the public mind which way we will."

To assist in this, his secret society would establish lyceum like institutions that would serve as "hidden schools of wisdom," which one day would "free men from their bonds." The human race will then become one family, and the world the dwelling of Rational Man." Our great secret is that "reason will be the code of laws to all mankind."

The Illuminists also went after the educators, the opinion shapers, and the intellectuals. Weishaupt told his followers "We must win the common people in every corner. This will be obtained chiefly by means of the schools, and by open, hearty behavior." He urged his followers to show condescension, popularity, and toleration of their prejudices, which "at leisure we shall root out and dispel." Secrecy and deceit were the hallmarks of the Illuminati. If a writer publishes anything that attracts notice and is in itself just, but "does not accord with our plans, we must endeavor to win him over, or decry him." Weishaupt knew that the secret to control was the dissemination information. He urged his followers to show condescension, popularity, and toleration of their prejudices, which "at leisure we shall root out and dispel." Weishaupt told his followers to sometimes speak one way and "sometimes in another, so that one's real purpose should remain impenetrable to one's inferiors."

It is apparent that the Illuminati approach has abetted the cause of liberalism. It has also served as the nexus for the creation of several best selling books within the past year. As if he were re-inventing the wheel, newsman Bernard Goldberg awoke one morning to find out that his profession had been hijacked by a pernicious liberal "Bias." Ann Coulter used hundreds of examples to illustrate how conservative and Republicans ideas and leaders had suffered "Slander," while Mona Charen portrayed fifty years of liberal outrage and complaint as the work of communism's "Useful Idiots."

In anticipation of the French Revolution Weishaupt wrote, "Salvation does not lie where strong thrones are defended by swords, where the smoke of censers ascend to heaven or where thousands of strong men pace the rich fields of harvest. The revolution, which is about to break, will be sterile if it is not complete." He wanted to "direct all mankind," and influence "all political transactions." He yearned for the day when "princes and nations shall disappear off the face of the earth." Weishaupt foresaw the time "when men will have no other laws than the book of nature. This revolution will be the work of the secret societies and that is one of our great mysteries."

Weishaupt was a forerunner of world government. He was the first utopian to think in a global scale. He wrote: "With the origin of nations and peoples, the world ceased to be a great family." Nationalism was to take the place of human love. His vision of a superstate began with the abolition of private property, social authority, and nationality. He dreamed of a world without a "patriotism, nationalism, and the family."

Unlike anarchists who sought an end to all government, Weishaupt's Illuminati sought a "Novus Ordo Seclorum," a world government, dominated by "human-centered rationalism," administrated by a "dictatorship of the elite." Each leader would be likened to a god in his own realm. In the spirit that any liberal could be proud, Weishaupt taught that his followers "must direct all of mankind." Humans would automatically live in harmony and universal brotherhood, based on free love, peace, spiritual wisdom, and equality. Each would be linked to a god in his own realm. When the illuminati rule the world, Weishaupt reasoned "each member becomes a ruler." This was his group's major attraction. Weishaupt wrote, "we must direct all of mankind . . . The occupations must be so allotted and contrived that we may, in secret, influence all political trisections." He organized hgis Order," so that it could "be secret and to work in silence for thus it is better secured from the oppression of the ruling powers, and because this secrecy gives a greater zest to the whole . . . The slightest observation shows that nothing will so much contribute to increase the zeal of the members as secret union." The hidden meaning of language was also a very important part of his strategy. "One must speak sometimes in one way, sometimes in another, so that our real purpose should remain impenetrable to our inferiors."

Men are not bad except as he is made so by arbitrary morality. Men act badly because religion, the state, and bad examples pervert him. They chose blind faith above their own reason. Weishaupt wanted to replace the Christian religion with one of "Reason." This corresponds perfectly to Jean Jacques Rousseau and his "Philosophes." As Weishaupt wrote "the rational, illuminated mind sees that the society, the environment, and not the criminal is at fault for the actions of the individual." He also presaged the revolutionary ideas of Antonio Gramsci who would reroute dialectical materialism as a "long march through the culture," in the twentieth century.

Weishaupt was just twenty-eight, when he founded the sect but did not make much progress until Baron Von Knigge joined him in 1780. Friedrich Ludwig Baron Von Knigge, whose secret name was Philo, was the only other central figure in the Illuminati. He was a person of great energy and possessed a strong imagination. These two rapidly spread the gospel of the Revolution throughout Germany.

Weishaupt was shrewd enough to realize that his could not be an "open conspiracy." It had to take place quietly and in secret. Afraid that the German authorities would suppress them when they learned of their subversive activities, they grafted their group onto the Freemasons and worked their nefarious plots under their guise. He thought the German Masonic lodge would be the perfect nursery for his revolutionary seedbed.

The reason the Masonic Lodge was chosen was because it already had a reputation as a secret society. It had always been part of his plan to infiltrate the Masonic lodges so as to establish a foothold on all of Europe. He wanted "a Masonic lodge of our own . . . . We shall regard it as our nursery garden . . ." The Masonic lodges were deigned to serve as the Illuminati's incubator where Weishaupt's ideas would grow and gain acceptance because they could easily meld with the basic ideas of the lodges. The lodge in Munich was an excellent choice for Weishaupt's plan of infiltration. French revolutionist, Mirabeau underscored the real reason for the early success of the Illuminati, in that the Lodge Theodore de Bon Conseil at Munich "where there a few men with brains and hearts, were tired of being tossed about by the vein promises of Freemasonry." To most people, Freemasonry is a family-oriented benevolent society. Few are aware of its religious and political underpinnings. Author Malachi Martin demonstrated the sinister side of Masonry in his powerful 1996 novel of papal intrigue, "Windswept House."

Weishaupt's first contact with a Masonic lodge dated back to 1774. He had been extremely disappointed by their lack of real knowledge of the occult significance of Masonry and most of its members knew nothing about its pagan symbolism. In 1777, Weishaupt was inducted into the Mason Order, the Lodge Theodore of Good Council, in Munich. It was Von Knigge who brokered a "shotgun marriage," with Freemasonry at the Congress of Wilhelmsbad in 1778. It was at the Congress of Wilhelmsbad, a much-publicized meeting, where the Illuminati abandoned their claim of descent from the Knights Templars. This meeting proved a significant turning point for the order.

Their assembly held its first formal meeting on July 16, 1782. The secret assembly represented over three million secret society members all over the world. All attendees were sworn never to reveal, under pain of violent death, any of the assembly's proceedings. Although attendees were sworn to strict secrecy, the Count de Vireu later wrote in his autobiography, "the conspiracy, which is being woven, is so well thought out that it will be . . . impossible for the Monarchy and the Church to escape." A year later Von Knigge and Weishaupt split up. Since he had effected the fusion with the Masons, Von Knigge felt that entitled him to be co-ruler with Weishaupt. When Weishaupt refused to share his power, Von Knigge quit the order in 1784.

The Illuminati moved their headquarters to Frankfurt where they could receive financing from the Rothschilds. It was from the Frankfurt Lodge, where author William Still wrote the Illuminati "plan of world revolution was carried forward. Frankfurt became the seedbed of illuminated Freemasonry, a symbiotic union that bred evil for many generations to come. It spread like wildfire throughout the German principalities, Saxony, Prussia, then into Sweden. Later its thinking appeared in Scotland, England, Italy, Austria, and all throughout Europe, even Russia. It was Dr. John Robison who acknowledged with great regret that a number of British Masons were seduced by Illuminati rhetoric. By 1785, France was ripe for moral and political subversion. It even spread to America. They established a chapter in Virginia in 1786. They established the Cato-Italian Society in America and some referred to themselves as Jacobins.

It was during their ill-fated attempt to overthrow the Hapsburg government in 1784 that eventually led to their banishment. In July of 1785, disaster struck when an Illuminati courier named Lanz, racing through Ratisbon, now Regensberg, was struck and nearly incinerated by lightening. His pouch miraculously remained intact and extensive documents outlining the Illuminati's plans for revolution and world domination were retrieved. Four of Weishaupt's followers came forward to give evidence of the sinister nature of their secret society before by the Court of Enquiry. Their accounts left no doubt about the diabolical nature of Illuminism. They admitted that their goal was the annihilation of all religions, love of country and loyalty to sovereigns. It was revealed that the Illuminati possessed dreadful poisons, including a powder, which produced blindness. It was clear that they were not afraid to use this weapon of human destruction to silence an enemy or advance their cause.

Among the captured documents by the Bavarian police was Weishaupt's correspondence and other documents that included his "Essay on the Sect of the Illumnists," which was published in 1788. In it, Weishaupt described in lurid detail the process of initiation. Marks were made with blood on the prostrate nude body of the candidate. His testicles were bound with a pink and poppy-colored cordon. He then renounced all other human allegiances before five white-hooded phantoms with bloody banners after a "colossal figure," appeared through a fire. Then the bands and the marks were removed and he had to drink blood before seven black candles. It was later revealed that the Illuminati possessed dreadful poisons, including a powder, which produced blindness. It was clear that they were not afraid to use this weapon of human destruction to silence an enemy or advance their cause.

The Bavarian government realized that the Illuminati posed a direct threat to their society and condemned it as such. The Elector of Bavaria officially condemned Weishaupt's Illuminati. Weishaupt had no choice but to flee the country. By 1790 its two thousand members had simply fled to other countries while retaining their loyalties to the group's teachings. The Bavarian government published a series of documents entitled "Original Writings of the Order of the Illuminati" and distributed all over the Continent. But their warnings fell mostly on deafened ears. Weishaupt found sanctuary with Duke Ernst II in Gotha. From there, he continued his malevolent activities against God and His Church. He died on November 18, 1830.

It was easy for the Illuminati to go underground since they had merged with Continental Freemasonry earlier in the decade. Masonic historian Waite tried to distance Freemasonry from the Illuminati by writing "The connection of the Illuminati with the older Institution is simply that they adopted some of its Degrees and pressed them into their own service." Unfortunately, the rest of Europe refused to take Illuminism seriously. This is especially true of France.

It would be in France where eighteenth century Illuminism had its greatest success. The standard interpretation of the French Revolution is that it was the spontaneous action of the peasants. It was left to Weishaupt's spiritual heirs, revolutionaries, such as

Auguste Comte, Saint-Simon, Count Mirabeau, Robespierre, and Danton, to pick up his baton and continue Weishaupt's social and moral revolution. While these progenitors of the French Revolution were not officially Illuminati, they surely traveled on their same broad highway of revolution. They had all supped at the Weishaupt's banquet table of blood, violence and sexual perversion. All the revolutionary leaders of the revolution were members of these illuminati lodges.

Voltaire spread through the Grand Orient Lodge of Freemasonry. All the revolutionary leaders of the revolution were members of these illuminati lodges. The Illuminati seedbed of revolution in France was centered in the town of Lyons. It was the Duc d' Orleans who became its first Grand Master. There were many contrived grievances that contributed to the start of the French Revolution. The Duc d' Orleans, a member of the Illuminati, purchased large quantities of grain to cause the French people to take their grievances to the King. The Illuminati spread the rumor that the king had hoarded the grain. He eventually fell victim to the Revolution and lost his head on the guillotine. It is apparent that the Illuminati had infiltrated the Masonic lodges but there were other forces at work in France.

Auguste Comte, the "Father of Sociology," was another who picked up Weishaupt's baton. It was he who perpetuated the search for a science of society through a three-step theory of progress. Comte believed that mankind moved from a theological era through a metaphysical one into a "positive" era. Though essentially apolitical, positivism relied on the intellectual elite to inform and direct the transitions. This was the first intelligentsia that would populate and promote all the liberal schemes of the next two hundred years.

Saint-Simon was one of the first to popularize the notion that truth was not absolute but historical and is realized, not in individual thought but in social action. He was truly a seminal intellectual force. Like Weishaupt, Saint-Simon wanted a new religion. His real faith was in science but his death in 1828, left his followers in doubt as to whether his "New Christianity," was to be the moral basis of his new society or just fill the void until the masses were sufficiently educated to accept the new scientific religious doctrines.

Another prominent revolutionary was Count Mirabeau, who was reputed to have been an Illuminist, as were many others such as Garat, Robespierre, Danton, Desmoulins, and many others. In 1782, Mirabeau had announced that he was a member of a secret organization, influenced by the Knights Templar, whose goal was to destroy the Catholic Church and the crown, so that a religion of love could be established in France.

It is obvious that the revolutionary spirit of world change and the overthrow of the establishment, especially the clericalism of France, appealed to both the Illumnists and the Jacobins. From the time the first Jacobin club was organized, the club system grew to over a hundred and fifty by 1790. A year later they had a honeycomb system that stretched all over France. They brought a perverted sense of order to the chaos that was revolutionary France. Weishaupt's disciples, such as Bode and Baron de Busche, were able to influence many of these clubs and further the cause of dogmatic atheism.

Mirabeau has been reputed to say when the Bastille was stormed on July 14, 1789, "The idolatry of the monarchy has received a deathblow from the sons and daughters of the Order of the Templar. The Masonic tenets of equality, liberty, and fraternity became the battle cry of the mob with the red banner, a Masonic symbol of universal love. It was openly carried in the streets during the bloodshed. When Louis XVI lost his head, it was heard that de Molay is avenged!" The entire plan of the French Revolution was found within the papers of Mirabeau, the Freemason and Illuminati. An important document, "Croquis ou Project de Revolution de Monsieur de Mirabeau," was seized at the home of the wife of Mirabeau's publisher. Mirabeau demanded that they "overthrow all order, suppress all laws, annul all power and leave the people in anarchy . . ." To accomplish this, Mirabeau urged his followers to "caress their vanity, flatter their hopes, promise them happiness." To him "the people are a lever which legislators can move at their will, we must necessarily use them as a support and render them hateful to them everything we wish to destroy and sow illusions in their path." He was for subsidizing writers in that "we must also buy all the mercenary pens which propagate our methods . . ." He would destroy the clergy "by ridiculing religion, rendering its ministers odious, and only representing them as hypocritical monsters." He would enlist "Libels must at every moment show fresh traces of hatred against the clergy."

Whether they were actually card-carrying members of Weishaupt's group, it is clear that the spirit was the same mixture of blood, violence, and sexual perversion. Mirabeau had been an observer at their convention at the Grand Masonic Convention in 1782 in Wilhelmsbad, where the plan for the revolution was laid out. He also confessed that he subscribed to the Albigensian heresy whose aim was to destroy both the monarchy and the Catholic Church and replace it with a religion of love in France. By 1788 supporters of Weishaupt who were actively spreading his dogma had infiltrated every lodge in the Grand Orient. By this they meant the abolition of the monarchy, policies of terrorism against the state, religious freedom, sexual permissiveness and social equality.

Unquestionably there is a lot of truth to that perception. As trends, they have been real enough. The obvious explanation is that a ruling or political class has long sought these goals, has advocated them openly and has succeeded in getting enough control over the machinery of government to go a long way toward implementing them. They created the Zeitgeist. In order to do this, they did not have to meet secretly at any point. The Illuminati wanted to destroy finance, demean religion and God, destroy the family, and eventually reduce the world to slavery, which is really the goal of any megalomaniac conqueror. Weishaupt believed it was important that all the State's efforts be directed toward breaking the link between mother and child. In essence, Weishaupt's revolutionary thinking laid the philosophical basis for Marxism a generation later.

One interesting figure in Illuminati history was the Comte Cagliostro, whose real name was Joseph Balsamo. Born in Palermo,

Sicily in 1743, Cagliostro traveled through Greece and Egypt and was familiar with the occult secrets of the Jewish Cabala and had been a Rosicrucian at one time. He was also a Jacobean and attended the Grand Masonic Congress in 1785 when plans were made for fomenting the French Revolution. Cagliostro had become a Freemason while in Germany and had much to with wrecking European Masonry and changing it to an instrument for producing carnage. He was an intimate of King Louis XIV's as his court magician. He lived in Paris for several years and decorated his living quarters with effigies of the gods and goddesses of ancient Egypt. He detailed how German Illuminati had infiltrated the French Freemason lodges for years and by 1789, stating that "the 266 lodges controlled by the grand Orient were all 'illuminated' without knowing it." Contrary to popular opinion the attack on the Bastille and the ensuing events of the French Revolution were carefully orchestrated from behind the scenes. Brigands and prostitutes from the South were recruited to serve as the agitators. William Still says that for the first time in history, "grievances were systematically created in order to exploit them."

Cagliostro was also the focal point in the infamous "Diamond Necklace Affair," which was an Illuminati plot, designed to discredit the monarchy. Cardinal de Rohan, a French priest who dabbled in the occult and had fallen for Marie Antoinette, asked Cagliostro to purchase a diamond necklace for her on his behalf. De Rohan had been duped into thinking he was corresponding with the Queen, only to have his letters intercepted by the Comtesse de la Molte who pretended to be the Queen. The stone was purchased and delivered to the Comtesse instead. She and her accomplices broke the necklace into stones and sold them in Paris and London. When word of the plot was leaked, they were all arrested, including Cagliostro and thrown in the Bastille. Foolishly the king decided to have them tried by the Estates General which was strongly anti-royal because of Masonic infiltration. Cagliostro was the only one who escaped a guilty verdict. Unfortunately for the king, the tawdry affair stoked the flame of hostility for both the Church and the monarchy.

The radicalism of many of the lodges, especially against the throne had alienated many of the aristocrats who resigned from these lodges. The Inquisition had arrested Cagliostro and he tried to save his life by talking. He told them of the international conspiracy of Illuminati, the neo-Templars, and the Freemasons to start revolution all over Europe. Their goal was to complete the work of the Knights Templar and overthrow the papacy in Rome by quite possibly, infiltrating the College of Cardinals and electing one of theirs as pope. He also claimed that the House of Rothschild had financed the Revolution and they were acting as agents of the Illuminati. Writer Michael Howard thinks it was a figment of his imagination. He says there is no evidence. However his primal fear extended to England where Parliament debated the Unlawful Societies Act, which would have prohibited Freemasonry. It failed because many aristocrats were members and the Craft had never involved itself in politics. He moved to London, living at 50 Berkeley Square reputed to be the most haunted house in London.

Cagliostro's mentor was the legendary Comte de Saint-Germain, an occultist, alchemist, spy, industrialist, diplomat, and Rosicrucian. While studying the occult in the East Saint-Germain, he was introduced to the secret rites of tantric sex magic, which provided him techniques for prolonging his youth. He performed many tasks for the Royal family and was involved in several international intrigues and plots. While Saint-Germain was an Illuminist, he did not share all their revolutionary ideas. As early as 1780, he had warned Marie Antoinette about the international plot to overthrow the throne. Many French Masons remained loyal to the monarchy. Among some of these liberal elements there was some opposition to these secret societies.

Fortunately for posterity, there were individuals who were cognizant of this conspiracy at the time it happened. The man who uncovered the Illuminati was John Robison (1739-1805). A distinguished scientific writer, and professor of natural philosophy at Edinburgh University in Scotland and a Freemason, Robison was asked to join the Illuminati. He declined because he did not like their revolutionary agenda. He felt they were founded for the "express purpose of rooting out all the religious establishments and overturning all the existing governments . . . the leaders would rule the World with uncontrollable power, whole all the rest would be employed as tools of the ambition of their unknown superiors."

Using their own words to expose them, Robison wrote the book "Proofs of a Conspiracy Against All the Religions and governments of the Europe Carried on in the Secret Meetings of the Freemasons, Illuminati and Reading Societies." Published in 1798, it became the definitive work in exposing their tyrannous plots. Robinson described in detail how the Illuminati had infiltrated the Freemasons and helped foment the French Revolution. He strongly believed that Freemasonry was an association for the purpose of rooting out all of the religious establishments and overturning all the existing governments of Europe. He says that Illumination surfaced in "Die deutsche Union," which gained influence over Freemasonry and in turn plotted the French Revolution. Robison was defending English Freemasonry from the scourge of French or European Freemasonry. To him the Jacobeans were just "Illuminati in action." He sent a copy to George Washington, who said that he was aware of them in America and said they had "diabolical tenets."

History's "most important "student of conspiracies" was Augustin de Barruel (1741-1820). He was a French ex-Jesuit and an abbot who wisely took refuge in England after the fall of the Bastille. He was also a former Mason, who wrote that the Masons believed the death of Christ was a tragedy because with it the birth of Christianity took place. They despise that day and anything to do with it. Barruel was inspired by Robison's book. He was the first to present conspiracy theories in an orderly and intellectually punctilious fashion. He produced a monstrous work on the Illuminati and Free Masonic influence on the French Revolution, in four volumes, published from 1797-1798. These "Memoirs" fully illustrated "The History of Jacobinism," which contained three main elements—the Philosophes, the Illuminati, and the Freemasons. He believed that the French Revolution was about private property. The book is widely considered as the "greatest classic of conspiracy theory," a veritable "Bible of secret society mythology and the indispensable foundation of future anti-Masonic writing."

In the first volume, Barruel wrote about the anti-Christian Voltaire and others who plotted to overthrow the Catholic Church. In the second volume, he treated the conspiracy of the Sophists and the Rebellion against Kings." The last volume was his singular grand vision of history beginning with the Mani, the Iranian prophet of dualism and culminating in the French Revolution. According to Barruel, Michelangelo Buonarroti was the man who organized secret societies. He participated for five decades, starting with "Babeuf's Conspiracy of Equals," which lasted long after his death. It was the bogeyman with a paranoid mind, which meant doing more than anyone to give reality to the specter of the universal conspiracy, which leaped from the secret society to the national conspiracy was or fear of government was. Anti-imperialism started this, that is, the kind of thinking that goes from the clandestine nature of the secret society to the CIA or MI5. In the modern world, secrecy has been irretrievably broached. The government has become the new secret society. For his efforts, Barruel has been posthumously maligned, slandered and attacked for exposing the truth of the French Revolution by the denizens of the modern liberal establishment.

Illuminism and Freemasonry have had their many defenders. Dr. Albert Mackey, an American Mason and a 33rd degree Mason wrote in his "Encyclopedia of Freemasonry" that Illuminism was a "good thing." Its basic goal was the elevation of the human race. But he also described Weishaupt as a "radical in politics and an infidel in religion." Mackey said his main purpose in establishing the Illuminati was to overturn "Christianity and the institutions of society," which presumably were also "good things."

The late Richard Hofstadter saw the Illuminati within the context of the paranoia rampant in American society. He abruptly dismissed the Illuminati as "no more than another version of Enlightenment rationalism, spiced with an anti-clerical animus that seemed an inevitable response to the reactionary-clerical atmosphere of 18th century Bavaria." It was this same kind of pseudo intellectualism that allowed other scholars to quickly dismissed or deny the depravities of the Stalinist regime during the thirties. He also called Illuminism a "somewhat naive and utopian movement which aspired ultimately to bring the human race under the rules of reason." Herder, Goethe, and Pestalozzi fell under its influence later. He characterized Robison's book, as "fantasy" saying that Robison's French Revolution was "one great and wicked project fermenting and working all over Europe." He saw it as libertine, anti-Christian, given to the corruption of women, violation of property rights. He had a tea that caused abortions and a secret substance that "blinds or kills" when spurted in the face.

Thomas Jefferson, a contemporary of Barruel, had another view of Weishaupt. The future president saw Weishaupt as an "enthusiastic philanthropist," whose thinking was consistent with that of Jesus Christ. Jefferson understood Weishaupt as focusing on Christ's precepts of "love of God and the love of his neighbor." Weishaupt's major objection was with organized religion. It is believed that his contempt for organized revolution started when Pope Clement XIV suppressed the Jesuits on July 21, 1773. The pope had been pressured to do this because the governments of France, Spain, and Portugal were convinced they were meddling in the affairs of state and therefore were enemies of the government. They were denounced as "traitors." Jefferson felt he was a Jesuit who vowed to destroy the Catholic Church. They were finally re-instated by Pope Pius VII in August of 1814. John Adams wrote to Jefferson, "If ever there was a body of men who merited eternal damnation on earth . . . it is this Society." Jefferson replied "Like you I disapprove of the restoration of the Jesuits, for it means a step backward from light into darkness."

Others saw through Weishaupt's false rhetoric. Another contemporary, the Marquis de Luchet, who supported the revolution claimed, was quoted in 1789 as having said, "There exists a conspiracy in favor of despotism, against liberty, of incapacity against talent, have vice against virtue, of ignorance against enlightenment. This society aims to govern the world."

Tom Bethel, in the "National Review," talks of the Illuminati as being engaged in an "alleged plot." Bethel is wrong about the Illuminati conspiracy being alleged. He also tries to undermine the passing of the "revolutionary idea," from the Illuminati to the Communists. He strongly believes that in order to keep the conspiracy going, elderly Illuminati must have met at some point with fledging Communists, to turn over the keys to the mystery. His arrant attempt at sarcasm betrayed an unschooled naivete that detoured his arguments from the pathway of reality. The Illuminati were the custodians of an idea that was as old as evil itself. Their demise had little or no bearing on the transference of their ideas.

To dispute Bethel, one need only to turn to James Billington, the chairman of the left-leaning Woodrow Wilson International Center of Scholars, affiliated with the Smithsonian Institute. He is no conservative dupe. In his classic 1980 book, "The Fire in the Minds of Men: Origins of Revolutionary Faith," he captured the spirit of the Promethean fire that burned in all young revolutionaries from Karl Marx through Nicolai Lenin. Many of these revolutionaries looked back to the pagan days of old when there was not Christianity and no virtuous ideology or religion to dissuade them from enjoying the natural things of life. Weishaupt's spirit still lives in the ideas of Marx, Lenin and the disciples of the Communist revolution. This explains why liberal democrats have been so susceptible to the progressive enlightenment that has weakened the very pillars upon which American society was founded. Mozart captured this spirit in his "Magic Flute," which romanticized this plight of early man. This was a moral quest for many of these utopians. They viewed the historical struggle prophetically as "the unfolding of a morality play."

Flame is a symbol of this charring flame that Billington carried throughout the book. He says the Christian aristocrats transferred their candles of approval from the Catholic churches to the Mason lodges. The flame of "occult alchemists, which had promised to

turn dross into gold reappeared at the center of new circles seeking
to recreate a new golden age. Weishaupt and his Illuminati were a
vital part of his entire revolutionary thesis. The president of Harvard
University on July 4, 1812 saw the work of Illuminati in the War
of 1812. There is sufficient evidence that a number of societies of
the Illuminati have been established in this land. They are doubtless
striving to secretly undermine all our ancient institutions, civil
and sacred. Without the Illuminati, it is unlikely that the spirit
and energy that gave rise to Communism would have existed in
the powerful fashion that characterized it in the early twentieth
century.

Weishaupt was a German "Johnny Appleseed," sewing the seeds
of revolution that spread all over Europe. As Nesta Webster put it
so succinctly, "Weishaupt . . . knew how take from every association,
past and present, the portions he required and wield them all into
a working system of terrible efficiency." He was able to combine
the "disintegrating doctrines of the Gnostics and Manicheans,"
with the French Encyclopedists, the methods of the Assassins, with
the "discipline of the Jesuits and Templars." To this he added "the
organization and secrecy of the Freemasons, the philosophy of
Machiavelli, the mystery of the Rosicrucians into one coherent
revolutionary doctrine."

Weishaupt's ideas are still vibrant and alive. I have often
compared this transference of revolutionary fervor, to the itinerant
Coke bottle, in the Kalahari Desert, in the movie, "The Gods Must
be Angry." His unsettling and disruptive ideas have been handed
down from revolutionary generation to revolutionary generation,
like ideological family heirlooms. It does not require a great leap of
faith or to realize that an idea can remain dormant or inconspicuous
for years, maybe even centuries, before it is resuscitated. This attests
to the nuclear life of the Illuminati ideology. It may fall out of
favor or be lost for a long time, but eventually they come back and
influence new generations of people. The beliefs of the Illuminati
and the French Revolution are like that. Freemasonry kept
Illuminism alive, though in somewhat of a dormant state. The
revolutionary idea was eventually passed on to the League of Just

Men, which had Karl Marx as a member. This directly led to the Communist League, Progressivism, New Deal Democracy, and Liberalism.

As writer James Marrs writes, "Many researchers today believe the Illuminati still exist and the order's goals are nothing less than the abolition of all government, private property, inheritance, nationalism, the family unit organized religion." Winston Churchill put it best when he wrote, "From the days of Spartacus Weishaupt to those of Karl Marx, to those of Trotsky, this world-wide conspiracy for the overthrow of civilization, has been steadily growing."

It is apparent that the Illuminati, the Freemasons, and their spiritual heirs, an intellectual and moral amalgamation of liberals, environmentalists and New Age religionists want to undermine the Christian social order and mutate it into a one world government, army and one world economy under an Anglo-Saxon financial oligarchy. This would be in effect a world dictatorship served by a council of twelve faithful men. It is their goal to replace Christianity with an occult-inspired world socialist dictatorship, under which the world come under the domination of Lucifer and all of us would be inmates in a giant prison of the New World Order. This could explain why liberal democrats have been so susceptible to the progressivism enlightenment that has fought so hard against the very pillars upon which American society was founded.

4

A Nation of Frogs

"We have it in our power to begin the world again."
Thomas Paine's "Common Sense"

The Marxist mind is hard to fathom for the average Westerner for there is not even the most basic notion of arid humanitarianism in the Communist rulebook. They merely go along or encourage social action projects to infiltrate the Western social apparatus. It is what Dostoyevski and James Billington have called the "fire in the mind," that animates the champions and guardians of the Marxist mentality.

No one can seriously doubt that material dialectics or Communism is an actual conspiracy. The often-abused John Birch Society held in 1966 that the Communist Manifesto was just a codified version of Illuminati principles. Communism was also dependent on the secret society. The Communist league, which sponsored the Communist Manifesto, was a secret society.

There is little doubt that Marx had been influenced by the ideas of Adam Weishaupt. Born in 1818, Marx went to Paris in 1843 to study economics. It was there that he met Friedrich Engels. Engels was the son of a wealthy Lancashire, England cotton spinner. Ironically, Marx lived off Engels' largess for the rest of his life. He spent his life living off the capitalist rewards of cotton spinning.

When he was nineteen, Marx joined the Doktor-Klub in Stralau, Germany. This led him to the "Young Hegelians," such as Bruno Bauer and David Strauss. His life changed dramtically after this. Engels had studied under the "Communist Rabbi," Moses Hess. Marx gave some indication of his thinking in his "The Union of the Faithful with Christ," when he wrote "through the love of Christ we turn our hearts to our brethren for whom He gave Himself as sacrifice. This theme runs through his early writings.

The Young Hegelians seduced Marx of what was left of his religious belief. Marx believed "Before anything else we must rid ourselves of this myth about God." Echoing a strong Luciferian influence, Marx cried, "God is the great evil." He truly believed that it is the "ghost of God which prevents us from carrying through to the very end of our efforts to bring into existence that vision of which religion is only an abortive dream: the reign of justice and happiness, paradise upon earth." In his mind, "the number one exploiter, capitalist and robber of humanity is God.

After Marx lost his faith in God, he vowed to avenge himself "against the One who rules above." He joined a Satanist Church, grew his beard long in imitation of Joanna Southcott, a satanic priestess who said she was in contact with the demon Shiloh. Marx also hated the Jewish religion. He hated all religions because it protected private property, kept the poor downtrodden, and taught that each man should be self-sufficient. Marx believed that the unequal distribution of wealth was the cause for man's unhappiness. Religion taught that one should not take property of another by force. He saw that as wrong. Since he did not believe in sin per se, he blamed all evil on capitalism.

Marx had started his hatred of God at an early age. As a youth he composed a poem, in adoration of "Oulanem," a ritualistic name for Satan. He consistently took an anti-God attitude in his opposition to religion the rest of his professional life. Marx had no vision of world improvement. He merely wanted to bring it to ruin. Satanism led to his communism. Mysterious rites of black magic are still celebrated at Marx's tomb in England.

Since Marx had no real positive philosophy of life, it is not surprising as Malachi Martin states he "should have looked to the philosophy of another man to supply the superstructure of his own historical and social outlook." The irony here is that he used that of Frederick Hegel, who had passed from the scene before Marx was intellectually mature. Hegel was a devoted Christian his whole life and "his theories about human history were steeped in his faith."

All of his poems are directed to Oulanem, a favorite name that is used in Black Masses and Satanic hymns to denote the Devil. These poems revealed a delight in the destruction of men and women. The words of Mephistopheles in Goethe's "Dr. Faust," "everything in existence is worth being destroyed," became his constant mantra. The future, Pope Pius XII, Eugenio Pacelli had realized as early as 1929 that if one dug deeply enough behind a Marxist, one would find a Satanist. The Pope realized that to compromise with Marxism was to open the culture to Communism through the portals of thought, politics, and economics.

Both Marx and Engels flouted traditional sexual morality. When Marx married Jenny Von Westphalen, the daughter of a rich and respected Prussian official, they were given a maid as a wedding gift from her parents. In his book "The Intellectuals," author Paul Johnson uncovered the fact that Karl Marx, the so-called champion of the proletariat, knew was the only proletariat in his life, his maid Lenchen, whom he treated like a domestic sex slave. Marx's research on the proletariat was as phony as was his notion of the workers' paradise. She bore him several children, most of whom died in poverty. It was Marx's father-in-law, Ludwig Von Westphalen, who taught him collectivist thought. He had studied Fourier, Hegel and had been enamoured of Proudhon's term, "scientific socialism." Marx's person lineage did not fare so well. Marx allowed two of his six children to starve to death because he could not provide for them. Two other children committed suicide.

Hegel said all progress proceeded from the dialectic of thesis, anti-thesis, and synthesis. It was the engine that continually drove the history of mankind in what Father Martin calls a "a dialectic of spiritual transcendence," by which man was able to rise above the material limits of his nature. In a total contrast to this plan of God's as seen by Hegel, Marx gave the world a dialectic of materialism that was based on the oppression of the worker in a class struggle that would purify mankind of its basest elements. It was the proletarian class, the workers who were the driving engine of the dialectic.

Marx's atheism severely altered Hegel's paradigm. Hegel believed in God but by putting philosophy over religion and writing of the all-encompassing "world spirit," he left the door open for Marx to drive God from the scene and substitute his material dialectic. Marx believed in Prometheus, who took fire away from the gods. Marx's plan to use the public schools to destroy the family could probably have been expanded to include the churches as well. Marx wanted to abolish the traditional family. As an institution, marriage has lost most of its legal, religious and social meaning and authority. The 2003 Lawrence Decision in Texas, which removed all the major obstacles for homosexual marriage, was just another nail in the coffin of traditional marriage. Communism abolishes all religion and all eternal truths. Existential man was the only measure of things.

When Charles Darwin proposed his theory of evolution years in 1850, Marx regarded it as a scientific vindication of his own thinking. It proved to him conclusively that there was no kingdom of Heaven, only "the kingdom of matter." Darwin had underwritten Marx's rejection of Hegel's belief in the soul, in the spirit of God as the ultimate goal of human history. To Marx Darwin had done for anthropology what he had done for sociology. Only matter was eternal. Marxism was a geopolitical theory that applied to everyone in the world.

It was essentially a flawed worldview. Since Marx believed that all religion was nothing more than an opiate to keep the people afraid and oppressed, he was literally unable to see that people differed all over the world and could not be neatly put into the round holes of his deterministic board. Father Martin compares him to just another servant of the devil who had his own consecrated oath, "I will not serve!" The fortunate thing for Marx was that he was swallowed hook, line and sinker by Lenin and his Soviet comrades. Otherwise no one would have heard of his deeply flawed theories, which Martin called "mental flatulence."

Later Marx's hypocrisy also came out when he confided in a letter to an uncle, that he had made 400 pounds in the stock exchange. The time has come, he wrote to Engels, when "with very little money, one can really make a killing in London." The irony is that Marx had the mind of a capitalist but the soul of a communist. He could have easily earned a living with his doctorate from the University of Jena, even though it was nothing more than a mail-order degree.

Both Engels and Marx joined the Communist League in 1846. This group had been formerly known as the League of the Just, an offshoot of the Parisians Outlaws League, founded by German refugees in that city. There is a distinct probability that the original group could have had some members of Adam Weishaupt's dispersed Illuminati. At their Second Congress of the Communist League, they were hired to write its platform, "The Manifest der Kommunistichen Partei." They had to have it ready by February 1, 1848, in London for the "spontaneous revolutions" were planned for that March 1st. However all their planned revolutions failed. The group had thought they were ready to make their name and platform available to the rest of the world. Though the revolutions failed, it was the "Communist Manifesto" that has survived to play a subversive role in American history. Part of the Marxist legacy that has limited the advance and rising power of the United States has been the nation's tax structure. Both the graduated income tax, as enacted in the sixteenth amendment and the estate tax were two of the ten planks. Two other elements that would have deleterious effects on the nation were the central bank, which became law under the Federal Reserve Act of 1913 and taxpayer supported public school education. The obligatory public schooling would serve to undermine the culture with the godless teaching of a communistic humanism.

Karl Marx was one of the first intellectuals to link the Communist philosophy with Humanism. As a derivative of the

French Revolution, Humanism stood as the denial of God and the total affirmation of man. Humanism is nothing more than "Marxism with a kind face." Most Marxists are atheists. They have no need for God since ownership of the means of production determines everything. It is also the basis for the culture, which Marx described as its superstructure.

But this could not be just any government. It had to be a new, more populist government, in which the workers of the world would unite and throw off the last vestiges of the religious and aristocratic rule that had dominated Western Civilization for hundreds of years. Old Marxism erroneously taught that in a widespread European war, the proletariat would rise all over Europe and overthrow the bourgeois and aristocratic governments.

There has never been a humane Communist regime. One need only look at their regimes in the Soviet Union, Eastern Europe, Mao's China, Ho's Vietnam, and bloody massacre of the Khemer Rouge under Pol Pot. Marxism is systemically totalitarian. It recognizes no moral limits on the state, or any restrictions on their power. It is a most convenient ideology for aspiring tyrants. It also has a utopian appeal for intellectuals and teachers, making the world a better place to live in as the rhetoric reads. They have proved equally skillful at rationalizing abuses of power and exculpating themselves.

As the most successful ideology of the twentieth century, Marxism has denied any divine element in man or the universe warranting modesty and restraint in the state. This meant the end of privacy and the government punishing its citizens for their thoughts. Communism may be dead in the Soviet Union. The Marxist spirit is alive and well, living within the liberal mind. Marxism has left its mark on the liberal political culture of the West, especially in the area of civil rights and political correctness. Hate crimes serve to criminalize motives as well as actions. As Joseph Sobran put it, in a 1998 newsletter "we are indebted to Marx for the general assumption that everything is the state's business and that even privacy is something that can exist only by the grace of the state' s rather suspicious permission."

Pat Buchanan's most impressive chapter in his latest book, "The Death of the West," dealt with "Four Who Made a Revolution." He pointed out how after the Russian Revolution the Communists attempted coups in several other European cities. These rebellions were ruthlessly crushed in Berlin, Munich, and Budapest. German war veteran quickly annihilated Rosa Luxembourg and her followers in the Sparticist uprising. Both she and Karl Liebknecth were clubbed and shot to death in Berlin by "Freikorps." Doctrinaire Marxists realized that Communism was not improving the lot of the German workers. They were not interested in being saved by the new philosophy because they had been indoctrinated by two thousand years of Christianity, which had blinded them to their true class interests. Until Christianity and Western culture, what Buchanan calls the "immune system of capitalism," was uprooted from the soul of Western Man, Marxism could not take root and the revolution would suffer betrayal by the very people it deemed worthy of help.

Most Americans believe that when the Berlin Wall went down with a thundering crash in 1989, it marked the end of the pernicious specter that had captivated half of Europe for over forty years. They believe that the country has nothing to fear from Communism any more. They have been conditioned to believe that the anti-communism crusade of the 1950s was nothing more the paranoidal ranting of Wisconsin Senator Joseph McCarthy. The fact is Communism is still very much alive and thriving in this country. It has taken on a more subtle, pernicious guise. The situation is analogous to the frog that is put into a pot of tepid water. If the cook were to quickly increase the temperature of the water, the frog would quickly jump out to safety. But the smart cook increases the temperature, only gradually, so that the poor frog does not realize it is being slowly, but surely, boiled to death. William Lederer once referred to America as a "nation of sheep." I believe America is more a nation of frogs.

Classical Marxism argues that ownership of the means of production has determined history. The cultural Marxists say that history is wholly explained by group identity. This identity politics as defined by sex, race, and sexual orientation results in aggrandizement of power over other groups. Because Western culture has been so predominantly white male oriented, its has oppressed all of these outgroups who are now throwing off the cultural chains that have bound them for centuries. While Classical Marxism preaches a classless society of equal economic conditions, cultural Marxism dreams of a different kind of classless society. Theirs is one where there is not only equal economic opportunity but equal results as well. Meritocracy has been replaced by an egalitarian system that rewards the lazy and the indigent as much as it does the productive. It is a system that inevitably leads to a police state. If those who produce do not comply, they will be coerced.

How did this happen? The place to start is with the writings of a Sardinian intellectual, Antonio Gramsci. Born in the village of Ales on the island of Sardinia in 1891, Gramsci became the most successful interpreter of Marxism. He left Sardinia for the mainland where he studied philosophy and history at the University of Turin. In 1919 he founded a newspaper in Italy, the "L"Ordinine Nuovo," or the "New Order." In 1921 with Palmiro Togliatti, Gramsci founded the Italian Communist party. When Italy adopted the Mussolini's fascism, Gramsci fled to Russia where he analyzed Lenin's adaptation of Communism. He was profoundly disturbed that Communist Russia failed to show any great interest in a "workers' paradise." Gramsci clearly understood that the Russian ruling class had maintained its hold on the workers by resorting to sheer terror and mass extermination. Communism had merely replaced one with the other.

After Lenin's death and the ensuing struggle for power, even Russia became a dangerous place for Gramsci. Lenin's successor, Stalin, eliminated anyone, suspected of deviation from his party line. Gramsci returned to Italy to struggle against Mussolini, was arrested as a likely agent of a foreign power, and imprisoned in 1926. He spent the remaining years of his life, expounding on his philosophy. It was here that he wrote his "Prison Notebooks," and "Letters from Prison," which have become extremely influential on the college campus. When Gramsci died after being released in 1937, he had produced a total of nine volumes on history, sociology, and Marxist theory.

Since economic Marxism was a failure, Gramsci reasoned that the only way to topple the repressive Western institutions was by what he called a "long march through the culture." He repackaged Marxism in terms of a bona fide "cultural war," not its doctrinaire class struggle. He was well aware that most people did not believe in the communist system. Their Christian faith was the big obstacle, preventing the necessary leap to Communism. Gramsci knew that the civilized world had been thoroughly indoctrinated with Christianity for two thousand years, so much so that civilization and Christianity were inexorably bound. It was the Christian character of the West that had provided an almost impenetrable barrier to infiltration. More than an opiate, religion was the peasants' lifeline that helped them endure the harsh realities of life. According to Pat Buchanan's book, "The Death of the West," Christianity was the "heat shield of capitalism." To capture the West, Marxists "must first de-Christianize the West," that is, destroy its religious foundations.

Gramsci understood the Christian nature of European society and its culture, which he saw as still vibrant and thriving in the lives of the people all around him. Not only did Christian society point to the divine forces and the presence of God around them, they also believed that things of the spirit mattered more than any of their material possessions. More than an opiate, it was the peasants' lifeline that got them through the harsh realities of life. He also realized that as long as the workers had a Christian soul, they would not respond to revolutionary appeals. Subvert and destroy from within was the method he instituted to overthrow the West.

Gramsci understood the idea of the "hive." He believed that the cultural Marxists should forge alliances with other groups on the left that included radical feminists, extreme environmentalists, "civil rights" movements, gay militants, anti-police organizations, internationalists, ultra-liberal church groups and so on. They should create popular fronts with intellectuals who shared a mutual contempt for Christianity and bourgeois culture, especially because of their influence among the nation's youth. It was precisely Sobran's metaphoric hive that captures the essential harmony of purpose between liberals and communist Marxists. They possess an active unity of purpose that serves to undermine the existing regime. There is no real pattern or plan here. It was natural of these different groups to act in the same way because their ideas and methodology flowed from the same fountainhead. As a result white males became the enemy, the chief repository of Western fervor. The white male was, according to this cultural theory, the progenitor of all oppression of all of these left-wing out-groups. In crossing Freud with Marx, these cultural warriors realized that just as under capitalism, the workers were systemically oppressed, so under Western civilization, blacks, homosexuals, women and everybody who was not a white male is automatically oppressed.

Along the same lines as Adam Weishaupt, Gramsci strongly believed that if cultural Marxists could gain control of the churches, schools, newspapers, magazines, the electronic media, serious literature, music, the visual arts, that is by "cultural hegemony," they could control the deepest wellspring of human thought and imagination. Like the slowly cooking frog, ordinary people would "love their servitude" without their knowing it as servitude.

Gramsci was not the first theorist to arrive at this methodology. He was restating a basic Leninist principle. His clarion call for "cultural hegemony" was also consonant with the general philosophy of the Fabian Socialists in England's plan for "permutation." The Coles, Margaret and her husband, G.D.H., who was a longtime leader of the Fabians explained in "The Story of Fabian Socialism," that through the practice of "permutation" society would pass "into collective control without there ever having been a party definitely and openly pledged to that end." What permutation meant, in accordance with the hive was "honeycombing." They worked to get their allies into key position of power and influence so that they could easily subvert a social institution from within. As William Jaspers said in "The New American," in 1999, the Fabians, who often worked not only hand in hand with the Communists but also the international corporate elite of America, "have carried forth the Gramascian strategy of subverting and transforming the entire cultural milieu."

This was not a Bolshevik revolution that seized political power. They usurped political power through a Cultural Revolution in which the culture just meekly surrendered to them. This would be a "bloodless coup," of the spirit. Gramsci devoted the nine remaining years of his life to expounding on his philosophy, producing a voluminous total of nine volumes on history, sociology, Marxist theory. His canon formed the foundation for a dramatic new Marxist strategy, as Father James Thornton says in the July 5, 1999, "The New American," "that makes the spontaneous revolution of Lenin, as absolute as hoop skirts and high button shoes." His thinking promised "to win the world 'voluntarily' to Marxism," since it is based on a "realistic appraisal of historical fact and human psychology, rather than empty wishes and false illusions. In essence as Fr. Thornton relates, Gramsci's main contribution is that he liberated the "Marxist project from the prison of economic dogma . . . dramatically enhancing its ability to subvert Christian society."

Gramsci hated marriage and the family, the very founding blocks of a civilized society. To him, marriage was a plot, a conspiracy if you would, to perpetuate an evil system that oppressed women and children. It was a dangerous institution, characterized by violence and exploitation, the forerunner of fascism and tyranny. Patriarchy served as the main target of the cultural Marxists. They strove to feminize the family with legions of single and homosexual mothers and "fathers," who would serve to weaken the structure of civilized society. As a general warning any time the word "oppressed," is used in political or social situations, there is strong indication that it comes from a Marxist formation or is echoing a Marxist world view.

The essential nature of Gramsci's revolutionary strategy is reflected in Charles A. Reich's sixties classic, "The Greening of America," in which he wrote, "There is revolution coming. It will not be like revolution in the past. It will originate with the individual and the culture, and it will change the political structure as its final act. It will not require violence to succeed, and it cannot be successfully resisted by violence." Reich proudly expressed his message that the revolution was now "spreading with amazing rapidity and already our laws, institutions, and social structure are changing in consequence." This is a revolution of the "new generation."

Much of Gramsci's influence took place under the guise of, what we call today, "secular humanism." As Hudson Institute scholar John Fonte writes in the "Policy Review," Gramsci believed in "absolute historicism." By that Gramsci meant, "morals, truth, standards and human nature itself are products of different historical epochs. There are no moral standards that are universally true for all human beings outside of a particular historical context." To him morality is just another social construct. Gramsci's modern disciples joined with Christian churches in brotherly dialogue and in common humanitarian ventures. But their real purpose was to confirm the new Christianity in its anti-metaphysical and essentially atheistic pursuit of liberation from material inconvenience, from sexual restrictions of any kind and finally from all supernatural constrictions as possible.

It was another cultural Marxist who brought the Gramascian strategy into the schools. George Lukacs was a wealthy Hungarian banker. He was reputed to have been the most brilliant theorist since Marx himself. Echoing the future sentiments of Jesse Jackson, Lukacs cried out "who will free us from Western civilization?" As Deputy Commissioner of culture in Hungary under Bela Kun, his first task was to put in radical sex education in the schools. He reasoned that this was the best way to destroy traditional sexual morality and weaken the family. Hungarian children learned the subtle nuances of free love, sexual intercourse, and the archaic nature of middle-class family codes, the obsolete nature of monogamy, and the irrelevance of organized religion, which deprived man of pleasure. If this sounds familiar, it is because this is what is happening in our public and even some Catholic schools today.

Lucas was the forerunner of President Clinton's libidinous Surgeon General, Jocelyn Elders.

Lukacs launched an explosive sex education program that should give every American pause for concern. Special lectures and supporting literature were developed to instruct Hungarian children the subtle nuances of free love, sexual relationships, the archaic nature of the bourgeois family and its moral codes, the obsolete nature of monogamy, and the irrelevance of organized religion, which all deprived man of pleasure. Children were urged to deride and ignore the authority of parental authority, and precepts of traditional morality. This undermining of the nation's youth was rivaled only by Lukacs' call for Hungarian women to rebel against patriarchy. As Pat Buchanan reminded us, Lukacs' purpose in promoting sexual deviancy among women and children was to "undermine and destroy the family, the core building block of Christianity and Western culture."

Gramsci and Lukacs' ideas came to fruition through the Frankfurt School or Institute of Social Research, as it was originally called. It was the child of Felix Weil, a German millionaire. He sponsored a "Marxist Work Week" in Germany in an attempt to overcome the divisions within German Marxist. This led to the establishment of a think tank in 1923 that led to the Institute at Frankfurt University in 1923. Weil wanted Marxism to become considered as a scientific methodology. In 1971 Weil revealed "that he wanted the institute to become known and perhaps famous, due to its contributions to Marxism as a scientific discipline."

Its researchers translated Marxism from economics into culture terms. One of the keys in the Frankfurt School was the merging of Marxist analysis with Freudian psychoanalysis and psychological conditioning. In mating Marx with Freud, the Frankfurt School developed its central thesis that rested on an analog with Western capitalism. Just as the working class is automatically oppressed, so under Western culture, blacks, homosexuals, Hispanics, and women, that is, everybody but white males, were automatically the objects of oppression. This is traditional Marxist terminology, which describes the owners, mostly conservative white males, as all being evil. They are all good and the white males are all bad. In her book, "Treason, Ann Coulter opines "our men are up to the job of protecting us from foreign enemies, but our women are losing the war at home." Coulter also points out that the radical feminists believe that if you are not with them, you are against them. There are no non-feminist women. All women support women's issues, such as abortion. The stay-at-home housewife, the homemakers—these are unauthentic women. This has become the official ideology, especially of the Democratic Party, liberals, and college professors. That's what hate crime and affirmative action laws are all about. Both use government power to enforce the ideology of political correctness, a subset of "Cultural Marxism."

The notion of group solidarity or what is called "identity politics" was designed to create a division, ultimately leading to violence and social anarchy. In order to undermine Western society, the cultural Marxists would constantly repeat the charges that the West was guilty of genocidal crimes against each and every civilization that it had ever encountered throughout its history, and the historical oppressions of mankind. The Frankfurt School gained a profound influence in American universities after many of its luminaries fled to the United States in the 1930s to escape National Socialism in Germany.

This intellectual merger evolved into "Critical Theory," which has served the left as its main weapon in the battle for the soul of American culture. The "Crits" employed destructive criticism of the main pillars of Western civilization, including Christianity, capitalism, authority, the family, including, morality, tradition, sexual restraint, loyalty, patriotism, nationalism, heredity, ethnocentrism, convention, Conservatism and especially the language. Critical Theory, which is endemic to all the major law schools in the country, holds that the patriarchal social structure should be replaced with matriarchy. The belief that men and women are different and have properly defined roles would be replaced with androgyny and with that, the heterodox belief that homosexuality is normal. The differences between the genders, not sexes, had to be minimized. According to Marxist feminists men and women were fungible and could be easily interchanged. Gender differences were nothing more than mere anatomical accidents.

The main consequence of Critical Theory has been a cultural permissiveness at worst or cultural indifference at best. Americans tend to be alienated from their cultural and religious roots because they do not want to be tainted by association with all these aforementioned historical crimes. These tendencies are very much in evidence, especially among American youth.

Critical Theory works hand in hand with political correctness. Its main goal is to impose a uniformity of thought and behavior on all Americans, making it totalitarian in nature. Its roots lie in a version of Marxism, which seeks a radical inversion of the traditional culture in order to create a social revolution. Political correctness is the key to understanding the plight of the American culture since the dawning of the sixties. A theory invented by Max Horkheimer, political correctness, or PC, represents the lead vehicle through which the Marxist mind has driven its cancerous ideas in undermining the genius of American politics and culture. Under the rubric of "diversity," its hidden goal is to impose a uniformity of thought and behavior on all Americans. The cultural Marxists, often teachers, university professors and administrators, TV producers, newspaper editor and the like, serve as gatekeepers by keeping all traditional and positive ideas, especially religious ideas, out of the public marketplace. One can easily see that happening in our society every day. As Raymond V. Raehn pointed out in his article, "The Historical Roots of Political Correctness," can be traced back to Friedrich Engels' 1884 book "The Origin of the Family, Private Property and the State." This polemic eventually gave birth to the radical feminist slogan, which holds "deep-rooted discrimination against the oppressed female sex was a function of patriarchy."

Multiculturalism and its twin sister, identity politics, are both intricately tied in with the concept of political correctness. Multiculturalism teaches that all cultures are systemically equal, yet in practice only West Civilization seems to pale in comparison.

Since the success of the Civil Rights movement of the sixties, black activists have used the Trojan Horse of multiculturalism to ingratiate themselves with the white elite classes, especially university professors, to foster the cause of black people. These novel ideas run through and energize the movement for civil rights for three distinct groups: blacks, women and gays. Both ideas served to create a new atmosphere of sensitivity to a person's race, gender, and sexual orientation. In many cases, this sensibility has evolved into a hypersensitivity that has paralyzed much of our civil and social activity. Incessant group demands have laid siege to the pillars and founding blocks of the nation's culture, such as the churches, the family, schools and legal structure. Consequently, each group has become an integrated theater in the culture war.

After the war, Horkheimer and Theodor Adorno returned to Frankfurt. A sociologist, philosopher, and musicologist, Adorno started out as a disciple of Schonberg, who developed the 12-tone system, which is explicitly a rejection of the whole harmonic basis of Western music. In a culture of alienation and repression, Adorno theorized that the art of that culture must reflect it. This is the core of Marxist fine art theory. All these must be unpleasant. With Horkheimer, Adorno wrote "The Dialectic of Enlightenment."

Another key ingredient in Cultural Marxism was Theodor Adorno's book, "Authoritarian Personality," which he published with Else Frenkel-Brunswick, Daniel J. Levinson, and R. Nevitt Sanford in 1950. Its central premise was that Christianity, Capitalism, and the patriarchal or authoritarian family created a character susceptible to racial prejudice and fascism. To them anyone who upheld the old traditional standards had an authoritarian personality that was basically fascist in nature. If a family adhered to Christian and capitalist principles, the children would most likely grow up to be fascists and racists.

Pat Buchanan called Adorno's book, "the altarpiece of the Frankfurt School." If fascism and racism are endemic to the culture, as Adorno believed, everyone who was raised in the traditions of God, motherhood, and family is in need of a psychological help. This is Orwellian logic that seems to have already established a beachhead in the American consciousness. Cultural determinism had replaced Marx's economic determinism. The book became a handbook for a national campaign against any kind of prejudice or discrimination on the theory that it can happen here. They threaten that there will be another Holocaust unless these hate-inspiring personality disorders are excised from the nation consciousness. A senior fellow at the Wisconsin Policy Research Center, Charles Sykes, describes the "Authoritarian Personality," as an "uncompromising indictment of bourgeois civilization." What the critics used to call old-fashioned, was now considered to be "both fascist and psychologically warped." It is obvious that the American left has internalized all of these ideas.

Adorno also developed his "studies in prejudice," a prejudice against anything that was critical of Cultural Marxism. Adorno and his disciples determined that America was ripe for its own social revolution. Not only was the United States hopelessly racist and anti-Semitic, but its attitude toward authority figures, such as fathers, policemen, clergy, and the military, was far too acquiescent. America was too self-absorbed in its religious sense, success, cleanliness, and had an inward pessimistic and puritanical view of humanity, a view which Adorno believed inevitably led to fascism.

It was Wilhelm Reich, who died in a federal penitentiary in Lewisburg, Pennsylvania in 1957, who provided an uninhibited sexual energy to the Marxist cause. He was known as the "Father of the Sex Revolution." A native Austrian, born in 1897, Reich's autobiography revealed a number of insights about his sexual development as an adolescent. Entitled, "Passion of Youth," he told of his adolescent obsession with sex. He witnessed a sexual act between his housemaid and a coachman that gave him "erotic sensations of enormous intensity." He had sex for the first time at age eleven with the cook. His erotic involvement included sex with farm animals, an addiction to brothels and so on. His mother committed suicide after having an affair with a younger man. Reich told his father and she killed herself. These inner demons played out in his life a she grew older. He transferred his mental torment to society in general. He thought society was sick and unjust and he did his best to right the situation.

Reich began his career as a psychiatrist, working with the laboring class in Berlin in the 1930s. He quickly adopted the principles of Marx, but was not having much success with his patients. He started talking about sex and quickly realized that it was a more effective organizing principle. He noted that he could exert great power and control over his patients by undermining their sexual morals. In his book, "The Mass Psychology of Fascism," he summed up this technique. "We, as Communists, used to debate the existence of God . . . I came to the conclusion that it was a waste of time. You are not going to debate away from the existence of God . . . if you get people involved in deviant sexual behavior, the whole idea of god just disappears automatically." Religion is where most people get their morals. Sexuality and sexual behavior is a function of morals. So when you "loosen people" from their morality, society gets an influx of adultery, divorce, abortion, homosexuality and radical feminism. The end result is the moral breakdown of society.

Reich's book "The Sexual Revolution" was a precursor of what was to come. His sex-economic sociology also attempted to harmonize Freud's psychology with Marx's economic theory. He attacked the traditional family, or what he called "the authoritarian family," which was nothing more than "a factory where reactionary ideology and reactionary structures are produced." He combined Freud and Marx into singular nostrum so that he could free the individual from his repression as well as society from its cultural inhibitions. If he could dissolve conscience then morality would go away also. He was the godchild of Jean Jacques Rousseau who thought Western Civilization was responsible for all the evil in the world, not original sin. Reich believed that the patriarchal family was the chief source of this repression. He defended children's 'and teenagers' right to "natural love." He even put his two children in a Marxist commune. He did not seem to realize that he was not freeing them from authority but merely substituting a group authority for that of a parent.

In 1939 Reich tried to find out what was at the core of his erotic impulses. He claimed that it was an unknown energy force, he called "orgone," that was at the heart of all matter. And the "basic life-stuff of the universe." Me intended to market his orgone in a box that costs two hundred and twenty-five dollars a box. When his scheme was exposed for the fraud it was, he was charged with fraud and sentenced to two years in prison for contempt of court and violation of the Food and Drug Act. His books were later burned. He called himself a healer but confessed that he could no longer live "without a brothel."

Reich believed that man was fundamentally a sexual animal and the child was an "agent of social change." Like Lukacs and Adorno, Reich believed that the way to destroy the family was through sexual politics and early sex education. Sex education courses became the main weapon in an ideological war against the family. Their fundamental aim was to "relieve" the parents of their moral authority. Consequently, teenage sex and abortion became auxiliary weapons as well. Battles over parental notification became central to undermining parental authority and responsibility. Former Surgeon General Jocelyn Elders was an able disciple of Reich's many arguments.

Eric Fromm was another key member of the Frankfurt school. He strongly believed in matriarchy. To him women have been forced into roles created by the oppressive Western culture. He said the essential differences between men and women were caused by a patriarchal culture. If society could eliminate all those brawny, Neanderthal men who played football, fought wars and marched to John Wayne's beat, then all Americans could enjoy a soft, happy, easy life in their modern Nirvana. Paterfamilias would transform into "materfamilias" with its emphasis on caring, nurturing, and compassion, as opposed to power, fighting, and self-defense. A nation can not stand when its men are weak and its women are part of the nation's self-defense.

Fromm's thinking has led to the virtual decline of most minor sports for men on most college campuses. His ideas have given birth to legislation, like Title IX, that, while it has advanced the opportunities for athletic endeavor for women, has as designed, decreased vastly those for male college athletes. Title IX legislates that women's sports have to be on a level with those of men, as if there were no difference in student and public interest, and levels of skill and performance. This has also further subverted the sexual orientation. Women's softball has become a haven and a den for lesbians, to the detriment of straight women. One need only read Yvonne Zipter's book, "Diamonds are a Dyke's Best Friend." She makes a convincing case that professional and college softball teams have long been the best way to meet other lesbians.

Probably the most important member of the Frankfurt School was Herbert Marcuse. He was largely responsible for bringing Cultural Marxism to the United States when he moved to New York City to escape the Nazi persecution in the thirties. In the sixties he became the guru of the New Left while a professor at University of California at San Diego. Marcuse was a full-blooded social revolutionary who contemplated the disintegration of American society just as Karl Marx and Georg Lukacs worked for the destruction of German society.

In his book, "An Essay on Liberation," Marcuse proclaimed the means for transforming American society. He believed that that all taboos, especially sexual ones should be relaxed. "Make love, not war!" was his battle cry that echoed through the ivy-covered college campuses all over America. His methodology for rebellion included the deconstruction of the language, the infamous "what does 'is' mean?" which fostered the destruction of the culture. By confusing and obliterating word meanings, he helped cause a breakdown in the social conformity of the nation, especially among the more uninformed young of America. He deliberately acerbated race relations by emphasizing the idea that white men were all guilty for slavery and blacks could do no wrong. Linguistic deconstructionists, Michel Foucault, and Jacques Derrida did this on a much grander scale.

These cultural revolutionaries were faced with a serious question raised by the Gramascian paradigm. If the proletariat was not the basis of the revolution, what was? Marcuse said that women should be the cultural proletariat who would transform Western society. They would serve as the catalyst for the new Marxist Revolution. If women could be persuaded to leave their traditional roles as the transmitters of culture, then the traditional culture could not be transmitted to the next generation. The idea that "the hand that rocks the cradle rules the world," is no idle statement. What better way to influence the generations to come than by subverting the traditional roles of women? The Marxists rightfully reasoned that the undermining of women could deal a deadly blow to the culture.

The cultural Marxists identified the American family as their main target with women as their focal point. According to Engels, all oppression against women originated in the patriarchal family, where the man was the head and the woman was tantamount to his slave. It served as a patriarchal dictatorship and incubator for sexism and social oppression.

Marcuse said that women would be the cultural proletariats who transformed Western society. If the women left their traditional roles as the transmitters of culture, then the culture is not transmitted to the next generation. Since the object is to destroy the culture, then this is the most important job to perform. It can strike the culture a deadly blow through its women. Now women do or think they can do anything a man does from being a fighter pilot, a combat soldier, policemen, firemen, priests, and all sorts of jobs that require manly strength or a masculine disposition. This could include even the presidency. Is America prepared for another President Clinton?

He knew he could speed up the destruction of the family by hastening women to the factories, free and easy divorce, or what we call no-fault divorce. He also advocated the abolition of sex roles, the transformation of housekeeping into a social industry, the communication of childcare, the elimination of the concept of "illegitimacy" and an open definition of family. It appears that Frederick Engels, were he alive today would marvel about how close his "prophesies," self-fulfilling prophecies were, a sesquicentennial ago.

Marcuse believed in a liberating tolerance, but a tolerance only for the ideas on the left. Marcuse was the facilitator who took an obscure school of thought and helped it permeate the Students for Democratic Action so rampant in the sixties. The anti-war protests of the sixties would not have been possible without the ideological ammunition and revolutionary fervor of his writings. His writings and ideas, which were widely disseminated among university students, lent him the status of a cult figure of the sixties.

In his book, "Carnivorous Society," Marcuse wrote, " . . . what we must undertake is a type of diffuse and dispersed disintegration of the system." As Pat Buchanan notes, what he means here is "the abolition of America." Like Gramsci, Marcuse had transcended Marx. He and his colleague aimed to end the corrupt Western Civilization, not by a violent overthrow but by cultural infiltration and subterfuge. In effect the death of the West would not be an act of mere suicide, as James Burnham and others have contended. This was to be more than an assisted suicide in the manner of Jack Kervorkian.

One of the heirs to this cultural strategy was Betty Friedan, the former Naomi Goldstein. A disciple of Marcuse's, Friedan's book, "The Feminine Mystique," served as the textbook in sabotaging the American family. Friedan's described the traditional housewife as a "parasite," who was forced to deny her true nature. To Friedan, the stay-at-home mom was a mindless robot devoid of a real brain. Friedan's hatred and disdain for men and patriarchy made her the "godmother of radical feminism." Her denigration of the traditional sex roles pulled the psychological underpinnings from under the family. Friedan's affect on the family has been devastating. Thanks to her ideas, millions of women have traded the domestic tranquility of family and the home for the power surge of the boardroom and the sweaty release of casual sex.

If women were the targets, then the Cultural Marxists scored a bullseye. They have lowered themselves from their lofty pedestals and sacrificed their natural moral superiority to men on the altar of equality and choice. In effect, they have let down society by descending from their historic pedestals to the snake pits of competition, violence, and social unrest. It is now the seven dollar an hour daycare worker who is rocking the cradles of too many of the nation's young children. Charges of sexual abuse, especially in Florida where incidences of oral gonorrhea in small children were common place, have dragged down the culture even further. This is just another accident with a purpose. Divorce statistics, wife and child abandonment, abortion and even spousal murder can be laid at Betty Friedan's doorstep to a large degree.

On a 2002 edition of my radio program, "The Right Stuff," Carolyn Graglia, the author of the book "Domestic Tranquility," lamented against easy divorce and what it had done to countless women and children all over America. What women have failed to understand is the fact that the feminist movement of the sixties was created by men for the benefit of men. Abortion, the linchpin of modern feminism, may get women out of crisis pregnancies but it relieves men of a great of financial, moral and social responsibility. And they do not have to bear the psychological scars of having attacked their own basic nature.

Abortion rights is one of the most powerful weapons the cultural Marxists have used to divide women and set many of them against their husbands and even men as a whole. And in doing so they have seriously impacted the family. Women think they have the right to an abortion. What they really have is an abortion privilege, given to them by seven old men in black robes. Since 1973, over forty million unborn children have had their nascent lives prematurely snuffed out.

The subversion of the family and the decline in respect for patriarchy has led to the increased feminization of the nation's cultural institutions, including the churches, schools, and universities, political parties and even the military and our police forces. According to Graglia, the "editors at Playboy could not have orchestrated the women's movement," any better. Today we have sadly seen the feminization of many of our cultural institutions from the churches, schools, and universities to politics and even the military. Men, in all walks of life, are suffering an extreme loss in self-confidence that can only impact American society in a negative manner. This accounts for a large part of the increase in the divorce rate in the last fifty years, the abuse of women and children and ironically the impoverishment of many women are the lower of the economic ladder. "Modern man," resembles more the saccharine sensitivity of an Alan Alda than the lusty bravado of a John Wayne.

After women had been "turned," that is seduced away from their traditional role as transmitters of the cultural imperative of Western Civilization, Marcuse focused his attention on the "children." Marcuse understood that Adorno's 12-tone system alone would not topple the culture. But a pernicious mixture of sex, drugs, and rock-and-roll could do the trick. While words and books might have undermined past civilizations, sex and drugs would serve as a better seductress for America's children. He envisioned a culture of "polymorphous perversity," a society hung up in "endless adolescence. In his book "Eros and Civilization," he urged a universal embrace of the "Pleasure Principle." One of the ways to do this was to unleash the sexual energy of a generation of young people. "Make love, not war" was the battle cry that Marcuse coined in the sixties, making him one of the leading gurus of the sexual revolution that has hurt us today.

E. Michael Jones, the editor of "Culture War Magazine," displayed a deep insight when he wrote "the synergistic effect of music and drugs has been known since the writings of Plato, both converged in inducing the trance-like state that was the goal of the orgiastic." He added that there is "something eternally appealing about the Dionysian triad of sex, intoxication and orgiastic music, and there always will be as long as there is such a thing as fallen nature."

Part of the success of the cultural Marxists has been the virtual eradication of the country's past. Left-wing historians have denigrated our revolutionary history, the memory of the founding fathers, who were all slave-holding racists, and the June Cleaver fifties with its antiseptic and honest culture of safe streets, drug free and sexually inactive teenagers and morally uplifting entertainment. Once the American past has descended down a

Marxist memory hole, according to Gramsci, nothing will be left to stand in the way of the new Marxist civilization. The inner man will be effectively "Marxized, as Malachi Martin wrote in his book "The Key of This Blood." Then it would be safe, Father Martin writes "to dangle the utopia of the 'Workers' Paradise before his eyes, to be accepted in a peaceful and humanely manner, without revolution, violence or bloodshed."

In the final analysis, Cultural Marxism, with its Orwellian inversion of the social order, is more pernicious than the economic Marxism that ruined Russia. Not only does the Gramascian Paradigm attempt to enslave people in a dictatorship of the passions and emotions, but also to drown society in flood of sexual perversion and matriarchal weakness. The Cultural Marxists were intellectual renegades and moral misfits who thought outside the box. They put into circulation the ideas that would eventually subvert the most successful way of life in America.

This is not to say that the cultural Marxists were the only ones who have contributed to the downward spiral of the American culture. Someone had to sponsor the work of these social Marxists. E. Michael Jones faults the Rockefellers and similar foundations that funded the anti-American social policies of the cultural Marxists. The foundations provided the necessary capital to the cultural Marxists to insure the political instability and drug culture that resulted. Many others have taken advantage of American post-war affluence and boredom to advance a negative culture that has become a very real threat to the traditions and morals of the American people. In the "American Arts Quarterly," editor James Cooper identified how extensive this cultural breakdown and control has become. "Through control of the culture, the Left dictates not only the answers but the questions asked. In short, it controls the cosmological apparatus by which most Americans comprehend the meaning of events." In effect, the Left controls and defines the parameters of the debate, throwing a few crumbs, such as a George Will or even a Rush Limbaugh to appear balanced and honest.

Only a few conservatives seem to know the truth of the matter. Their ideas have triumphed. There is no longer any conservative philosophy left that anyone takes seriously. Many conservative writers and authors, have either never heard of the Frankfurt School or glibly dismiss their significance as noted "conservative author," I conducted an interview with putative conservative Dinesh D'Souza on another edition of "The Right Stuff," in 2002. D'Souza, the author of "What's so Great About America?" said that the Frankfurt School was "just a lot of old Germans that nobody has ever heard of." This attitude is disquieting to say the least and symptomatic of what is inherently wrong with the loyal opposition in today" political culture. To paraphrase T. S. Eliot, our civilization will end, not with a big bang, but with a faint croak.

PART II

The Anatomy of a Conspiracy

5

Plato's Apostles

"Everywhere do I perceive a certain conspiracy of rich
men seeking their own advantage under the name and pretext
of the commonwealth." St. Thomas More

The concept of the New World Order is not new. The first
evidenced call for world government was the Italian poet, Alighieri
Dante, in his "DeMonarchia" in 1313. Sir Francis Bacon also
conceived of the idea of utopian planned society in the
posthumously published "New Atlantis." The movement toward
world government began in earnest with Comet de Saint-Simon.
In 1803, echoing Adam Weishaupt, Saint-Simon expressed his
belief in a universal association of all men in all spheres of their
relationships, who would evolve into a self-styled elite, socialist
and scientific in nature, would rule the people.

It would fall to an English entrepreneur and philanthropist,
Cecil Rhodes, who was known as the "African Colossus," or "the
Diamond King'" to formulate an ideological plan to effect this
utopian dream of a New World Order. He had many other imperial
appellations that would have sounded more appropriate for an
athletic hero, such as Jim Thorpe or even Babe Ruth. Rhodes
labored under "a monumental ego, ruthless ambition and an
incredible capacity for intrigue and conspiracy," said, William Jasper
in the February 6, 1998 issue of "The New American." He was a
determined, imperious sort of man who was greatly driven to power
in the name of humanity. He possessed a special chauvinism for

the British Empire, which he wanted to extend across the Atlantic to America. Ambitious to a fault, Rhodes had an uncanny talent for monopolistic organization. He was charming with a Clintonesque flare, yet he could be petulant, moody, and misogynistic. His strong attraction for young blond men gave every indication that Rhodes was an avowed homosexual. As one of his biographers relates, Rhodes was maudlin and "deeply morose toward the loss of two such young men, one to a horrible death from an infected knee and the other to a woman's arms." Both losses sent him into frantic depression and loud rages.

Cecil Rhodes amassed a fortune in the gold and diamond mines of South Africa with the financial support of the Rothschilds, an international banking cartel that has historically played an important role in the course to a world financial order. Rhodes was deeply worried that the responsibilities of world dominion would inevitably led to a watering down of the British intellectual and moral heritage. According to historian Carroll Quigley, "they feared that all culture and civilization would go down to destruction because of their inability to construct some kind of political unit larger than the national state." This failure was analogous to that of the Greek civilization in the fourth century B. C., which fell to destruction because of the Greeks' inability to construct some kind of political unit larger than the city-state. This fear animated Rhodes and his followers into developing the concept of the New World Order in a Commonwealth of Nations that he so aggressively pursued his undying legacy.

Rhodes explained some of his philosophy in his "Confessions of Faith," a document he prepared in 1877, which was the same year that he drafted his first will. He wrote, "I have felt that at the present we are actually limiting our children and perhaps bringing into the world half the human beings we might owing to their lack of country for them to inhabit . . ." It was land, the absolute lack of land that England had that severely limited the future greatness of the British empire. As he wrote, "if we had retained America there would at the present moment be millions more of English living." It was Rhodes' unvarnished opinion that "we are the finest race in the world and that the more of the world we inhabit the better it is for the human race."

Rhodes' vision is all laid out in his seven wills. All the originals now reside in the Rhodes house in Oxford. The first five contemplated the creation of a worldwide secret society to promote the British Empire. The sixth will, written in 1893, made the first provisions for scholarships. They were designated for "young colonists" in the furtherance of imperial unity. The last will, which was publicly released in 1902, specifically mentioned American scholarships. Though no direct mention was made of absorbing the United States into the British Empire in the last will, it was clearly his intent and part of his imperial vision.

It was his mentor, John Ruskin, who provided the philosophical underpinning for Rhodes' imperial dream. Professor Quigley, Bill Clinton's mentor at Georgetown University, was the only person whom he credited in his 1993 acceptance speech. It was Quigley who wrote the definitive book on how "the Insiders" worked. According to Quigley, the historic vision of world unity started in 1870 with the appointment of John Ruskin, as a Professor of Fine Arts at Oxford. According to Quigley's magnum opus, "Tragedy and Hope and The American Establishment," first published in 1966, Ruskin "hit Oxford like an earthquake because he talked about the empire and England's downtrodden masses." Gary Allen called Quigley, "the Joseph Valachi of political conspiracy," the noted Mafioso who was the first to break the bond of "omerta," silence on his fellow criminals. This is a weak analogy because Quigley's book praised the Anglo-American establishment that had grown up throughout the last decades of the nineteenth and the first few decades of the twentieth century.

Ruskin, the son of a prosperous wine merchant, had deviated from the commercial path of his forebears. He was an avowed Marxist, who suffered through a difficult lonely life that included frequent masturbation, and nympholepsy, an obsessive fondness for prepubescent girls. Ruskin failed to consummate his marriage to nineteen-year old Effie Gray in 1848. Six years later and still a virgin, she had their "marriage" annulled, a shocking development for those times. It is not surprising that Ruskin eventually lost his faith in God. The man, who influenced Rhodes and Alfred Milner and all those other globalists, was himself deeply influenced by the writings of Plato and Madame Blavatsky, the founder of the occult Theosophy Society. He was also deeply influenced by the books of homosexual Lord Edward Bulwer-Lytronn, one of Britain's "Apostles," and forerunner of the Salisbury Group.

Ruskin read Plato every day. He embraced Plato's notion of a "perfect society," as one that had its order imposed upon it from above. He believed in the ideal of a platonic state that would control the means of production and distribution and which in turn is controlled for the benefit of all those who are best suited by aptitude for the task. Plato wanted a ruling class with a powerful army and a society subservient to it. In his "The Republic," Plato advocated using whatever force necessary to wipe out the existing social structure. He wanted to eliminate marriage so that all women would belong to all men and vice versa. Children were to be taken and raised by the state. There would be just three classes, namely the ruling class, the military, and the working class. The ruling class would be the intellectuals who would decide what was best for everybody else. The state must take control of all means of production and organize them for the good of the whole community. Plato also advocated putting control of the state into the hands of an elite, presumably an "enlightened despot." He believed in personal superiority of an educated elite who knew how things should be run. He once wrote: "my continual aim has been to show the eternal superiority of some men to others." Marx and Engels were also students of Plato.

Ruskin told his select students that they were heirs of a magnificent tradition of education, beauty, rule of law, freedom, decency, and self-discipline. But this tradition did not deserve to be saved, unless it could be extended to the lower classes in England and to the non-English masses throughout the world. Ruskin's inaugural lecture attempted to ignite in his student a patriotic fervor for the Britain of old. Ruskin's chauvinistic teachings established a cult of "light, right and duty," around him. In 1870, long before Rhodes ever reached Oxford, Ruskin proposed a destiny for England, which was reputed to be "the highest ever set before a nation." He urged his students to make their country "again a royal throne of kings, a sceptred isle, for all the world a source of light, a centre of peace." He felt England had to do this or "she must perish." England was land poor and it had to seize "every piece of fruitful waste ground she can set her foot." In her colonies she must teach her subjects that "their first aim is to advance the power of England by land and sea." It was for him a magic brew, which justified and extolled "the fervor of imperialism." Ruskin's main disciples at Oxford were Arnold Toynbee, Andrew Lang, Alfred Milner, and Rhodes. Cambridge produced such Ruskin devotees as Reginald Balliol Brett, Sir John B. Seely, Albert Grey and Edmund Garrett. They would all spread Ruskin's ideas. They all would spread the Ruskin influence through their respective roles as historian, poet, statesman, and empire builder. Ruskin was like the Godfather of this imperial movement.

While still a student, Rhodes copied his mentor's inaugural address in longhand and kept it with him for thirty years. He formulated a detailed plan to put Ruskin's ideas into practice. Using his own money, Rhodes developed his elaborate plan for world federation, financed, and ruled by the English-speaking nations of the world. Rhodes' ideas were based on an incurable idealism that according to William Jasper in a 1995 article in the "New American," that "masks an ideological vacuum." For Rhodes, a personally troubled man with poor health and homoerotic tendencies, idealism had little to do with Christianity and its salvific teachings. His thinking was more akin to the current secular humanism that might fuel a group like Habitat for Humanity. His idealism also included a passionate belief in government as a positive force in effecting humanistic values on a worldwide scope.

Rhodes' idealism was not necessarily a bad thing. Oxfordian idealism, however, had more in common with secular humanism, collectivism, totalitarianism, Gnosticism, globalism, and elitism. These influences all may not be apparent but they are certainly implied within the history of the Rhodes scholar. Rhodes scholars believe in government more than anything. It is with and through government that the heirs to Rhodes' lethal legacy expect to effect his quixotic vision.

Rhodes' paramount design seemed to be mainly political, a policy of painting the world red—the color of British colonies. He was primarily an imperialist, though one with higher ideals and a grander design. His goal was world peace under a benign democratic world government, requiring society to promote social equality through social reform. He wanted to draw the United States and England in a league for the purpose of imposing peace or face the possibility of an Armageddon. The scholarship program merely served as a facade to conceal the doings of the secret society, or more accurately, as the instrument by which members of the secret society could carry out its function.

Rhodes was the progenitor of the modern secret society. It was the most important feature of this plan was his secret society, founded on the model of St. Ignatius' Society of Jesus. This is a page right out of Adam Weishaupt's playbook. They were to be called "Round Tables." The most important feature of the Jesuits was their requirement of absolute obedience to the Pope, the same idea that Weishaupt had used in founding the Illuminati. Rhodes and his successors were to be the pope, the objects of their members' undying loyalty and obedience.

The idea of a "Round Table" elite predates the intricate design of corporate directorships and tax-exempt foundations consisted of a maze of companies, institutions, banks, and educational establishments, which were almost unfathomable to the average person. The Round Table started out as a collection of semisecret groups, formed along the lines of the Illuminati and Freemasons with an inner and outer circle and a pyramidal hierarchy. It was an outgrowth of something Rhodes had instituted years before. He was worried that the general public would misunderstand his ideas and labored intensely to effect this global goal through a Jesuit-inspired "secret society." Unlike that of St. Ignatius of Loyola, Rhodes' Round Table was to be secret and decidedly anti-Christian.

To accomplish this he called on his closest and wealthiest confidants, who he labeled a "Circle of Initiates." This inner sanctum included the likes of Lord Balfour, Sir Harry Johnson, Lord Rothschild, Lord Grey and other scions of Britain's financial and aristocratic elite. Sarah Millin, a Rhodes biographer wrote, "the government of the world was Rhodes simple desire." Rhodes envisioned this as a great plan that for the next two centuries for the best energies of the best people in the world. His intellectual descendants would peacefully conquer the world and establish a Republic of the Intellect. Two members of Rhodes's inner circle included Lord Victor Rothschild and Lord Milner.

The name "Rothschild" would be of great significance for the New World Order. It was the Rothschilds' international banking firm, who financed Cecil Rhodes in Africa. With the cooperation of the Bank of England and the Rothschilds, Rhodes was able to establish a virtual monopoly over the diamond and gold output of South Africa with DeBeers Consolidated Mines and Consolidated Gold Fields, with an estimated annual income of about five million dollars.

Rhodes' inner group was ably assisted by Quigley writes of Rhodes' outer circle, an "Association of Helpers" that was reminiscent of the Illuminati concept of the double doctrine, or hierarchical structure of intimate knowledge. This group led, by editor William T. Stead, Reginald Brett, Arthur Lord Balfour, Milner, Sir Harry Johnston, Nathaniel Lord Rothschild, and Albert Lord Grey gained access to Rhodes' fortune. Using his money after his death in 1902, the Milner Group, also known as "the Kindergarten Group," was able to extend and execute his ideals. Socialist Christopher Hitchens, a classmate of Bill Clinton's at Oxford wrote in 1992, in "The Nation," the Rhodesian vision "imparts a definite sense of knowing what is best . . . for others. It has helped bestow a patina of refinement on the raw exercise of power, and has shaped the contours of the permanent party of government as it exists in law, lobbying, business, intelligence, diplomacy and the military."

As an aside, it should be noted that it was one of the Rothschilds who helped create the State of Israel. In 1917 Zionist Second Lord Lionel Walter Rothschild, a former Member of Parliament, received a letter from British Foreign Secretary Arthur Balfour expressing his approval for a homeland for the Jews in Palestine. This letter became known as the "Balfour Declaration." In 1922, the League of Nations approved of it, thus paving the way for the creation of the Israel. It was Baron Edmond de Rothschild who built the first pipeline from the Red Sea to the Mediterranean to bring Iranian oil to Israel and also founded the Israel General Bank. He was called the "father of modern Israel."

Eminent historian Niall Ferguson was allowed to publish the authorized biography of the Rothschild family in 1998. Unfortunately he was put under strict regulations that lessen the historical accuracy and substance of his work. He could only write the history up to 1848, the year, coincidentally, when Europe disintegrated into a fury of wars that forever changed its map and he could not quote from any source after March of 1915. Even then he discovered significant flaws and gaps in the "official" record. Being a self-described atheist from a Calvinist background, Ferguson paid scant attention to the metaphysical aspects of the Rothschilds, their knowledge of cabalistic tradition or their connection to the Freemasons and other secret societies.

The Rothschild Family was the major power behind the Second Bank of the United States, which was documented in Gustavus Myers' "The History of the Great American Fortunes." The Rothschilds learned early that if you control the credit of a nation, you control its economy. Meyer Amschel Moses Bauer started the Rothschild banking interests. He started as a clerk in the Oppenheimer Bank in Hanover and was eventually promoted to junior partner. After his father's death, he returned to Frankfurt to continue the family business, which had been identified by a red shield over the door. A "Roth Schild." He took this as his name. And added five gold arrows, held in the talons to represent his five sons. Their fortune began when they started using fractional reserve banking and turning manufactured debt into equity. His sharp business acumen allowed him to surpass his competitors. His sons expanded the business all over the world. They created an international independent financial empire that still continues to secretly maintain its internal control of global markets and financial dealings.

Wars have been very productive for them. Though not the only ones to do so, they have been able to work both sides of the military street. That why a central bank is so vital for success. He set up his five sons, each in a different country. Patriarch Amschel Rothschild used his sons, the so-called "Frankfurt Five," who were carefully groomed and schooled to advance the family's global banking interests. Meyer went to Frankfort and Solomon to Vienna. He sent Nathan to London, Carl to Naples, and James Rothschild to Paris. This allowed the sons to play one government off against another

The end of the Napoleonic Wars serves as an indication of the financial connection between war and global domination. It is common historical knowledge that the Rothschilds learned in advance the outcome of the Battle of Waterloo. This event is the best illustration of how they were able to amass a global fortune. Mayer Anselm had set up a courier system. The Rothschilds' red pouches were ubiquitous along the roads of Europe. Each brother exchanged financial and political intelligence with each other. They could cross national borders with a minimum of interference. Theatrics had much to do with pulling of this scam. Nathan appeared glum, sitting in the middle of the bond market, at the early news from Belgium. British investors thought Wellington had lost the battle. They rushed to sell every government bond they had. Nathan waited until the last minute when he purchased every bond available at a fraction of its face value. This allowed the Rothschilds to sink their tentacles even more deeply into the British government. They used pigeons to get across the Channel to get a jump on the market. This is a primitive example of "insider trading." The Rothschilds are a privately owned company, which means they don't have to report to any stockholders or public bodies.

The Rothschilds were no strangers to the necessity for a private intelligence network. They had been using such a sophisticated operation for more than a century. Amschel Rothschild had ensured his financial success by organizing a faster and more extensive spy service than the British government. His agents spied all the factions of European courts. The Rothschilds are part of the economic order and so have a vested interest in a world financial order. They loaned money to national governments and truly became the first known global banking structure in the world as they had branch banks in the major cities of Europe. They could and did use their power to extract interest and principle from their people if they ever got into trouble. Despite vain attempts to hide their prowess under the sordid mantel of anti-Semitism, it must be stated that the Rothschilds constitute a veritable international financial dynasty.

Their banks have intimately connected with the great power magnates in this country from the Rockefellers and the Morgans, to the Harrimans and the Carnegies. It was the Morgans and the Rothschilds that enabled Rhodes to establish his monopoly in South Africa over the diamond mines. They were his financiers.

Biographer Derek Wilson wrote in "Rothschild: The Wealth and Power of Dynasty," that opponents of judicial activism "resented them because its influence was exercised behind the scenes, that is in secrecy." In his novel "Coning," future English Prime Minister, Benjamin Disraeli, modeled his character "Sidonia" after Nathan Rothschild, by saying "he was lord and master of the money-markets of the world and of course virtually lord and master of everything else."

The American Civil War also serves as an example of the long reach of their international influence. In 1854, George W. L. Bickley founded of the Knights of the Golden Circle. He declared that he had started the war with an organization that spread succession among the slave states. J. P. Morgan studied in Germany in 1856 at University of Gottingen, where he probably ran into Marx who was writing and lecturing about his communistic ideas. According to John Reeves in his book, "The Rothschilds, the Financial Rulers of Nations," a pivotal meeting took place in London. The International Banking Syndicate decided that the South would fight the North. It was designed to get them to accept a national bank. The nation would not accept one without a strong reason.

The war would be that reason. By dividing the country, they employed the old tactic of divide and conquer. The Knights were established to accomplish this. Lincoln could see it coming. By issuing his own Greenbacks, Lincoln had crossed the bankers. The war was being fought to force the country to accept the national bank, run independently by the European banks. By issuing his own fiat currency, Lincoln had turned his back on them.

Congress passed the National Banking Act in 1863. This created a federally chartered national bank that had the power to issue U. S. Bank Notes, money that could be loaned to the government, supported not by gold but by debt. After the bill passed through Congress, Lincoln warned that the "money power" preys on upon the nation in times of peace and conspires against it in times of adversity. It is more despotism than a monarchy, more insolent than autocracy, and more selfish than bureaucracy is. Lincoln saw a crisis looming on the horizon that unnerved him, causing him to "tremble for the safety of the country." He knew that once corporations became enthroned, an era of corruption would swiftly follow. As a result, it would be the country's money power that would try to prolong its reign by "working upon the prejudices of the people, until the wealth is aggregated in a few hands, and the republic is destroyed," as quoted in H. S. Kennan's book, "The Federal Reserve Bank."

Lincoln depended on the blockade to keep the French and the English out of the war. One of the runners was Thomas W. House, reportedly a Rothschild agent who amassed a fortune through the war. He was the father of Col. Edward M. House, a key figure in the upset election of Woodrow Wilson in 1912, and the main instrument passage of the Federal Reserve Act. Lincoln needed an ally. He looked to Russia for help. Lincoln issued the Emancipation Proclamation because the Russians had freed their serfs in 1861. Lincoln felt it would encourage the Russian people to support the Union. The Russian fleet set sail to America, as a warning to the French and English.

Lincoln was no stranger to conspiracy ideas. He had anticipated an internal conspiracy as early as 1837, during a Springfield, Illinois speech when he said, "If destruction be our lot, we must ourselves be its author and finisher. As a nation of free men, we must live through all time, or die by suicide." Eight people were tried for killing Lincoln. Four were hanged including Mary Surrette, the first woman executed in this country. Other cabinet members and the vice-president were also targeted. Edwin Stanton, and his "Radical Republicans," who were frequently called Jacobeans, a throwback to the Illuminati, in effect took over Washington in an effort to find Lincoln's killer.

Booth had links to several secret societies in the South, including the Carbinari, the Italian branch of the Illuminati. Stanton blocked all the escape roads, except the road by which Booth escaped. Rumors abound that Stanton had allowed a Booth impersonator to be captured and killed allowing Booth to escape. The eighteen missing pages of Booth's diary included names of seventy prominent high government officials and prominent business leaders, who were involved in the assassination conspiracy. The diary was found in the attic of some of Station's descendants, as related in David Balsiger and Charles Sellier's book "The Lincoln Conspiracy."

So it is with this background that Rhodes sought to lay the pillars of his global legacy. His ultimate goal was to return America to the British Empire through a type of intellectual, economic, and social amalgamation. This would be a world power federation, dominated by Anglo-Saxons. By attracting the cream of the American crop each year, Rhodes thought it possible to control or greatly influence the course and direction of America's history. These leaders would all be "citizens of the world," who would break down America's Washingtonian tradition against deep world involvement. Isolationment was the term used to denigrate this historic stance and direction of America's dominant foreign policy since the days of George Washington. Today it is used to denigrate the ideas of traditional conservatives, such as Pat Buchanan.

Though this dictum was modified after Rhodes' death in 1902, money, power and dedication to the idea of world peace through a world federation provided the incentives necessary for members to foster lifelong adherence to the organization. Rhodes knew instinctively that only by controlling the wealth of the world could his plan come to fruition. That meant bringing the world's rich into the plan initially to finance it. The great foundations, such as the Carnegie, Rockefeller, and Ford foundations all signed up for this ambitious plan for a world government. After Rhodes death, Milner, Rothschild, and their international banking associates took control of the Round Tables. These secret societies seem to be following an intricate plan that was formulated years ago and included the ideas of many forerunners from Plato through Karl Marx and Edward House. Rhodes founded DeBeers in South Africa.

To effect this plan, the Rhodes Scholarships, as outlined in his will, became the main instruments whereby the most promising young people throughout the English-speaking world were recruited to serve Rhodes' plan. Like something out of a Robert Ludlum novel, Rhodes scholars were to infiltrate the major corporations, governments, and educational institutions of the world, subtlety exercising their undermining influence and power as they went. The Rhodesian legacy is indeed long and vast. His alumni read like a "Who's Who" in government, finance, journalism, academia and politics. The impact of the elect is incalculable. Rhodes scholars have permeated all elitist walks of life from the Presidency of the United States, cabinet positions, heads of influential businesses and industries, to commissions, federal judges, senators, and the president of the Carnegie Foundation.

There is a strong underpinning of Fabian Socialism behind Rhodes' idea of a one-world government. To understand both Ruskin and Rhodes, one must put them within the context of the Socialist atmosphere that permeated the upper echelons of English society in the latter half of the nineteenth century. The Fabian Society was founded in 1884. It was named after a Third-century Roman General, Quintus Fabius Maximus, who had defeated Hannibal in the second century B. C. Fabius learned patiently to wait before striking his enemy with a fatal blow. He greatly influenced Eduard Bernstein, the leading German Social Democrat exile. The secret to his strategy was to never directly confront the enemy in the open battlefield, but defeat him gradually through a series of small battle, running after each successful foray. Fabian socialists saw themselves as permeating every aspect of English society. In London in the 1890's and transferred across the channel in the early twentieth century. This incremental strategy is analogous to the frog in the vat of boiling water.

The Fabians decided that the free enterprise system was a superior philosophy and they could not afford confront capitalism with a frontal assault. They would content themselves with working slowly but surely, like the fabled tortoise, up against a capitalistic hare. They later changed this to a wolf in sheep's clothing, an image suggested by playwright George Bernard Shaw. They later aligned themselves with the non-violent wing of the Marxist conspiracy. To further their cause, Fabian founder, Sidney Webb created the London School of Economics to serve as an economic institution designed to indoctrinate the children of the very wealthy with the basic tenets of Socialism. Early funding came from the usual foundations, the Rockefeller, Carnegie United Kingdom Trust Fund and Mrs. Ernest Elmhirst, the widow of J. P. Morgan partner Willard. Prominent Americans, such as Joseph Kennedy' s sons, Joseph, Jr. and John studied here.

The major thinking behind Woodrow Wilson's Fourteen Points, originated from two Fabian publications, "Labour's War Aims," written by founder Sidney Webb and "International Government," written by Leonard Wolf. The Fabian texts were drafted into their Fourteen Points for Wilson by American columnist Walter Lippmann, a Fabian since 1909, and the notorious Edward Mandel House, who favored Socialism as envisioned by Karl Marx. It was the irrepressible Mr. House, who exercised near Svengalian control over President Wilson, in what has been described as the strangest friendships in history, who engineered the Fourteen Points. It has been written of House, a founding member of the CFR, that, "No other American of his time was on such close terms with so many men of international fame." House was one of its pioneers and it is a direct outgrowth of the British model, founded by Rhodes and his friends. The Council of Foreign Relations was founded on July 29, 1921 in New York City. It is not surprising that a group such as this, which usually meets in secrecy, has a roster of three thousand of the most powerful politicians, businessmen, and media moguls in the country. He envisioned a one-world economy, a one-world army, government, under a financial oligarchy founded on the Anglo-American model and a world dictator served by a council of twelve faithful men or "wise men."

In 1919 House's supporters founded the Royal Institute of International Affairs, at Chatham House. Its chief financial supporters were Sir Abe Bailey and the Astor family who owned the NY Times. They established similar institutes throughout the dominion and in the United States, especially the CFR. Quigley says the Rhodes coterie intended nothing less than to create a world system of financial control in private hands able to dominate the political system of each country and the economy of the world as a whole.

This leads to a discussion of the idea of convergence, something that Cecil Rhodes implied in his wills and "Confessions." In their 1968 work, "The Lessons of History," historians Will and Ariel Durant described this convergence as an historical inevitability. They wrote "if the Hegelian formula for thesis, antithesis, and synthesis is applied to the Industrial Revolution as the thesis, and to capitalism versus socialism as antithesis, the third condition would a synthesis of capitalism and socialism." This is the situation the country is in today. This begs the question of why businessmen would want to associate with a socialist power. In theory it seems to go against the grain of the stereotypical capitalist. While this may be true in a university economics seminar, in reality most large industrialists hate competition. It is a threat to their financial security. The natural order of things in the United States, with its monopolies and trusts, more closely resembles the Spencerian model of "survival of the fittest."

There are many parallels in history to illustrate this but the most interesting is that of Adolph Hitler and his Nazi Party. German industry recognized his power and strength in the 1930's and chose to pool their interests with the Nazis. They did this, not out of political or patriotic conviction, but because they realized the pragmatic nature of the situation. Hitler was their best hope of re-establishing the German industrial might and removing the Allied yoke from around their necks. It was a classic convergence of capitalism and socialism to produce a super state with strong military and industrial output. It nearly conquered the world. They were the stereotypical example of the "fascist state." Many of the same elements are presents within the United States military/industrial complex and the federal government, even today.

There is no such thing as "impersonal historical forces." People make history. It is very personal. Oliver North quotes at length Gabriel Kolko's study of the Progressive movement, the "Triumph of Conservatism," published in 1963. He argued that the liberal, reformist rhetoric of the Progressive period was in fact "a cover for big business that used the power of the Federal government to establish monopolies that became insulated from price competitions from newer more innovative firms." The late Murray Rothbard and his Chicago School of Economics came to the same conclusions.

It is widely assumed that the Morgan interests took advantage of the unsettled economic conditions in 1907 to cause a business and banking panic. This put many of their competitors out of business. Woodrow Wilson, then the President of Princeton, made an address in which he said that all this trouble could be averted if we appointed a committee of six or seven public-spirited men like J. P. Morgan to handle the affairs of the country. The main thrust of the explanation about the causes was that the country dearly needed a central bank, to prevent the abuses of the Wall Street bankers. The dealings take on the mystery of an old Robert Ludlum novel. Perhaps it could be called "The Morgan Protocol," or "The Jekyll Island Memorandum."

When government interfered in the halcyon days of big government and trust busting, business learned early that if they could not beat them, the best route was to infiltrate and undercut their ideals from within. It proved to be even more advantageous because now they would not have to resort to shady business practices and even violence to protect their interests but could merely attract the best politicians and justices that money and influence could buy. Contrary to the reforms of the Progressive Period, big business has taken control of government or at least unduly influenced it for its own ends. This has led to a virtual partnership that would have made Hitler and Mussolini proud.

Many of these economic reformers in the United States turned to Karl Marx's formula to set up the structure for their assuming a controlling interest in the affairs of state and economy. Frederick Howe detailed the strategy in his 1906 book, "The Confessions of A Monopolist." He stated the rules of big business, which are reducible to a simple maxim: "Get a monopoly and let society work for you." The best thing for business is "a legislative grant, franchise, subsidy, or tax exemption," which is worth more than "a Kimberly or Comstock Lode, since it does not require any labor . . . for its exploitation." Howe was discussing what today is called "welfare capitalism." It was an affirmative action policy for the select businesses that have the ear and the consent of the president and key members of Congress. It is what has made this country run and it is basically inconsistent with a strict rendering of the nation's Constitution. It was no odd coincidence that they used to call Senator Robert Dole, the "Senator from Arthur Daniels," because of his close association with the company. It effect this idea has fostered a corruptive influence on American business and government.

Central to Rhodesian economic thought was the idea of the idea of the central bank, as written in Karl Marx's Communist Manifesto. The very notion of the central bank had historically caused great dissention in the United States. It had militated against the parochial nature of many of the founding fathers, especially Thomas Jefferson and later Andrew Jackson. Careers had been made and destroyed over this volatile issue. A central bank would serve as the vehicle to best institutionalize the relationship between government and state. Its role as that of a Trojan Horse through which the nation's most powerful bankers could seize a monopoly over our monetary system. Rockefeller and Morgan felt the best place to do this was in the political arena.

What the monopolists wanted was a central bank of issue, similar to the Bank of England or the Reichsbank of Germany, that is, a federally funded but privately controlled institution, whose notes would be legal tender. This structure is just an invitation to power and greed beyond comprehension. According to Marx and Engels, the purpose of a central bank was to give international banking cartel access to control of the money system. This would allow the bankers to manipulate the economy anyway they want with little or no interference from politicians. J. P. Morgan went to London in 1869 to form the Northern Securities Company, which made him the Rothschilds' representative in the United States.

The Rothschilds had not set up any of their relatives in New York. It was an omission they gravely regretted. The NSC would act as their agent in this country. The need for the central bank came about because there was a great growth in new regional banks after the turn of the nineteenth century. In the first ten years of the new century, twenty thousand new banks had been formed. The New York banks were suffering a decline in revenue.

Secrecy is an elementary part in any idea of a conspiracy. Adam Weishaupt said "Of all the means I know to lead men, the most effectual is a concealed mystery." There have been several secretive or closed-door meetings that lend credence to some of these conspiracy theories. The clandestine 1910 meeting at Jekyl Island fits the mold. It did take place and it included clearly a quarter of the wealth of the world. While they did conspire in a personal and perhaps, immoral sense, to pass the proper enabling legislation that implanted the Federal Reserve System into place, they broke no laws in meeting. Benjamin Strong became its first Chairman of the New York bank. The first Governor of the Board of Governors was Paul Warburg.

The Jekyll Island Club exists today as the ingenious solution of the difficult problem of finding profound seclusion and congenial companionship in one and the same spot. So read the Preamble of the Jekyll Club in 1916 just five years after the famed secret meeting.

Jekyll Island is one of eight small barrier islands south of Savannah where wealthy families like the Vanderbilts frolicked in the winter sun. It is like most of Georgia's coastal areas, rich in history and tradition. The Island has been at various times occupied by Indian tribes, Spanish missionaries, English soldiers, French setters and finally by a coterie of the nation's financial elite. By the time General James Edward Oglethorpe established the first permanent Georgia settlement in 1733, making Georgia the thirteenth colony, the Guale Indians, the island's first inhabitants and the Spanish missionaries who had followed them, had all disappeared from Jekyl. The following year, Oglethorpe renamed the Island, "Jekyl," in honor of his friend and benefactor, Sir Joseph Jekyl.

The Civil War and subsequent Reconstruction destroyed the Island's plantation economy. It was at this time that wealthy Northerners flocked to the Island, seeking a winter's respite from the formidable northern weather. Jekyll Island, now spelled with an extra "l" became the winter retreat for the leading forces behind the American business and technological boom. The names Morgan Rockefeller, Pulitzer, Astor, and Vanderbilt all associated here for some time. Its members also included James Renwick who designed St. Patrick's Cathedral in New York City and Madison Square Garden, builder, David H. King and the attending physician during President U. S. Grant's terminal battle with cancer as well as the assassination of James Garfield.

It was a more important meeting that laid the basis for the new National Bank that would totally revolutionize American fiscal affairs and lead us into the clutches of the New World Order. It was at Jekyll Island that some of the major scions of the world met to formulate their plans for the future economic, political and social paradigm of the world.

Morgan spent two years touring the central banks of Europe, presumably learning all their financial secrets. In November of 1910 he boarded a train in Hoboken, New Jersey for a ride to Jekyl Island, Georgia for the most important meeting of his life. The roster of his fellow passengers for that storied meeting read like a directory of the world's wealthiest financiers and politicians.

The list included such financial luminaries as A. Piatt Andrew, Taft's Assistant Secretary of the Treasury, and Frank Vanderlip, president of Kuhn-Loeb's National City Bank of New York. Henry Davidson was a Senior Partner of J. P. Morgan while Charles Norton was the President of Morgan's First National Bank of New York. Benjamin Strong was the President of Morgan's Banker's Trust Company.

Paul Warburg, a leading partner in the banking house of Kuhn-Loeb & Company, was the architect of the system. He wrote what the guiding standard of the new bank would be. His people want a "flexible currency," whose value would fluctuate, "not in accordance with the amount of gold, but with the amount of commercial bills in the market . . ." Gold was a limiting, but stabilizing facet of the monetary system. Big Business liked the volatility because it could give them the opportunity of making huge profits as the small investors would panic every time the economy took a nosedive.

Collectively they represented one-fourth of the world's wealth. They were sworn to secrecy on this trip by Senator Aldrich and asked to refer to each other by only their first names. This became known as the "First Name Club." The result of their meeting was the infamous "Aldrich Plan," which eventually became the Federal Reserve System.

Vanderlip later revealed his role in the Jekyll Island meeting in an article in the "Saturday Evening Post." He expressed his fears apprehension before the meeting when he wrote " . . . in 1901 when I was as secretive, indeed as furtive, as any conspirator, I do not feel it is any exaggeration to speak of our secret expedition to Jekyl Island as the occasion of the actual conception of what eventually became the Federal Reserve System." The "conspirators," all rode in Aldrich's private railroad car. They had to avoid the name "Central Bank" because it had an ominous ring to it. So they came up with name of "Federal Reserve System." It had a milder, gentler aura to it, even if it failed to relate to any specific reality. It was to be owned by private individuals who would draw profit from their ownership of shares. They would have the lofty power of being able to control the nation's money supply. They would also get tax-free dividends. In effect they had stripped Congress of its Constitutional authority to regulate financial affairs. The system had twelve regional banks but only one director who controlled all the banks. He had control over the nation's financial resources. This privately owned cartel of banks does and has controlled the economic and political destiny of this country for seventy years now. To excuse their concentration of power in the name of that it was not illegal is to miss the magnitude of what these few insiders have accomplished in a short period of time. It matters little how these insiders of the establishment have garnered their power. They have it, which they intend to use for their own ends.

Aldrich was the only non-banker present. He was a Mason, and the maternal grandfather of David and Nelson Rockefeller brothers. He was appointed to a National Monetary Committee and charged to make a thorough study of financial practices before formulating banking and currency reform legislation. When he entered Congress in 1881, his net worth was around fifty thousand dollars. When he left several years later, he was worth $30 million. President Taft had threatened to veto the bill. The Aldrich Act failed to garner support and was soundly defeated. Taft had to go! This was accomplished when the financial powers enlisted former president, Theodore Roosevelt to run against his own successor. The power elite realized that Woodrow Wilson, their hand-chosen candidate, did not have the support to win in a two-horse race. The Morgan interests chipped in with several million to launch Roosevelt's campaign.

On March 16, 1998, I took a bus tour whose first stop was the Jekyll Island Club Hotel where it all had began nearly ninety years ago. The fortress-like structure gave off the air of wealth, highs finance, and intrigue. The so-called secret meeting that gave us the Federal Reserve System is no secret any more. The Club emanates an air of big money and high finance. Without any mention of the concentration of moneyed power, the brochures and the surroundings suggest their non-cognitive approval of what transpired behind closed doors in 1910. The tour took us around the grounds, pointing out Morgan's favorite table in the northwest corner of the luxurious Grand Dinning Room. I walked past meeting rooms with the ominous names of J. P. Morgan and the Federal Reserve Room. The embossed initials "J.P." were ubiquitous.

In his book, "Wall Street," Dr. Anthony Sutton says the Federal Reserve System is "a legal private monopoly of the money supply operated for the benefit of the few under the guise of protecting and promoting the public interest." The reason the bankers fought for the Federal Deposit Insurance Corporation was so that they could have a tighter hold on the taxpayers, who would inadvertently support their reckless behavior.

What most people do not realize is that the federal government has little control over the Federal Reserve Banking System. It is not a government-controlled system. The Fed is a privately owned institution is divided, broken into twelve parts, but that was merely a public relations tool. Paul Warburg warned the participants at Jekyl Island in 1910 that the American people would never go for a central bank, so they had to give it the appearance of a series of regional banks. They all knew that the New York "branch" carried the most weight. The Federal Reserve is virtually autonomous. While the president, with the Senate's consent, appoints its members, they serve for fourteen years, staggered so that only one member's term expires every two years. They are not required to seek the approval of any of their actions from any branch of government. An astonishing fact is that in the nearly ninety years it has been in operation, the Fed has never been subjected to an independent audit.

Tax reform is the other side of the Marxist coin. Led by the Rothschild agents in this country, these financial forces had been trying since the 1880's to get an income tax and a central bank. Such basic changes would facilitate greater government control over the American people. They created an alliance between politicians and businessmen, which is still very vital today. The businessmen wanted government support and protection for their businesses, especially in case of bad loans. By having a graduated income tax structure, they would have a large reservoir of capital from which they could tap if ever anything when wrong. The tax structure and the central bank would act as their safety net provided by the government and paid for by the American taxpayers. This was a conspiracy of greed, bringing out the worst instincts of American business. As Ferdinand Lundberg observed in "The Rich and the Super-Rich," the income tax eventually became "the siphon, gradually inserted into the pocketbooks the general public." As government got bigger more money was transferred, not to the poor, but to the wealthy friends of big business. Frederic Morton wrote in his 1961 book, "The Rothschilds," about how the "wealth of the Rothschild consists in the bankruptcy of nations." Nothing much has changed. H. G. Wells, a Fabian Socialist, felt the same way. "Big Business is by no means antipathetic to Communism . . . It is the upper road of the few instead of the lower road of the masses to Collectivism."

The first major move was the income tax which was sold to the nation as a "soak the rich" scheme. In 1908 Rhode Island Senator, Nelson Aldrich of Rhode Island introduced the legislation that was destined to be the sixteenth amendment. He was the "authentic" voice of the Morgan banking interests. When this same idea had been first introduced in 1894, Aldrich had denounced it as "Communist" in nature. He had changed his tune with this form of government and business marriage.

Another agent of the Rothschild banking interest was Colonel Edward Mandel House. For the first thirty years of the twentieth century, House was the facilitator of the New World Order. He was dialectically close to the leading international bankers but also authored a book, "Socialism as Dreamed of by Karl Marx." House also wrote another fascinating book, "Philip Dru, Administrator," published in 1912. The plot of his novel revolves a meeting in 1925 between John Thor, described as a High Priest of Finance and Senator Selwyn, who found out that government was run by a few men, and that outside of this little circle, no one was of much importance. Selwyn wanted to be part of the inner circle. He wanted to secretly govern the country with an absolute hand.

Dru, who is not involved directly in the plot, recruits a half-million man army and marches to Washington as President

Rockland flees the country. Selwyn is appointed acting president and surrenders the country to Dru. Dru keeps Selwyn as president but assumes powers of a dictator. He is now in a position to give the country a new and better form of government. He arranges for several key Marxist programs, such as the graduated income tax and a punitive inheritance tax. As president he then abolishes the right to sell anything of value, in effect severely limiting private property. He starts making decisions as if there were in Al Gore's words, "no governing authority." He also re-writes the obsolete and grotesque Constitution of the United States. He then hopes for great changes in Russia, that despotic land with great potential.

House later admitted that this book reflected his ethical and political faith. He saw himself in his hero, Philip Dru. It was his "Mein Kampf." One only has to study his relationship with President Woodrow Wilson to see how much of his philosophy he was able to inflict on the American people. Franklin Roosevelt wrote to Colonel House, " . . . as you and I know, that a financial element in the larger centers has owned the government ever since the days of Andrew Jackson . . . The country is going through a repetition of Jackson's fight with the Bank of the United States— only a far bigger and broader basis."

Wilson was an important and enigmatic player in this "Open Conspiracy." He once admitted that there was something un-American, something rotten in Denmark. "There is a power somewhere so organized, so subtle, so watchful, so interlocked, so complete, and so pervasive that they better not speak above their breath when they speak in condemnation of it." He did not identify this group as the Masons because he was part of it. Another Mason who read this book was Franklin Roosevelt. It is possible that he later called his addresses to the nation, "Fireside Chats," because Dru sat smugly, smoking by a log fire in his library.

Most of the international bankers of the world live in this country yet they have no real allegiance or patriotic fervor for this country. They are only concerned with making money and insuring the power to preserve and extend their moneymaking ability. Their essential purpose is to so alter our monetary system to make it easier for them to control all monetary systems all over the globe. President Clinton enjoyed his high approval ratings during an unprecedented litany of personal and governmental scandals and accusations, primarily because the economy was robust, buoyed by the low-interest rates, high employment manipulations of Federal Reserve Chairman, Alan Greenspan.

In order to drum up public support, business needed to influence the editorial policy of many of the country's dailies. In the Congressional Record for February 9, 1917, Representative Oscar Callaway described how big business controls their public image. They infiltrated the newspaper business by getting twelve men high up in the newspaper world and employed them to select the most influential newspapers in the United States and sufficient number of them to control generally the policy of the daily press of the United States. The twelve selected 1879 newspapers and then began an elimination process to secure enough to unduly influence the whole industry. They found that they had to purchase a controlling interest in just twenty-five and insert their own editors, to effectively control the editorial policy of all the nation's newspapers with their own liberal attitudes.

Not everyone was fooled by what amounted to an unconstitutional power grab. One man who opposed this legislation was Congressman Charles Lindbergh, Sr. He warned the American people the Federal Reserve System was created to foster economic emergencies. He felt it was an instrument of economic destruction. Another Congressman, Louis McFadden, complained that the Congress did not foresee a world banking system was being set up, controlled by international bankers acting in concert to "enslave the world for their own pleasure." After the Stock Market Crash in 1929 had run its course, McFadden complained that the money and credit resources of the United States was now in the complete control of the banker's alliance between J.P Morgan's First National Bank group and Kuhn, Loeb's National City Bank. On May 23, 1933, McFadden brought impeachment charges against the Federal Reserve Board. "I charge them with having taken over eighty billion dollars from the United States Government in the year 1928 . . . I charge them with having arbitrarily and unlawfully raised and lowered the rates on money . . . increased and diminished the volume of currency in circulation for the benefits of private interests."

McFadden also charged them with having conspired to transfer to foreigners and international moneylender's title to and control of the financial resources of the United States. Unsurprisingly there were two assassination attempts on McFadden's life by gunfire. When he died a few hours after attending a banquet, "there is little doubt that he was poisoned," wrote Martin Larson in his book, "The Federal Reserve."

Years later, Chairman of the House Banking Committee, Wright Patman succinctly described what the Federal Reserve Act had done. He knew that in the "United States today we have in effect two governments . . . We have the duly constituted Government . . . Then we have an independent, uncontrolled and uncoordinated government in the Federal Reserve System, operating the money powers which are reserved to Congress by the Constitution."

By the end of the 1930's, several countries had central banks. The grand scale in the New World Order was to have a universal central bank for the entire world. J. P. Morgan was responsible for the Bank for International Settlement, under the Hague Agreement in 1930, an international bank for all the world's central banks. In "Tragedy and Hope," Quigley said that the aim was to "create a world system of financial control in private hands able to dominate the political system of each country and the economy of a world as a whole." The system was to be controlled in a feudal fashion by the central banks of the world acting in concert by secret agreements arrived at in frequent meetings and conferences. Basel, Switzerland was to be the apex of this international system through the auspices of the Bank for International Settlement. In an August 5, 1995 article for the New York Times, Keith Bradsher wrote "In a small Swiss city sits an international organization so obscure and secretive . . ." Control of the institution, the Bank for International Settlements, lies with some of the world's powerful and least visible men: the heads of thirty-two central banks. Their officials are able to shift billions of dollars and alter the course of economics at the stroke of a pen.

This Eastern Establishment, with a pervasive Rockefeller influence, has effected a substantial unauthorized takeover of the national government, which in a country with a written constitution implies, a silent coup de tat. Many will disagree with this idea but it does go a long way in explaining why the nation seems to be on an unalterable course to the brink of financial ruin when most Americans favor making substantial changes in the course and direction. It also explains the poor and anti-national interest decisions our leaders have been making since the conclusion of World War II. Our closet socialist leaders have been leading us on a utopian path to world governance, totally ignoring the tensions that exist between the popular, sentimental idea of nationalism and those of an elite worldly idealism. These leaders have done great harm to this nation by defining the national interest in terms of, not the sordid, violent realities of the Realpolitik but rather in terms of an interdependent world order in which the anachronisms of conflict and war will be finally discarded.

The Rhodesian legacy still haunts us today. It has evolved into a global network of Rhodes scholars that stretches through all levels of world government, even the White House. Writer William Jasper says that his most significant legacy, the secret society for world government, which he established in 1891. It was through the "Round Table" that he exercised his megalomaniac obsession for power. It is ironic that even though he died in 1902, the twentieth century is inarguably marked with his vision of imperial conquest through subterfuge. His secret society was the principal fixture of his life, magnifying his influence way beyond other malefactors of great wealth. His graduates went on to dominate the American government, especially the State Department. The global context of American foreign policy since the 1930's is clearly visible. Their world bias was clearly evidenced as they worked tirelessly to effect a future world government and global unity.

The Association of American Rhodes Scholars numbers about sixteen hundred alumni who have become part of our new democratic ruling elite. This power elite includes such leading thinkers as economist Lester Thurlow, Sinologist, the late John K. Fairbank, Nicholas Katzenbach, Senator Bill Bradley, and the late

Howard K. Smith. The late Senator, J. William Fulbright, who like his protégé, Bill Clinton considered himself a "world citizen," was the very epitome of the Rhodes Scholar. Carl Albert, the late Speaker of the House, the late Dean Rusk, Michael Kinsley and historian Daniel Boorstin are some of the others in this influential elite. There were at least twenty Rhodes scholars in the Clinton administration alone, including Strobe Talbot, Ira Magaziner, and Robert Reich. Rhodes had planned that by the year 1920 there would be just under three thousand men in the prime of life scattered all over the world, each of whom would have been specially gifted toward the Rhodes' imperial goals.

6

The Brotherhood of the Flesh

"The chains of habit are too weak to be felt until they
are too strong to be broken." Samuel Johnson

English novelist Aldous Huxley let the proverbial cat out of
the bag in 1938 when he revealed that the real reason intellectuals
of his generation embraced modernism was because of the
unrestricted sexual freedom that it guaranteed them. Most
biographers of great modernists, such as Jean-Paul Sartre, Margaret
Mead, or Sigmund Freud have all but ignored their sexual
proclivities. Since the time of Luther and Descartes, the West has
accepted the notion that what people do with their bodies have no
effect on how they use their minds. E. Michael Jones, the editor of
"Culture Wars Magazine," focused on this liberal contradiction in
his book, "Degenerate Moderns." Sex is an appetite of unusual
power, especially when it is not properly controlled. Undisciplined
sexual behavior leads to compulsive behavior, which is the antithesis
of rational behavior. Jones conclusively established the link between
the private behaviors and public philosophies of its liberal
luminaries.

Mead's book, "Coming of Age," did much to underpin the
Sexual Revolution epidemic of the sixties with her emphasis on
the free love tendencies of the Samoan natives in their natural state.
Jones relates how Mead wrote her book, partially as a justification
for her promiscuous life style. Mead, who was married, was involved
in two lifelong affairs—one with a man and the other with

anthropologist Ruth Benedict. Jones argues that Freud's famous Oedipus Complex was just a rationalization for his incestuous relationship with his sister-in-law, Minna. By developing the theory that such illicit desires were universal, he projected his guilt feelings onto the world at large, avoiding self-blame for his misbehavior. All modern philosophies can be understood in light of the moral disorders of their founders, proponents, and advocates. Jones also clearly demonstrated how the intellectual's revolt against the moral law, is in effect, a rebellion against truth itself. Jones has shown, without reservation, how the twin creeds of modernity, that is, personal hedonism and social utopianism, are the products of the disordered lives of middle class intellectuals.

Probably one of the most degenerate human beings ever to walk the face of the earth was Aleister Crowley. Crowley was called the "King of Depravity and the "Wickedest Man on Earth." If the idea of a "Renaissance Man" invokes an image of one who is well versed in many intellectual and moral issues of his day, then Crowley might properly be called an "Apocalyptic Man," because his entire life embodied a journey into deep human degradation and perversity. Crowley once said, "to me every dirty act was simply a sacrament of sin, a passionately religious protest against Christianity, which for me was the symbol of all vileness, meanness, treachery, falsehood and oppression."

Born in England in 1875, his real name was Edward Alexander. He later changed it to "Aleister," to avoid sharing the same first name as his father, who died when he was eleven. As a child he was fond of torturing cats in horrible ways to see if they really had nine lives. He surrendered his virginity at age fourteen to a household maid. At seventeen he got his first case of gonorrhea from a prostitute. At Cambridge he studied alpine climbing, living in the life of an aristocrat. Crowley also enjoyed as much sex as humanly possible, showing no preference for women or men. This was in strict contrast to the behavior of his parents, who were strict fundamentalist. He was a self-centered child who had disliked his mother. He called her a "brainless bigot." It was his mother who called him "the Beast 666 of Revelation." He adopted the name as a form of rebellion against his earlier Christian formation. Crowley had almost no capacity for natural affection. He showed great indifference toward the death of his first two children and the mental illness of his wife Rose. In his autobiography, "The Confessions of Aleister Crowley," he admitted that much of his later depravity was a revolt against the moral strictures of his childhood. His religious upbringing had equated sex with sin and since his sex life was intense and varied, he had to refute and disavow that influence. His entire life became the embodiment of this rebellion, especially with regard to sexual sins. To him religion became the oppressor of the human soul, the blasphemer who denied the supremacy of the individual will. The only religious faith Crowley ever displayed was an antinomianism, which was the belief that Christians were freed from obeying the moral law because of grace and faith. Crowley personified the writings of the Gnostics and Rosicrucians on sexual expression. He was a pansexual, as was Alfred Kinsey. Hugh Hefner limited his sexual activities to beautiful women.

Crowley's strong Biblical formation left him with a deep disdain for Christianity. While at Trinity College at Cambridge University he met George Cecil Jones, who was a member of the Hermetic Order of the Golden Dawn, which was an occult society, with Rosicrucian roots. The Order's contribution to western Magical Tradition is worth noting. It was their synthesis of the Kabbala, alchemy, astrology, divination, numerology, Masonic symbolism and ritual magic into one logical and coherent system that led them to influence countless future occult societies.

Crowley was initiated into the Order in 1898 and quickly rose among its ranks. He traveled extensively through Asia and the Middle East, learning and practicing Yoga and Oriental mysticism. Crowley later became involved with the Ordo Templi Orientis (O.T.O.). This group of high-ranking Freemasons had claimed to discover the supreme secret of "practical magic," which was taught in its highest degrees. Crowley's experimental methods got him expelled from the Golden Dawn.

Crowley later wrote the "Book of Law," which explained his philosophy as "Do What Thou Will." The writings of Rabelais and William Blake greatly influence this book. It was his Koran and he was its chosen prophet. He believed that the epoch of God and demons must get out of the way for the new area, which was at hand. This new era was one in which man stopped thinking of himself as a mere creature and stood firmly on his feet. This was the enlightened rationalist idea of secular humanism. Crowley did not stop here. He took a Nietzschean leap forward to a position where man must see himself, not merely as human but as divine. "The Book of Law," was his attempt to write a semi-biblical text, like "Thus Sapke Zarathustra." George Bernard Shaw evoked this same idea in his play "Man and Superman," written about the same time. While Nietzsche emphasized the "will to power," Crowley was more interested in transcending sexual expression and the liberation of men from the dreaded restrictions of religious faith.

Crowley liked magic because it was the direct and empowering contact with the divine. Crowley had developed a philosophy that revolved around what he called "sexual magic." It was the secret behind much of his thinking. To intensify his sexual release, he employed the sacred techniques of the ancient tantric practices, which include cosmic couplings, such as the passive emulation of Shiva and the energetic Shakti. Crowley usually assumed the "female" role in his sexual relations with other men. As part of his ritual, he sodomized Victor Neuberg in Paris in 1913, as part of a magical ceremony. Neuberg later married and settled down but remain obsessed with Crowley for the rest of his life. Crowley had cursed him when they broke up and Neuberg attributed his life of bad health to that curse. Crowley's "The Scented Garden," was the most frank and impassioned exploration of his own sexuality. Surprisingly, critics have failed to rank it as a classic example of gay literature. He had been practicing sexual magic since 1911. He described it as the "art of producing phenomena at will."

Crowley was a staunch defender of every vice known to mankind. He developed his own Gnostic Mass, replete with multiple speaking parts, choreographed ritual that was to parallel the Catholic Latin rite Mass. Crowley carried sexual magic and traditional tantric practices even further. For him the object was not limited to a mystical union with the goddess or god, but could involve any form of concentrated inspiration or it could even manifest itself as a magical child. This could occur in any form, such as a talisman, or even a human baby, or a newly spiritually transformed adult man or woman. This inspiration would eventually lead to the creation of the "divine self," fully released from the human soul.

Crowley felt that the sexual organs were the image of God. The best way to free the hidden powers of the subconscious mind was through sexual magic. Crowley felt the church's sexual restrictions were unhealthy and they placed a destructive restraint on his sexual freedom because the phallus was "both symbolically and functionally the microcosmic human manifestation of the power of divine creation." Crowley strongly believed that orgasm was good for one's health. He was all for students deciding what form of life or moral code they would follow. In sexual magic, one had to experience the physiological phenomena in order to understand it. This constituted the true esoteric secret of the act.

Crowley practiced sex magic with whomever he could get to join him. One such coupling included a gaggle of Russian chorus girls, called the "Ragged Ragtime Girls." Crowley's sexual antics often included sadomasochism. One partner had to be beaten violently before she could be satisfied. To intensify his sexual release he even sharpened his canine teeth so he could inflict love bites on the wrist, and the throat with his fangs. He called this his "serpent's kiss." His biographer, John Symonds, wrote that Crowley defecated on carpets, because he believed even his ordure was "sacred." Crowley emphasized the complementary roles of the "Beast" and his female lovers, who were known as "Scarlet Women." The way he described his actions demonstrated a blending of the "Christian, Taoist, and Thelemic symbolism." Crowley was the "a Sun, giving Light and Life," while his mistress was "their guide in darkness, making them pure, single of heart, awake to the Highest."

Thelema, which is Greek for "The Will," was the name he gave to his "religious abbey," where he practiced his sexual magic.

Crowley covered his walls with pictures of people having sex in every imaginable position and demons of all kinds. He called the studio," the Chamber of Nightmares." These pornographic paintings provided Crowley with the sensual atmosphere he needed to put his conquests in the mood. The Abbey did not have any lavatories. His philosophy of Thelema would admit the natural propriety of homosexual relationships but it would not go so far as to champion its acceptance into the societal mores.

When one of his students, Raoul Loveday died after some weeks of Crowley and his rituals, Italian dictator Benito Mussolini, ordered him to vacate Thelema. He fled to Tunis, where he acquired a small black boy with whom he performed more acts of sex magic. Crowley's homosexuality began as an act of open defiance of convention rather than actual preference. By this time, it seemed to be just another nasty habit.

For one who thought he was God, Crowley could not even master his own life. He would eat and drink until he became bloated and then deliberately starve himself back to a normal weight. His body started to deteriorate from chronic bronchitis and asthma. His many sessions with mescaline, hashish, cocaine, heroin, and opium also greatly worsened his health. He never developed an interior strength and throughout the last quarter of his life he was addicted to drugs and alcohol. He died in 1947 at the age of 72.

Aleister Crowley passed on his baton of sexual depravity to a meek and outwardly man whose early interests centered on his gall wasp collection. This was Alfred Kinsey, who would revolutionize the sexual mores of the American people. One illustration should prove how far out of the sexual mainstream Kinsey was. One night during a moment of despondency because his Institute for Sex Research had lost its major funding from the Rockefeller Foundation, Professor Alfred C. Kinsey looked at the exposed pipes in his basement office in Wylie Hall. He tossed a rope over the exposed pipes. He fastened one end around his scrotum and tugging hard while he masturbated. For years he had boosted the pain he inflicted on himself with urethral insertions, sometimes using a toothbrush to stimulate himself. As Dr. James Jones, a professor of history at University of Houston, relates in his seminal study "Alfred C. Kinsey: A Public and Private Life," this was a typical activity for the man who helped destroy the traditional moral strictures of the Christian code of personal ethics. With Kinsey as a guide, it is not too difficult to understand how American society has lost its way into the sexual wilderness that characterizes the country's "anything goes" mentality toward sex.

Like Crowley, Kinsey considered religion a major source of human misery. He also had an abiding animus against Catholics. Religious people struck him as the "most wretchedly conflicted group." In words that were laced in anger and spite, Kinsey said the Catholic Church "has always emphasized the abnormality or perverseness of sexual behavior, which occurs outside of marriage." In his abject criticism, Kinsey displayed a chutzpah that often characterizes E. Michael Jones' degenerate moderns. Kinsey believed that the Church was responsible for the breakdown of the family because of its relentless hostility to human passion and its strident efforts to control the sexual behaviors of family members. He opposed certain "aspects of Catholic dogma that were very repressive," such as birth control. Kinsey was a "eugenicist in his thinking." He thought, "the wrong people were having too many babies."

Kinsey's whole professional and private life was a frontal assault on traditional morality in a revolutionary attempt to dismantle the cause of his own self-torment. He suffered great pangs of conscience and guilt over his sexual yearning and his incessant masturbatory sessions as a young man. As an Eagle Scout, he often used his love of the outdoors to parade around naked in front of his fellow scouts in a veiled attempt to initiate sexual activity.

Kinsey's dedicated assault on religious and moral tradition also utilized the academic surroundings of his very popular marriage course at Indiana University in Bloomington. It was here that Kinsey perfected his technique of the personal case history. He interviewed everyone he came into contact with, including many inmates from area prisons. His casual manner undressed his subjects of their inhibitions against detailing their innermost sexual secrets. Kinsey catalogued their sexual histories into what he considered meaningful data. He used his "scientific: data re-institute pagan and modernistic attitudes about sex, marriage, and homosexuality that are at the very heart of the culture war today. In a very real way Kinsey was one of the pioneering members of the sexual vanguard that would assault the Christian code that had characterized American society for nearly two hundred years.

Kinsey was a firm believer in moral relativism. "What is right for one individual may be wrong for the next." What is sin and abomination for one "may be a worthwhile part of the next individual's life." Kinsey believed that "the range of individual variation in any particular case is usually greater than is generally understood." He thought man and woman were no better than the gall wasps he collected and studied for the first part of his professional life. So-called crimes against nature, such as masturbation, oral genital contacts and homosexual practices were common among many mammals. Society may condemn them on moral grounds, but it was impossible and unscientific to call them unnatural. With logic only George Orwell could fathom, Kinsey declared that the great distortions of sex are the "cultural perversions" of celibacy, delayed marriage, chastity, and asceticism. Kinsey viewed himself as a defender and protector of the institution of marriage. By stressing the need for premarital sexual intercourse, he erroneously taught that it would strength the marriage bond later.

In his book, "The Age of Consent," researcher Robert H. Knight demonstrated how American culture has descended from the time when the society had a moral consensus with the Ten Commandments at the focal point. Since the 1950's, the moral tenor of society has declined into a state in which personal gratification is the defining factor. What Knight calls "New Age Relativism" has not produced a neutral common ground but a general leveling of the defense of civilization itself. This is especially true on college campuses where professors of the "old school," are losing their positions to a new wave of radical Marxists whose clarion call of "political correctness," is the new standard.

Dr. Kinsey's sexual research, which included a voyeuristic collection of thousands of case histories, unscientific methodology, and the observance of the sexual abuse of children, revolved around the theory that deviance is the engine of social and biological processes. While Kinsey's personal sex history is still secret, biographer Jones made an impressive case that he, too, was justifying his own inner leanings, if not behaviors, by his research. This is perfectly consistent with E. Michael Jones' "degenerate moderns," thesis.

Kinsey was the high priest of liberation, an iconoclast popular morality. It was his sexual ministry. His belief was that all sexual desires are normal and should be acted upon without inhibition or guilt. He wanted to extend his ministry to the prisons where many people were unjustly imprisoned because of their sexual behavior. He reasoned that current sexual legal prohibitions were based on Talmudic proscriptions and not the product of rational scientific judgments. Kinsey saw himself as a modern day Martin Luther or John Calvin, who had proclaimed the Protestant Reformation to anoint each individual as his own priest. Kinsey had come to proclaim a secular revolution that would wrest control of the most intimate and private of affairs from the perversions of religious faith and ordain all people to the "priesthood of their own genitalia." Liberation from sexual morality has had an enslaving aspect that has addicted millions of males through what Gustave Flaubert has called the "groined archway."

The basis of Kinsey's science was his own homosexual compulsions. He was compelled to witness bizarre sexual behavior, to personally engage in it and then to justify it by claiming that large segments of the population were doing it themselves. He was looking for ways to justify his own sexual behavior. Kinsey toured the gay scene wherever he traveled from Rome through Paris. He felt Spain was "a priest-ridden country." He learned that other European nations had handled sexuality without all the prudery and prohibitions this country did. He took 7,985 case histories and created a large store of erotica, which still resides in his archives in Bloomington.

Kinsey had sexual relations with anyone who would submit to him. But it was mostly with men, especially in sado/masochistic circumstances that really excited him. Kinsey believed that the main cause of homosexuality was society's failure to condone premarital heterosexual relations. Kinsey's open admission that he was a homosexual came after years of claiming that he was a devoted family man. He was, according to his biographer James Jones, a "crypto-reformer," who turned "voyeurism into science." He was a "covert revolutionary," involved in a "furtive attempt at social engineering." Kinsey excused his own sexual perversions in the name of science. He hated "normal" sexual relationships so much that he did everything he could to discredit and undercut the norm.

Kinsey was a scandal just waiting to unfold. The horror of his personal life, which was repeatedly covered up by his institute and the foundation, is only rivaled by the horrific lives of those who followed his example in the name of liberation. Kinsey was a sexual addict, masquerading as a scientist, in a nation that was shallow enough to listen to him. Those that followed his advice are still paying the price. His institute is still engaging in a cover-up to protect his image and their grants.

Deviance, according to E. Michael Jones, "clearly takes on a metaphysical if not a theological role in Kinsey's philosophy." As his obsessions became more dominant, Kinsey became determined to find a connection been evolution and homosexuality. Evolution had become for him the matrix for deviance or the point where something new develops. To Kinsey homosexuality was an evolutionary step above heterosexuality. Darwin legitimized Kinsey's deviant behavior. His scientific license eradicated society's outmoded moral norms.

By mid-summer of 1939, Kinsey was spending every weekend in Chicago where he had gained entry into the nether world of homosexual culture. Homosexuals in the late 1930's and 1940's were like a secret society, engaging in criminal behavior. This underworld, on like Rush Street and other area locales, resembled some dark and dreary scene from the pages of Dante's Inferno.

Kinsey followed an "anything goes" approach that provides excitement and pleasure. Kinsey's adventures, not only intrigued him, but caused him to deepen his crusade of exposing the anti-homosexual prejudices of the general public. Kinsey often indulged his own sexual urges at these hangouts. He found "gays" to be special people, who knew how to dance, laugh and, of course, love without restraint. Kinsey sought to restore their dignity, and their self-respect that the custodians of the culture had taken from them. Unlike a priest in confession, Kinsey was their secular priest who was there to defend, approve, console, and encourage them to be themselves. Kinsey developed such a strong kinship with Chicago's homosexuals that straight society's rejection of them enraged him. Homosexuality completed the jigsaw puzzle that was Kinsey's life and legacy. He was an unabashed "pansexualist."

His inner feelings led Kinsey to some early involvement with the Mattachine Society, an early homosexual rights advocacy group, founded by Harry Hay. If one were to mate Karl Marx with Alfred Kinsey, Harry Hay would be the product. Hay, who died in San Francisco on October 24, 2002, at the anomalous age of ninety, was the Gay Movement's founding father. For well over a half century Hay chased his dream of a "golden brotherhood." He organized the Mattachine Society, a group of seven gay men who began to meet secretly in a Los Angeles basement in 1951. This society constituted an early homosexual rights organization that laid the foundation for what would become the National Gay Rights Movement. Its original members included many left-wing political activists, including several members of the Communist Party and the radical fringe of the labor movement. Named for the medieval jesters alleged to have been homosexuals, the Mattachines wore masks while fomenting rebellion against the monarchy. Their modern namesake, the Mattachine Society was committed to the revolutionary idea that "no boy or girl approaching the maelstrom of deviation need make that crossing alone." By 1953 they had tow thousand members in California, with a solid base in the Bay Area.

Kinsey's entry into the underworld of homosexual sex had given a new direction to his research. Kinsey taught that homosexuality was not a glandular disease but was an acquired taste. As he plodded more deeply into his perverted addiction, Kinsey vowed to make society pay for the harm it had inflicted on him by making him hide his homosexuality and live the sham of a life he had with his wife Clara. He had exchanged the lab coat for the flasher's raincoat. The science laboratory had now became the toilet stall. Because of his immersion in Darwinian theory and the minutiae of insect taxonomy, Kinsey had seriously undermined the concept of the norm, both social and personal, in the area of sexual morality. Science is the protective mantle that excuses anything that traditional morality had previous condemned.

Kinsey's most depraved subject was a Mr. X who was the product of a home corrupted by cross-generational sex. He had sexual relations with both his grandmother and his father when he was still a young child. Over the years he had sex with seventeen of the thirty-three relatives with whom he had personal contact. As an adult, he was obsessed with sex. He was "a walking id with polymorphous erotic tastes." By the time Kinsey interviewed him, he had had sexual relations with hundreds of prepubescent males, young girls, numerous adults of both sexes, and even with animals of different species.

He also had a repertoire of masturbatory techniques that he was willing to demonstrate for Kinsey. He boasted that he could start from a flaccid state and ejaculate in exactly ten seconds. Kinsey and Pomeroy were skeptical but ten seconds later he had proven them wrong. Mr. X also confessed how he had masturbated little children, including infants, and even penetrated small children. Casting an indifferent eye, Kinsey took notes and made this predatory pedophile's life part of his scientific database.

Mr. X was college educated and had a responsible job with the government that required extensive travel. He also had a sizable collection of erotica and personal notes on his conquest, which he readily shared with Kinsey. He also carried a tool kit with him, including drills that allowed him to observe the sexual behaviors of all the people who happened to have rooms near his on these trip.

Kinsey's sexual research had turned a fateful corner with the inclusion of data about sex with children. Before he started his investigations, Kinsey reflected much of the traditional taboos about sex with children. Over the course of his studies and interviews with the likes of Mr. X., Kinsey gradually came to the conclusion that sex with children was not that bad and could even serve as a benefit for the child in the long run. He softened Mr. X's words by saying euphemistically that he had stimulated these infants and babies, instead of "molested." He made reference scientists and other adults studying children's sexual responses over long periods of time. The word "torture" is the choice of Dr. Judith Reisman.

In his crusade to combat prudery and celebrate Eros, Kinsey had crossed the line. At best his research made him an accessory to the crime of child molestation. He described orgasms in children in graphic detail, replete with frenzied excitement and violent convulsions. These kids were clinically described in his literature as "partners." Since there were no moral boundaries in his thinking, why should children be exempt from sexual pleasure, he logically reasoned. As degenerate moderns often do, he rationalized what had been repugnant to the general population really didn't hurt anyone and was of no threat to public safety. Kinsey started to question society's condemnation of pedophilia. Kinsey's perverted behavior had taken its ghastly toll on him.

As it is the basis of homosexual recruitment and initiation, children became the next battleground that Kinsey prepared to conquer. It is the sleeping sentinel that allows sex educators to subvert the early moral pillars of children under the rubric of "education." Sex educator, Edward Eichel, has identified "heterophobia," as the "hidden agenda" of sex education courses. Their primary function is to break down the child's innate sense of modesty and his natural aversion to homosexual behavior. By doing this it could open up the whole range of sexual activities. Kinsey extolled the normality and frequency of sex between adults and children. He believed that there should be no age or relationship barrier to sex. Kinsey taught that children were all sexual and potentially orgasmic from birth. He claimed that two-month old infants were capable of multiple orgasms. All forms of sodomy were natural and healthy. Children are not harmed by incest and may benefit even from it.

Kinsey's studies accelerated the rate by which children were being integrated into the sexual revolution. That's the logic of the revolution, which is really a redefinition of human nature in defiance of God's law. The gay lobby, especially its most deviant wing, NAMBLA, the infamous, Man/Boy Love Association, is constantly reminding the culture that pedophilia was widely tolerated in pre-Christian pagan societies. Acceptance of this goal would signal the final stage in the de-Christianization of the West. Pedophilia is the manifest destiny of the sexual revolution. There is no principled reason why sexual freedom should stop with adults. If there is nothing sacred about sex, there is nothing sacred about any arbitrary age of consent.

The aim is to lessen the country's resistance to having their children, especially their adolescent children, especially their sons, involved in sexual relationships with adult men. The media and the universities are rising to the challenge. Holland's sexual "emancipation" serves as the model for Judith Levine's book, "Harmful to Minors: The Perils of Protecting Children from Sex," published by the University of Minnesota. It is an enlightened alternative to the country's moral standards on sexual morality. According to Levine, "the threat of pedophilia and molestation is exaggerated by adults, who want to deny young people the opportunity, for positive sexual experiences." Like Kinsey did, Levine insists "The research shows us that in some minority of cases, young—even quite young—people have positive (sexual) experience with an adult."

Like the cultural Marxists, Kinsey was an avowed enemy of American civilization. He seemed to think it was important that children be able to climax at age three and four. His thinking was echoed in much of the verbal detritus that emanated from Jocelyn Elders, Bill Clinton's ill-fated Surgeon General. Her lobbying argued for the positive aspects of teaching masturbation to six-year-olds proved to be her undoing. It is this kind of neo-Marxist thinking that underscores how these perverted minds intend to subvert our society and control our kinds, through increased sexual behavior at ages when the deep creative and psychological aspects are not at all present.

The "Big Lie" of Kinsey scientific research was that Kinsey had no sexual predilections. He portrayed himself as an open-minded scientist just interested in the truth of human sexual behavior. For Kinsey, the beauty of his research was that it allowed him to disguise his voyeurism as science. Decades later research scientists, such as William Masters and Virginia Johnson, would convert Kinsey's approach into a thriving business that liberated millions of Americans from their religious convictions and their "Puritan" attitudes. Respected newspapers, such as the New York Times, blatantly advertise scientific videos about improving one's love life through technique and sensuality.

Kinsey had very distinct ideas about how people should behave sexually. His seminal volume, "Sex and the American Male" had many veiled references and thinly disguised opinions, as well as polemical stances, all designed to attack and challenge the traditional attitudes and mores of American society. His associate Paul Gebhard remarked years later about how the detached scientist was really a passionate reformer. Kinsey believed that people were pansexual, like him, a mixture of both sexes. Consequently, relationships with either should be natural and fulfilling. He felt that binary labels, such as homosexual and heterosexual, could not capture the rich diversity of the human species. Sex was a wonderful thing that should not be restricted by monogamy and marriage. He thought knowledge would cure society of its ills and everyone would be happier. His research and that of those who followed used the orgasm to reduce sex to quantifiable physiological data and there is nothing more subversive to the traditional morality marriage bond.

Many thought Kinsey was the twentieth century's answer to Charles Darwin. He wanted to change the world. His team included men with less than conventional attitudes on sexual relations. One was a lowly factotum, named Clyde Martin, another a covert Don Juan, Wardell Pomeroy and the third, Paul Gebhard a free spirit who saw human sexuality as an anthropologist's next frontier. One of his followers, Vincent Nowlis, was reported to have said that their demimonde was "a submarine, moving in a self-contained world with a commander directing every movement and the crew utterly dependent on him and each other because the craft was so vulnerable."

Kinsey's "scientific methods" were dubious at best. The Reports were not a record of what Americans did sexually as advertised and promoted by a generation of social scientists. His book was an accurate recording of Kinsey's mad obsession with sexual deviancy. His insatiable prurient interests were the reason he spent an inordinate amount of time with sexual deviants—homosexuals, prison inmates and prostitutes. Kinsey showed that sex was not merely a fixed pattern but more of a human mosaic of human variation. Questions about normalcy seemed blurred and imprecise. The scientific falsehood of his study was that Kinsey had stacked the deck and directed his research to arrive at these preordained conclusions, all in the name of irrefutable science. And the American people bought it. Kinsey's book "Sexual Behavior in the Human Male," published in 1947, rivaled the sales of Margaret Mitchell's "Gone With the Wind," published a decade before. "The Kinsey Report," as the public quickly dubbed it, cost $6.50. It was difficult to read with its 804 pages, brimming with "a dreary morass of technical jargon and statistical charts."

Kinsey saw quickly the erotic possibilities of using film to document his scientific research. He enticed most of his staff and their wives to perform sexual acts for the benefit of the camera, sometimes alone and sometimes with a partner or in a group. In his attic, Alfred Kinsey attempted to establish his own sexual utopia that would be free from any moral or legal restraints. Arbitrary rules and religious taboos would not bind members in his inner circle. Unfettered sex would be the rule of the day with the sole exception that Kinsey had to approve of every sex act performed. He urged the men to have sex with anyone's wife, with each other or engage in the "solitary vice." Women could do whatever they wanted, and with whomever they wanted. They were free to refuse but there was the inherent threat of loss of status within this free love community. Kinsey believed that since this was all to benefit science, there should be neither shame nor repugnance among the participants. Kinsey went so far as to filmed himself performing some of his sado/masochistic techniques.

Kinsey often brought suitable partners into the group, mostly for his own S&M pleasure. Kinsey urged a Mr. Y to have sex with his wife Clara. She dutifully complied. Kinsey would also indulge himself with Mr. Y. As he later wrote, Kinsey and "I would be having sex upstairs and I go down (stairs) and have sex with Mac (Clara) in the same house." They were a wonderful couple and she accepted everything he wanted her to do. She knew if she didn't she would lose him. Mr. Y was stunned by the household's complete lack of jealousy or possessiveness. They totally accepted what the other one did. Mr. Y said that Kinsey did not seem to enjoy himself when having sex. He had a lonesome, forlorn look on his face. Kinsey was displaying all the clinical symptoms of a sex addict.

Clara's supplicant behavior is one of the most incredible sections of Jones' biography of Kinsey. It is amazing that such a rather plain woman with lively eyes could have joined him in his wife-swapping experiments, and allowed his sordid homoerotic behaviors to take place under her very own roof. Unquestioning, Clara literally stood by her man, no matter how perverse nor how degrading his demands were. It was as if his hypnotic charm had emotionally lobotomized her. Kinsey had liberated his wife from her brain and maybe even her soul. Ironically, she was the example of the stereotypical example of the subservient wife, whom the Betty Friedans and the Gloria Steinems so detested in American women.

Kinsey later published the "Sexual Behavior in the Human Female." In it he depicted women as sexual beings who did not need the male penis for orgasm or sexual fulfillment. He was a pioneer in separating sex from procreation. Now women had their own study that put them on the same sexual plateau as men.

"Newsweek" called it the season's most sensational best seller. The two years following its publication saw over five hundred magazine and journal articles about the Kinsey Report. Virtually all were favorable because the journalists sensed that Kinsey was providing for the license to do whatever they pleased and with anyone they pleased. "People Magazine" later described Kinsey as a man with few conventional vices. Actually there is an ambiguous truth to that statement, since he did not smoke or swear. His mastabatory and sado/masochistic vices were certainly not conventional.

The enlightened thinking that gave us Kinsey and his imitators jettisoned Christianity in favor of science as a better moral guide than either religion or morality. All the while they thought they controlled him when all he had to ask is if they wanted to see "naked women dancing on the mountain to shift the balance of power." When his sponsors and critics came to Bloomington, Kinsey showed them his growing pornographic library, all protected under the rubric of scientific research. Many executives of the Rockefeller Foundation unwittingly gave him their sexual case histories. This provided Kinsey with leverage over them and they were compelled to grant him money to fund his sickness. The same mechanism worked on the members of the press. Kinsey threatened to use his information to blackmail them if they dared to criticize his institute.

Their funding gave Kinsey access to build a staff, travel, add books and drawings to his collection of sexual literature and other materials for his library. They wanted to use his information, with its academic imprimatur as a means of controlling the American people. They were into biological engineering, something that seemed more germane to a communist dictatorship than a constitutional democracy. Initially they hoped to use his data to defeat the Nazis but later turned the smoking gun on the American people themselves. Population control and family planning, including abortion services, became the hallmark of the union of ideas and policies between the Kinsey Institute and the Rockefeller Foundation. They saw his eclectic mind as one that would compile scientific data that others could use to develop social and economic policies that would impact the sexual habits of the world population in such as way that would more easily advance their global ideology.

Without the millions in funding from Rockefeller and Ford, Kinsey and his Institute would have merited not even a footnote in a thin history book. They provided the acclaim and the resources so that his views could be promulgated throughout American society. What the foundation did not understand was they had engaged a perverted social revolutionary, who had his own agenda of razing the sexual edifices of American civilization. It was not until some of his more bizarre, even kinky practices started to leak out, that the new president of the Foundation, Dean Rusk, a member of the Council of Foreign Relations, and future Secretary of State under John F. Kennedy, took office that Kinsey lost their formal support.

Like Crowley and later Hefner, it was the pleasure principle that dominated Kinsey's adult life. Kinsey's behavior had a deleterious affect on his physical health. During much of his professional life, he suffered from a lengthy list of illnesses that included orchitis, an inflammation of the testicles and hypertension. Kinsey took a lethal cycle of drugs for stimulation and tranquilizers that eventually led to heart disease. Kinsey died on Sunday August 25, 1956 from an embolism that resulted from a bruise from a fall in his garden.

The distorted Kinsey image continues to live on. Francis Ford Coppola plans to bring out a biographical drama of Kinsey. He has gotten with some very strong opposition from, Dr. Judith Reisman who has called Kinsey the "most infamous pedophile propagandist in scientific history." Homosexual director Bill Condon, who gave us the homophile "Gods and Monster," plans to bring out this "art-house," movie about the deviant sexual researcher. Condon has also written the screenplay with the working title of "Kinsey's Report." Empire Online, which calls itself the UK's No. 1 Website, says of the proposed movie, "With production ready to start in March, ready yourself for a touch of sexual perversity, a measure of gender confusion and every kind of reproductive action. All in the name of scientific research, of course."

Liam Neeson, the talented actor from "Schindler's List," currently heads the list of actors who are deeply interested in playing Kinsey. Condon has already received rejections from leading actors, such as academy award winners, such as Russell, Crowe, Tom Hanks, Kevin Spacey and Harrison Ford." They all flirted with playing Kinsey but their better judgment finally got the better of them. Reisman has repeatedly warned Neeson not to play Kinsey. To do so would place him in a "hideously inaccurate role, much like playing the monster Mengele as a mere controversial figure." Condon put Kinsey into perfect perspective when he said, there would have been "no Playboy or Dr. Ruth with Kinsey's liberating effects."

Kinsey fueled the sexual revolution of the 1960's, which was a blatant attack on the cellular structure of society. Under communism, free love, including abortion was the only freedom left. It was the only freedom that was compatible with dictatorship. Sexual freedom has come to mean sexual anomie or the total breakdown of norms or standards, supported by irresponsibility. Parenthetically, the state releases its citizens from their duties and responsibilities to their families as it increases our allegiance to the state. You can divorce your spouse, leave your children, abandon or euthanize your parents, abort your unborn children but you can never divorce the state. It owns you. The state provides just two options. If one refuses to be dependent, he must pay taxes to support those who are living off the largess of other people's taxes. This is legal plunder. What is illegal is refusing to pay taxes as one of my callers sternly advises all Americans to do.

The third member of this sexual axis of evil, is Hugh Marston Hefner, the founder of Playboy Magazine. While Kinsey was a strong admirer of Crowley, Hefner often voiced his great debt to the Kinsey Report. With Kinsey as his inspiration, Hefner launched a soft porn industry that rocked American mores and influenced several generations of American males and a few females.

Born in Chicago in 1926, Hef, as his intimates call him, is considered the patriarch of the sexual revolution. His father was a Methodist and a direct descendant of puritan patriarchs. Like a figure in a Hegelian textbook with strong Freudian overtones, Hefner emerged as the self-absorbed son of a repressed Chicago Methodist couple. His was a typical dysfunctional household that was marked by an emotionally stunting lack of physical affection. Hefner grew to believe that sexual prudery was the root of all social evil. He dedicated his life to dispelling the social norms that he believed had created such an uptight situation. He was an underachiever in high school, despite an I.Q. of 152. Doctors advised his parents to show him more physical affection. His mother's response was to allow him to post sexy pinups of Vargas girls on his bedroom wall.

It was during college that Hef discovered Kinsey. Kinsey was "a revelation for me," he said in 1999. It was Kinsey's sex survey that inspired Hefner to shed the moral shackles of a repressive Puritanism and experience his sexuality to the fullest. "It confirmed the hypocrisy for me, the gap between what we said and what we actually do." As he put it, "The sexual revolution began with the Kinsey Report. I have said it many times that Kinsey was the researcher and I was the pamphleteer."

After a stormy courtship, marked by her infidelity, Hefner married Millie Williams, his college sweetheart in 1949. She had been the only girl he had ever been intimate with at this point in his life. After two children, Hefner's uneasiness with domestic life and monogamy wore him down, so he left Millie. They divorced in 1959. Hef had always wanted to be a cartoonist. He went to work for "Esquire Magazine," the closest to acceptable men's magazine around in the early fifties. When they refused to give him a five dollar a week raise, Hefner left and went in search of fulfilling his dreams and fantasies. With just six hundred dollars of his own money and over seven thousand from friends and investors, he launched what later became a quarter billion industry.

When the cultural Marxists, such as Marcuse and Reich, were dreaming up ways to subvert the West they must have had someone like "Hef" in mind. In his eternal search for pleasure, Hefner unleashed the uncontrollable beast that lay within the heart of every red-blooded male in America. He founded "Playboy" in 1953 and scored a real coup in publishing original calendar photos of a very lascivious Marilyn Monroe that he had purchased years before from her photographer. It was an instant hit and when the first issue sold over 50,000 copies straight from the newsstand, Hefner knew he had hit the jackpot.

The magazine did not publish the hard core pornography that had been relegated to the back rooms and lavatories of seedy bars and houses of ill repute. Hefner gave respectability to female nudity. He brought women's bodies out in the open in a soft core setting that excited and titillated but did not disgust or repel normal men. His models were clean, almost pure in their nudity. "Playboy" went a long way in legitimizing the once sleazy profession of nudie magazines by displaying idealized nude photos of girls who seem to project the purity of the girl next door, surrounded by articles with a modicum of intellectual content—the so-called "magazine within the magazine." Hef parlayed this new freedom and openness about one's body, especially the female body, into a veritable empire that has revolutionized the sexual mores of the country. Unlike the common pornographer, Hefner had more than a hunger for financial gain. He wanted to change America's repressive sexual code. Hefner presented himself as a publisher in the liberal humanist tradition of the French Enlightenment. He was a "rebel with a cause." Ending society's sexual hypocrisy became the mission for the rest of Hefner's life. "Playboy" served as his "bovine pulpit." Hefner was a moral and social iconoclast who attacked Puritanism, which was his code word for Christianity with its outdated concepts of modesty and marital fidelity.

There was much more to the Playboy Empire than nude pictures. Hefner not only fulfilled male fantasies but he also offered intellectual justifications for his revolutionary style of "photojournalism." He developed the "Playboy Philosophy," which was not much more than a reflection of his solipsistic need to change the religious and moral values that pained his own conscience. Another example of E. Michael Jones' "Degenerate Moderns," Hefner became the de facto "Playboy of the Western world." He personified the Playboy Philosophy as an urbane sophisticate, who read intellectual books, discussed Nietzsche, and Picasso, liked jazz, and usually smoked a pipe. Hef also had a penchant for fine wines, and always wore silk pajamas. He was liberal on issues, such as abortion, gun control, and the death penalty. To him, organized religion was a dinosaur that had outlived its usefulness.

Hef loved women, all kinds of women. He was free and easy with his own body and expected his ladies to be the same. Marital fidelity was limiting. It cramped his style of freedom and mellowness. Hefner felt that if he gave American men a break from the pressures of the business world and their family lives and even the atomic age and all of its concomitant fears and anxieties, he had provided a great service to society. Hef was old fashioned, in that he expected his "dates," to be faithful to him but he was free to sample all the fruit of the yum-yum tree. He would project women as a thing of beauty when the real lure for his readers was pure unadulterated naked flesh. Hefner prided himself on being an early advocate for women's rights, especially abortion, which in reality favored the swinging bachelors who impregnated their girl friends.

Hefner became almost bigger than life. He was living, at least in his own mind, every man's fantasy. To concretize this he established, in Chicago, the Playboy mansion, replete with swimming pools, waterfalls, spas, naked and semi-naked vixens that fawned and hung over all him, like a pulchritudinous security blanket. He threw lavish parties that attracted Hollywood stars, such as Tony Curtis, Peter Lawford, James Colburn, Sammy Davis, Jr., James Caan, and many others. Hefner worked from his round bed, on which it is estimated he had sex with at least a thousand beautiful women, sequentially or sometimes in small groups. He also used his bed to carefully scrutinize every photo that would appear in his magazine. Women did everything imaginable to become a "Playmate," that is bare all for his magazine. He resurrected the careers of aging starlets, such as Joan Collins, Farrah Faucet and even Patricia Reagan, who did "artistic" spreads for his magazine.

An integral part of the philosophy was the Playboy Bunny. The bunny, a cocktail waitress in an undersized costume with a cute little cotton puff attached to her derriere, became an international symbol of the free-loving woman of the post 1950s generation. Bunnies were a combination courtesan and Geisha girl that served as not only candy for the eyes but also gave the impression of being there, primarily for a man's pleasure and sexual gratification. The Playboy attitude permeated American society to the extent that Hefner's idea of sexual liberation became acceptable within the mainstream culture.

The Playboy philosophy is not new. It dates back to the ancient Greek philosopher, Epicurus, who enunciated the ethical philosophy called "hedonism," the Greek word for "pleasure." Hedonism committed its followers to a life of pleasure. It ranked pleasure as the sole good. Pursuit of pleasure is the guiding star for millions of young people in the West today. The underlying principle to this philosophy is that pleasure is alone the only good in life and should be pursued at all costs. Hefner has succeeded in creating a new American male, one who had put off or disavowed the accepted standards of wife and family. Society now had millions of single men who enjoyed dozens of new naked women each month.

Hefner believed that polygamist bachelorhood is the ideal that every male should shoot for. Many men bought the myth of his philosophy and the American family has paid dearly for this revolution that was started by one man's obsession with sexual relationships and physical pleasure. Sexual liberation was his main drive. To him naked women were not pornography but sensuous displays of beauty. Hefner suffered from what is sometimes called, "Casanova Syndrome," an over-compensation for an early deficit of love. In reality the Playboy is really living in an unreal world, an alternate reality that underscores his inability to grow up. Hef is the prototype of the heterosexual version of arrested development, a modern Peter Pan who never got over his fascination with the genitalia of women. As he has grown older, only the names have changed from Barbie and Christie to Mandy, Sandy, and Brandy.

After a stroke fell him in 1985, Hefner made several modifications in his life style at least for the moment. His daughter took over the management of the company in 1988 and Hefner tried domesticity again as he married one of his "Playmates of the Year," Kimberly Conrad. Hef's second fling with marriage lasted only nine years and produced two sons before the call of the wild and his chemically aided libido seduced him again. One woman has never been enough for Hefner. He credited much of his former and present successes on two pills, the birth control pill, developed by Dr. John Rock and the Viagra pill. The one virtually nearly eliminated the fear of pregnancy, for him at least, and the other gave new and restored vigor to his waning sex life. At last count, Hefner was "dating" seven blonde vixens at the same time. He admitted that blonde was his favorite color. He once said that Picasso had his blue period. "Well I am going through my blonde period." His motto was "To thine own self be true." This solipsistic rendition of Shakespeare says it all. Despite his objectification of women, feminists of all stripes, such as Betty Friedan, joined Hefner in attacked the traditional American family, and suburban life. Without even knowing it, Hef had been a very successful Cultural Marxist.

Hefner has had many rivals and imitators that displayed so much raw sexuality that Hef, "the liberator," was caught off guard. Panderers, like Bob Guiccione of "Penthouse Magazine," and the thoroughly despicable Larry Flynt of "Hustler" fame took the loss of safeguards to their great depths. Hefner had opened the doors and chased out the Puritan gatekeepers but by his own admission he had opened a Pandora's box that let so many low lifes in that it degraded what he was doing. In an attempt to compete with these more daring imitations, Hefner's nudes started revealing some pubic hair and even pudenda. Like the stripper in the play "Oklahoma," the Centerfold "had gone as far as she could go."

An interesting hole in the Hefner armor appeared in the June 2001 issue of "Philadelphia," magazine in Ben Wallace's essay, entitled "The Prodigy and the Playmate." In this article, Hef's former girlfriend, and Playboy cover girl, Sandy Bentley, along with her twin sister, Mandy described in graphic detail, Hefner's sexual practices. She said that Hefner "had trouble finding satisfaction through intercourse." Instead he liked the girls to pleasure each other "while he masturbated and watched gay porn."

Masturbation seems to be a habit that dominated the lives of Crowley, Kinsey, and Hefner. They were all united in a perverted brotherhood of the flesh, a proverbial axis of sexual deviancy. It not surprising that Hefner should resort to this type of sexual gratification, since his magazine was the dean of the "one-handed" genre. Hefner's use of gay porn is not also surprising. All pornography is homosexual in that it is a sign of arrested development. Pornography reduces spiritual desire to Newtonian mechanics. This is something Playboy and pornographers have had in common. Pornography is really a man's thing. Women only provide the heterosexual protection for the issue, so that he can fend off any suggestions of overt homosexuality. In the Playboy's world, that is, in Hugh Hefner's world, equality for females has come to be synonymous with males. For a woman to be acceptable she must be always available and she must be childless in name if not in fact. His idea of sexual relation was the pursuit of pleasure without children. Abortion is a necessary bedfellow for the playboy. It is not surprising that one of Hefner's liberal causes has been the through his Playboy Foundation, the goal of maintaining the easy access to free and easy abortions. The soft porn culture of the playboy philosophy demands women who are unrealistic expectations of the normal culture. To the playboy, women must have skinny bodies, huge, augmented breasts, and sterile wombs.

Dr. Judith Reisman agrees that pornography promotes homosexuality. In her 1994 analysis "Kinsey, Hefner & Hay, the Indoctrination of Heterophobia in American Men & Women," Dr. Reisman explains: "Playboy manifests a blatant homosexual ethos." Its heterophobia is sustained by a utilitarian analysis of "Playboy" images and philosophy." She goes on to show how important imagery is to the fertile mind. The church has used holy cards, stained glass windows, and plaster statues to initiate, instruct, and indoctrinate people in a religious faith. Hefner's sexual images similarly work on his readers, leading them down the road to indoctrination in the tenets of its religion, its homosexual morality. According to Reisman, pornography expresses a "vicious hatred and contempt for the dignity of all men in that it treats men as nothing more than an appendage to be manipulated by the twisting and exploitation of female sexuality." In treating women as sex objects, Hefner degrades them. The sexual act is reduced to just another hedonistic pleasure that can as easily be satisfied by another man.

It not surprising there is a Satanist connection to the Playboy philosophy. To the Satanist, the promotion of the Playboy philosophy was critical in numbing the conscience of society to the evils of pornography by advocating a Crowleyesque, "Do What Thou Will," mindset. In his article on Jayne Mansfield, who appeared like clockwork in Hef's "Valentine Playmate" every February, from 1957 through 1964, Jason Kovar details her satanic convictions that eventually led to her own decapitation in an auto accident outside of New Orleans in 1967. Mansfield rigorously pursued this throughout the course of her life. Crowley's claim that free sex would mark the attitudes manifesting themselves in the New Age definitely, was also advocated by Jayne Mansfield. She completely advocated his idea of liberated free sex under the Antichrist. She once said, "I love sex . . . It should be animalistic. It should be sadistic, it should at times even be masochistic . . . There are few rules and moral conventions." According to Kovar, Mansfield "sold sex better than any performer in the world." She reveled in the lust that she evoked in men. It gave her great feelings of power and control. Eyewitnesses spoke of her full compliance with evil. She would stretch out "nude upon the altar of the Black Mass," and then she would "open herself up to the devil." As a disciple of Anton LaVey, who founded the Church of Satan, Mansfield believed in the destruction of Christianity and its influence in society. As a Satanist, her desire was, like Mae West's before her, to "emancipate mankind from the biblical concept that sex outside of marriage was sinful."

What is Hefner's legacy? It has degraded the spiritual side of sexual relations, to the extent that as Mercer Schuchardt says "even the horniest old Viagra-stoked goat is unable to physically enjoy the bodies of nubile young females." Like the old joke, Hefner was "a solitary master baiter," who single-handedly stroked the American id into "accepting his adolescent fantasy of false desire and technological gratification, a legacy that amounts to our generation's toxic dump." Who knows what Hefner thinks about an afterlife? Maybe he expects some good sex the other side of the grave. Years ago he has purchased the crypt next to Marilyn Monroe in Westwood Memorial Park. Some clever man beat Hef to the spot directly above her.

7

The Judas Complex

"The Catholic Church is the only thing which saves a
man from the degraded slavery of being a child of his age."
G.K. Chesterton

Catholics will be surprised to learn that by their very nature
they are conspiracy theorists, that is someone who believes that
anti-Catholic groups are more than they say they are. If Catholics
are called to follow the teaching authority of the Church it becomes
a truism. Much of the Church's teachings are found in its papal
encyclicals. "Humanum Genus" is one of those encyclicals. Written
by Pope Leo XIII on April 20, 1884, it condemned Freemasonry
as the center whence all secret societies go forth, and whither they
all return. The Freemasons, like their Gnostic forbears, the
Manicheans, are by their nature secretive and conspiratorial. They
conceal themselves from the public, admitting no witnesses but
their own members. They have consistently held that "a regard for
religion should be held as an indifferent matter and that all religions
are alike." This manner is "calculated to bring about the ruin of all
religion and especially the Catholic religion."

Most importantly Freemasonry "attempts to undermine morals
and use sexual license as a form of political control." This is the
Augustinian "Libidio Dominandi," that E. Michael Jones has so
brilliantly intoned in his many articles and books about cultural
sexual seduction. It is what has happened to this country since the
sexual revolution of the 1960's and the Second Vatican Council.

This has led to a siege on the Catholic Church which has seemed endless. The Church has faltered and staggered under the assault precipitated by many of its priests and bishops over the improper handling of several allegations of sexual misbehavior and child molestation that has dated back for decades. Daily revelations of adolescent molestation and child rape have shocked Catholics in the pews like nothing ever seen in American Catholic history. One would have to return to tales of the sixteenth century sale of indulgences to find anything that even rivals this crisis for its severity. This begs the question of how could this happen to a Church that has been led by the saintly likes of Pope John Paul II and the late Blessed Mother Teresa of Calcutta?

The Church has suffered through a period of secularization that has seen its holy offices infected with intellectual cancer of Gnosticism. In Gnostic writings this is the lesser supernatural agent who created the world, and in some ways is the creator of evil in the world. The real danger to the Church is modernism or what we call secularism. The more the Church becomes like society, the more she disdains her historic Christian mission. The late Malachi Martin called secularism "a spreading disease of the modern world." The Enlightened ignored God, relegating Him to the outer limits of the moral universe. The twisted, demonic mind of Frederick Nietzsche upset the conventional wisdom when he wrote, "Men can not be good without God." But of course, he later argued "God is dead." Most ignored Nietzsche's twisted reasoning. They just accepted his derivative notion that the traditional teachings of God were all based on doctrinal superstition. The existence of God was affirmed but he was a powerless, uninterested deity. God was identified with mankind and the human cosmos. God was in each individual and all men were all gods. This is the reasoning of the modern Gnostics. It was what cemented people together in common humanity. Father Malachi Martin said that "so complete is the secularist distortion of God's image, and so completely does it leave man to His own devices, that it constitutes a subtle and cunning blasphemy and sacrilege."

American Gnosticism has begun to serve as the theological linchpin of cultural and even political liberalism. For two centuries the chief opposition to orthodox Christianity came from atheistic humanism or agnostic scientism or any other thought process that categorically excluded the supernatural from consideration. Now that has all changed as Gnostic roots pop through the intellectual surface. The very people who have nearly destroyed American civilization with a handy diet of social pathology, moral relativity and religious indifference are claiming a moral exclusion and sort of a supernatural sanction. The anti-religious people who control the basic institutions today are more arrogantly pious than their predecessors were a century ago. Modern Gnosticism has plans not just for the destruction of society, as we know it but also for its future reconstruction.

Secularism is ubiquitous in American society. It has infected every aspect of the culture. It eliminates the force of moral obligation to an authority believed to be outside human consciousness and above even the subjective will of men. It creates blindness to the things of the spirit. To the extent that the Catholic Church buys into the core of modern liberalism, it risks losing part of the eternal heritage of its core doctrine. In many ways, the Church has given birth to the child of Gramsci's ghost, a completely secularized society. As Father Martin wrote "in what is still called the 'spirit of Vatican II' John Paul II's worldwide Roman Catholic institutional organization has been both midwife and wet nurse to that child."

Pope John Paul II has made it one of the goals of his papacy to reunite Catholicism with as many of the church's "separated brethren" as possible. His ecumenical agenda has not worked out as intended. What we have experienced is not really a union of religions but a religious union of the liberal sects within various sects. The Vatican knows that it can get nowhere with those denominations who believe they possess the real truth. So they have engaged the progressive wings of many religions whose main concern is that we "all just get along." In 1966 Father Joseph

Ratzinger, a progressive theologian boasted that thanks to Vatican II, "conversion of non-Catholics has been replaced by 'convergence with' non-Catholics." This secularization has quietly and subtlety substituted for its salvation teaching and guidance, a romanticized, and virtual deification of the poor. The transcendent has bowed to the material. The American Catholic Bishops have adopted much of the statist philosophy of the Democratic Party in an unholy alliance that has warped its fundamental role in human history. The Church has been seduced by the enticements of federal dollars that have seriously derailed its historic and prophetic mission in salvific history.

At the heart of the attack on Catholicism is a vicious frontal assault on patriarchy. Its vehemence is reminiscent of the French attack on the bourgeoisie. It is a major element in the social structure and feminism is the means to drive a wedge through it. This is just another way that the Cultural Marxists have been able to use women to further their satanic ends. Women have also been willing tools in the attack on the Church and its priesthood. When coupled with homosexuality, there exists a double-edged sword through which the Left may fatally piece the heart of the church. It is a studied loathing of ordinary life not because it is evil but because it exists.

In the absence of eternal verities, the constant pursuit of pleasure appears to be a popular idea. Society then becomes riven with people whose lives have been broken through the social pathologies of divorce, abortion, drug abuse, venereal disease, pornography, alcoholism, crime, child abuse, and crime. As researcher Robert Knight put it, "the latter part of the twentieth century might best be thought of as a massive, brutal hangover from the God-is-dead party."

In "The Age of Consent," Knight demonstrates how among liberals "virtue is found in the pursuit of—not resistance to—vice." This is an Orwellian idea that underscores the extent to which our civilization has turned its collective back on its origins and its eternal essence. Situational ethics provides an excuse for self-indulgences, leaving children vulnerable to those predators who would liberate them with sex and drugs, thus beginning the cycle all over again. This leads inexorably to moral relativism or "freedom of conscience," which has had a deleterious affect on the churches. During the last century, many churches have ceded their claim to absolute moral authority. They have given ground to world philosophies "based on human whim." Many have become the driving forces for all progressive causes "from the sexual revolution to Marxist economics." According to Knight, moral relativism or "freedom of conscience" has had a deleterious affect on the churches.

Father Malachi Martin calls this the "Judas complex." It is difficult to comprehend the motivations of this gross betrayal. Judas was not an evil man. He shared the religious fervor and noble idealism that so motivated Jesus' hand-chosen apostles. Along the way, he started seeing reality through his own eyes and thought that his plan for feeding the poor and performing good works was superior to that of Jesus. This complex is the compromise of one's basic principles in order to fit in with the modes of thought and behavior that the world regards as necessary for its vital interests.

What does this have to do with the decline in the priesthood and the periodic revelations about pederastic priests? In keeping with the idiomatic structure of the hive, Gramsci's strategy of cultural subversion rested on the use of several disparate but parallel groups that would serve as what Lenin called "useful idiots." They would undermine the Church, not because of some great commitment to Marxism, but through some other, more self-serving cause such as feminism or homosexuality. Most of these fallen away conservatives, Catholics and other lovers of freedom, succumbed to the ideological temptation that they could serve a higher good. Their love of humanity had taken on divine attributes. A culture war could be launched with just a few well-placed Judas goats. They would serve to bring down the Church's moral and spiritual influence and with it the culture that looked to the heavens for guidance and solace.

This is right in line with the Gramascian paradigm for a new form of Marxism. He wanted to reduce all men's expectations of any salvation from on high in art, literature, science, medicine, social work, politics, finance or virtually every expression of cultural life. It was a thorough and total materialism. In 1916, Gramsci remarked that Socialism was precisely the "religion that would overwhelm Christianity." In the New Order, he explained that Socialism would triumph by first "capturing the culture via infiltration of schools, universities, churches and the media by transforming the consciousness of society."

Gramsci was, according to Father Martin, "far more advanced than either Hegel or Marx in his understanding of Christian metaphysics in general, of Thomism, in particular." In practical terms, Gramsci felt he had to get individuals and groups in every class and walk of life to think about social problems without reference to the Christian transcendent, without any reference to God and his commandments. This is what author Thomas Molnar called "the Humanist Tradition." Christianity could be subtlety driven from the marketplace of ideas. It could be relegated to the backseat of the bus that would limit and eventually terminate its moral and spiritual influence upon western society.

John J. Reilly illustrated many of these points in his 1997 review in "Culture Wars Magazine," of Peter Jones' perceptive monograph, "Spirit Wars." The theme of his book is that "Traditional religion is often the enemy of the cultural Marxists." The very existence of the Church is an affront to their sensibilities. It is a reminder that there can be eternal consequences for rejecting God and embracing sin and vice. The only way to deaden the conscience, outside of drugs, is to make the Church disappear or so soften its message as to be meaningless in the cosmic scope of things.

The stark truth is that a large number of American theological establishments have abandoned traditional Christianity and adopted a spirit of Gnosticism. Jones' book is a serious guide to this new religion, showing how it fits into the intellectual landscape of the late twentieth century America. It is written from an evangelical perspective. It describes the "progressive paganism" of the leadership of the mainline churches in America. It connects Gnosticism with the main trend in Biblical studies, which is the deconstruction of the Bible. This is a throwback to the idea the Nazis instituted in the 1930's. It has created the intellectual universe in which the transcendental monotheism of orthodox Christianity has become quite unthinkable for many people who are well educated. It has been replaced in some circles by historicism, which means that biblical accounts are recast in ideological terms.

Modern Psychology proved to be another useful weapon in the undermining of the Church. One of the most ardent anti-Catholics was Carl Gustav Jung. Jung was born on July 25, 1875 to Paul Achilles Jung, a Protestant minister, and Emilie Prieswerk, both of whom were the thirteenth child born to their parents. By 1912 he was totally absorbed into an erotic way of life, fueled by his deep interest in the occult. In this same year, Jung denounced Christianity, saying that only the new science of psychoanalysis could offer personal and cultural renewal and rebirth. To Jung, honoring God meant honoring the libido. For Jung the libido became the "vital force" or even God. When we feel that vital force within us, we are really feeling the "god within."

It was in the first quarter of the twentieth century that Swiss psychologist Jung began sending his apostles out from Zurich to Britain and the United States to preach a Gospel, diametrically opposed to that of Christ. Jung's teachings amount to what psychologist Dr. Richard Noll called an "anti-orthodox Christianity cult of redemption in the Nietszchean mold." Jung's theories found fertile ground among disenchanted Catholics. Noll explained in his 1994 work "The Jung Cult: Origins of a Charismatic Movement," that Jung's entire life was motivated by a desire to destroy the Catholic Church, whose religious doctrines and moral teachings he considered the source of all the neuroses that afflicted Western man. Jung hated the Catholic Church and he felt that he could destroy it by unleashing the power medium of disordered sex.

To aid him in this crusade he enlisted the financial backing of some major foundations, including the Rockefellers, who had played such an important role in funding Alfred Kinsey at Indiana University. It is a truism that the foundations led by the Rockefeller clan were most instrumental in making certain that the "killer bees" in the hive had ample funding to produce their liberal destructive honey. He also attracted the aid of several of these self-interested groups, such as libertines in the media, the universities and government. His plan to deconstruct orthodox Christianity became the handbook of the managerial elite of the new planned society that took the western world by storm in the 1930's.

"Wanderer" columnist, Paul Likoudis quotes the "Wandlungen," the first liturgical exegesis that contains core Jungian concepts, which held that "Having a god within could lead to the experience of becoming one with God, or merging with this God-force in some way." Jung felt that the central experience of transformation "in the ancient mystery cults of the Hellenistic world involved just such a process or experience of self-deification." Noll summed up Jung's philosophy in this way. "Two thousand years of Christianity makes us strangers to ourselves. In the individual, the internalization of bourgeois-Christian civilization is a mask that covers our biologically true religion, a natural religion of the sun and the sky."

"Culture Wars Magazine" publisher, E. Michael Jones has also pinpointed Jung's hostility to Christianity as a result of his adulterous relationship with his patient Sabina Spielrein. He needed a kinder and gentler religion that would not condemn him because of his sins. It was Jung's mentor and confident, German psychoanalyst Otto Gross, who influenced Jung to lead a life of "life-enhancing eroticism." He reasoned that just as one has several friends, he could have several lovers to enhance his daily life and yet still remain faithful to his spouse. It can be quickly deduced that this is the same verbal deconstruction that led a former president to question the meaning of the word "is." Jung's battle cry became "free love will save the world!" He firmly believed that the only way to overthrow or undo the cultural underpinnings of the Judeo-Christian world was to establish a new religion of psychoanalysis whose underlining basis would be sexual liberation. This would inevitably lead to a repudiation of organized traditional religion and the adoption of a new religion of personal spirituality.

Jung and Gross sometimes spent all day analyzing each other. Jung wrote approvingly of his mentor's use of sex orgies to promote pagan spirituality. But he cautioned that "the existence of a phallic or orgiastic cult does not indicate 'Eo ipso' a particularly lascivious life any more than the ascetic symbolism of Christianity means an especially moral life." Before he committed suicide in 1920, Gross prophetically wrote that the "coming revolution is the revolution of matriarchy." This statement effectively underscores what would become the working engine of the Frankfurt School in overthrowing the West.

According to Likoudis, Jung has been behind the "quiet revolution," that has taken place within the Catholic Church for the past sixty years. Jung borrowed many of his ideas from the Aryan spirituality and occultism of his times. Jung swiftly became the putative "apostle of adultery." He hoped his teachings would eventually replace those of Jesus, St. Paul, Augustine, and Thomas Aquinas. It has been his apostles, such as Dolores Leckey, who headed the U.S. Bishop's Marriage and Family Life Office in their national conference for twenty years who have been responsible for the gradual erosion of traditional sexual morality. To a large degree this has been the case in the mainstream of Catholic education in seminaries, convents, colleges and universities, as well as retreat programs and spiritual formation courses. God has become the code world for "self." Likoudis points out that it is "spiritual seduction as a way of enacting sexual abuse." Dr. Wallace Clift, an Episcopalian minister and President of the Jung Society of Colorado, said that Jung "was a trailblazer in recognizing that the old form of externalized Christian ritual and belief had given way to a new form of religion." He described this as "a discovery of the God within." It is apparent that the Jungian cult within the Catholic Church is everywhere from Boston to San Francisco. Its teachings and secrets have indoctrinated entire groups of priests, religious and Church leaders.

Jungians treat the spiritual realities of life as psychological realities that are mere projections of the psyche. Christianity then is not valued for its revealed truth about man and his relationship to God but for its usefulness in mapping and exploring the unconscious. His disciples interpret scripture subjectively with Christ losing His uniqueness as Incarnate WORD and mediator between God and man. By pushing God beyond the range of human knowledge, that is, beyond the ideas of good and evil, they have created a Manichean god who is both good and evil, a mere projection of the human mind, under whose image spiritual forces come to lord over human lives. The abandonment of the quest for holiness and spiritual transformation leaves the path open for the "spirits of sexual bondage, and phallic demons."

The first crack in the Church's moral edifice occurred many years after Gramsci's death. At the dawning of the Second Vatican Council, Pope John XXIII emasculated the Church' s historical opposition to World Communism. At the insistence of Nikita Khrushchev, the Pope agreed that his upcoming council would not issue a condemnation of Marxism and Communism. This was a historic reversal of Church policy. It was the price the Pope paid to get the Communists to allow two Russian clerics to attend the Council as observers. Consequently the Pope's decision undermined its traditional opposition to this evil force. American Catholics all but stopped their consistent and dedicated support for ant-Communist policies and détente became the catchword in religious as well as political dealings. It has had serious ramifications in the United States.

Under John's successor, Paul VI, the Church set on a course from which it has not yet recovered. Pope Paul VI said that the Church was now dedicated "to serve man, to help him build his home on earth." On a metaphysical level, the fundamental struggle in which all Catholics were engaged in was no longer the personal battle between Christ as Savior and Lucifer as the Cosmic Adversary of the Most High in the quest for the souls of men. The struggle had degenerated from the supernatural plane to a sociopolitical battle on earth. The class struggle was really a cultural battle, a veritable culture war. Since the Council, the Church has been intent on creating a universal habitat for humanity on earth in imitation of its secular counterparts. This new paradigm of social action and religious liberty for all faiths seriously distracted the hierarchy from its chief obligation of promoting the salvation of the souls under its care. Paul VI's emphasis on human welfare hastened the call for reducing traditional liturgical sacrifices and prayer. Theologians called for new forms of worship, endangering belief in the Real Presence, and the efficacy of the sacraments. The Catholic Church started to resemble some large Protestant denomination in its devotions and adherence to traditional doctrines and teachings. Gramsci could not have written a better script for what Martin called "the de-Catholicization of the Roman Catholic hierarchy, clergy and faithful."

This new approach infected the lifeline of the Church, namely its priesthood. The Cultural Marxists had already enlisted women to effect their nefarious aims. It was also through motherhood that they strove to weaken the Catholic priesthood. Women have nearly ceased to influence their sons to become priests. Many seemed more intent on opening the priesthood to their daughters instead. The old adage that the hand that rocks the cradle rules the world could prove no truer than in this context. Through family limitation programs and the pressures of the materialistic times, women opted for smaller families. They married later, had their careers, and thus severely cut the amount of childbearing years available to them. This meant that there were fewer young Catholic men reaching maturity. When women had larger families, there would always be one or two sons that would be steered to the Church.

Women have tended to feminize their sons more. They have sought to purge them of their natural tendency toward patriarchy and aggressiveness. Mothers wanted their sons to be kinder and gentler. They lobbied against the Vietnam War, the death penalty, and sports that appeared too violent. One example will suffice. In a heated pennant race, closer Jason Isringhausen of the St. Louis Cardinals left his team in Atlanta during a crucial series to be with his wife while she experienced childbirth for the first time. Twenty years ago, his teammates, and the public would have laughed him off the field. Now there is nothing wrong with male sensitivity and it is nice to see that a man loves his wife and is supportive in her time of need but he is also the breadwinner and his job does have to take precedence in many cases.

The first sign of a bankrupt spirituality is a disordered sexuality. Many of these men put out by this increased feminization have a leaning and an innate attraction to members of their own sex, fostering a homosexual dichotomy. Homosexuality has plagued the Church for the past eighty years and it has only now crystallized to the extent the Church's influence and moral weight has been severely damaged if not destroyed. In an interview with former president of the John Birch Society, John McManus which appeared in the June 9, 1997 issue of the "New American" Magazine the late Father Martin, a former member of the Jesuit Order, revealed a great deal. The interview revolved around his novel, "Windswept" which depicted a Catholic Church, nearly at war with itself over the demons that did apparently fly in the open windows of Vatican II. Published by Doubleday in 1996, the book dramatized political and religious intrigue by a small group of highly placed Church officials within the Vatican who wished to steer the Church into the New World Order. Martin stated that while his novel was fiction, eighty-five percent is based on fact and that "most of the personages appearing it are real enough, although I have given them fictional names."

Father Martin believed that there was another network throughout the mainline Church. One was determined to gradually transform the meaning of the sacraments and deconstruct the church to become "Earth festivals," cultivating man's relationship, not with a loving God but with his own earthbound destiny in the global village to come. New Age religion is the religion of Lucifer. It is based on materialistic utopian principles and mystical language. Judas' "city of man," had become more important than the "city of God." Thomas Molnar is the author of "Christian Humanism: A Critique of the Secular City and Its Ideology." In it he warned that compromise would inexorably cause a "transition from a civilization with a strong religion-inspired sense of reality, to an anti-civilization where man's worst urges are allowed free course, in view of no other purpose than more pleasure."

Father Martin has called the system "The Process," which was both an evolutionary and inevitable historical process with the aggrandizement of power as its central feature. The Church as the means for uniting all the nations of the earth under what was to be a spiritual form of geopolitics has accepted this "process." According to the new liberal doctrine all ills were caused, not by original sin but by poverty and a lack of education. In a true liberal spirit, the Catholic bishops established the "preferential option of the poor," and new ideas of "social justice" emerged that forged an emotional and rhetorical alliance with socialist, communist and even terrorist groups.

This leads us to a discussion of the idea of a homosexual network. It is apparent that this nurturing of a homosexual underground within the Catholic Church dates back to the late 1920's and early 1930's. It was the "Cambridge Apostles," led by homosexual Marxist spy, Anthony Blunt, which included such notorious spies as Kim Philby, also a homosexual, who were determined to seize control of the major institutions, especially the churches, newspapers, cinema, universities, museums, government cultural agencies and radio stations. Television would have its media message added to the list when its impact became self-evident. If this seems incredulous, one should merely read the late John Costello's masterful biography of Blunt entitled "Mask of Treachery," written in 1988. The book provides copious documentation of this plan, which is consistent with the Gramascian dictum of marching through the culture. Their history illustrates that secrecy was necessary for the Victorian Apostles who played a leading role in opposing the doctrinaire authority of the Church of England. "The Bloomsbury Group," a clique of English intellectuals, served as a cover for the covert Apostles and their devious conspiracies. They held that homosexual relations were a necessary reflection of individual freedom.

According to Costello, the "homosexual network reached out like a cobweb across the pinnacles of the British Establishment, with connections in Whitehall ministries." He says that historians have never really investigated this network and its vast influence of personal favors and private machinations. It had a deleterious effect on national policy and enables someone like Blunt to betray his country to the Soviets.

With regard to infiltration within the Catholic Church, some insight may be found in Stephen Knight's book "The Brotherhood." Not long before his mysterious death, Knight wrote "I have discovered that there is a deliberate policy in operation within the English hierarchy of the Roman Catholic Church to keep its members in ignorance of the true standing of the Church on the question of Freemasonry . . . . I have evidence that the Vatican itself is infiltrated by Freemasons." Ex-Communist and another celebrated convert, Douglas Hyde, revealed long ago that in the thirties the Communist leadership issued a worldwide directive infiltrating the Catholic Church in America. There is also the Congressional testimony of many former Communists in the United States, such as Manning Johnson and Dr. Bella Dodd, who told how they encouraged more than a thousand communists or fellow travelers to enter the Catholic seminaries in the 1930s.* This is reminiscent of the Masonic manual, "Permanent Instructions of the Alta Vendita, which mapped out an entire plan for the infiltration and corruption of the Catholic Church. The Alta Vendita was the highest lodge of the Carbonari, an Italian secret society with links to the Freemasons. Johnson was a prominent black functionary and a member of the Communist-infiltrated American Federation of Labor, while Dodd was a teacher and labor representative

It was Dodd who confirmed his charges when she testified before the House Committee on Un-American Activities in the 1950's, and also in a lecture given at Fordham University, "In the 1930s we put eleven hundred men in the priesthood in order to destroy the church from within." The theory was for these men to be ordained and progress to positions of influence and authority as Monsignors and Bishops. A dozen years before Vatican II, she said, "Right now they are in the highest places in the Church," where they were feverishly working to bring about change in order to weaken the Church's effectiveness against Communism. Dodd said that these changes would be so drastic that "you will not recognize the Catholic Church."

Dr. Dodd unveiled what would seem as an uncanny and incredulous prophecy. She outlined a step-by-step battle plan for Communist subversion of the Catholic Church, which was the only religion that the Communists feared in the entire world. Dodd, who converted to the Catholic faith in 1952 through the influence of Bishop Fulton J. Sheen, told how the Communists sought a clerical fifth column that would not destroy the institution of the Church. They were far more subtle and sinister than that. They wanted to undermine the faith in the minds and hearts of Catholics through the promotion of a pseudo-religion. In other words the people would be given something that resembles Catholicism but would lack its core beliefs. Once the Catholic faith was destroyed, there would be a "guilt complex introduced into the Church that would label the pre-Vatican Church as "being oppressive, authoritarian, full of prejudices and arrogant in claiming to be the one true Church." They would develop openness, that is, a more tolerant attitude through the ecumenical recognition of other beliefs. The Communists would exploit this to the detriment of the Church. When planning to infiltrate the Church, it is logical to assume that the Communists realized that the all-male priesthood could be susceptible to a homosexual influx that would undermine its basic requirements and tenets of faith.

While there is little or no direct proof as to how many Communist moles and sympathizers made it into the priesthood, it is logical to assume that the current church crisis had its makings during this time. There is also no way to find out just how many of these "recruits," were de facto homosexuals and what their specific influence was. It can, however, be easily assumed that their presence served to mitigate against the true mission of the Church and served to weaken it from within. It can also be assumed that some did make it and that the "coincidence" of this gradual decline had something to do with their efforts.

Knowledge of this homosexual network came to light with the publication of Father Enrique Rueda's book, "The Homosexual

Network: Private Lives and Public Policy," in 1983. Columnist Joseph Sobran has written that this book was "so shocking in its allegations that even sympathetic readers found it hard to believe." Fr. Rueda charged that militant homosexuals had already infiltrated the Church and had achieved considerable power, including the control of many seminaries. They had become a "lavender Mafia." The "National Review," in its February 11, 2002, "The Sins of the Fathers," talked of an al-Qaeda like network that needs to be torn out root and branch like its parallel terrorist organization.

The first objective of the network, according to Father Rueda was to "foster the homosexual ideology among clerics and religious." Their second goal was to offer as an "alternative the possibility of rationalizing homosexual behavior within the confines of Roman Catholicism." They wanted to force the Church's hierarchy to redefine scripture and its teachings in line with their gay ideology. Rueda detailed a growing network, replete with referrals, support groups, counseling, newsletters, and its own Website. The network was particularly active in the late 1970's when most of the damage had been done. Since then their lobby has been very successful in removing the stigma associated with homosexuality. It has expertly manipulated public opinion under the mantras of sensitivity and tolerance.

Chicago was at the epicenter of homosexual infiltration. A Catholic advocacy group, the Roman Catholic Faithful, first learned of the Communication Ministry, Inc. from a message posted by a Father James Mott, of San Diego on the e-mail list of St. Sebastian's Angels. St. Sebastian's Angels was a notorious Website for homosexual priests and brothers, on which they promoted the gay agenda throughout the Church in defiance of traditional Catholic teaching. Fr. Mott was later removed from his parish when his involvement with St. Sebastian's became public. CMI, a Pennsylvania corporation since 1983 describes itself as a "network of gay, lesbian and bisexual clergy and religious bound together by the common journey of living toward healthy integration of sexuality and spirituality." Its charter said it was to be exclusively "for charitable, religious, educational and scientific purposes." It effectively served as a message board, clearinghouse, and information center for the homosexual network informing them of meetings, "retreats," and information.

Father Andrew Greeley, the author of many popular novels generally with Catholic themes, noted in his non-fiction book, "Furthermore! Memories of a Parish Priest," the existence of an underworld in Chicago that rivaled anything that Al Capone ever put together. On page eighty of his book, Greeley relates tales of a "ring of predators" about whom he wrote in the paperback edition of "Confessions." It remains "untouched." There is no evidence against them because their fellow priests have not denounced them to the authorities. Those who were removed were for the most part, single offenders who lacked the skills to cover their tracks. The ring "is much more clever." According to Greeley, "They are a dangerous group." There is reason to "believe that they are responsible for at least one murder and may perhaps have been involved in the murder of the murderer." Fr. Greeley expressed no fear of this group for his own safety because he had secretly deposited information that would implicate them, should anything happen to him. When his book was published, no one in the Archdiocese of Chicago made any reference to his candid revelations nor made any effort to refute his charges.

The murder Greeley referred to was probably that of Francis E. Pellegrini. In May of 1984, he was found stabbed to death in his Chicago apartment. His dog had also been stabbed. He was an organist and the choir director at All Saints-St. Anthony of Padua Catholic Church. He was also an Assistant Professor of Sociology and Social Science at City College. Some believe he was about to expose the "Boys Club," an alleged group of pedophile clergy operating in Chicago.

In his perceptive book, "The Amchurch Comes Out," Paul Likoudis, an editor for "The Wanderer," makes a powerful argument that the Protestant Revolution was a milestone event in starting this homosexualization process of the self-destruction of the Catholic Church. He quotes at length the book by English historian and Catholic apologist, Hillarie Belloc, "Europe and the Faith," published in 1920. In it Belloc states that the most evil effect of the Reformation was what he called the "isolation of the soul." Protestantism stressed the individual conscience and the private interpretation of the Bible. It caused a "loss of corporate sustenance," that is, a demise of the "sane balance produced by general experience, the weight of security and the general will." Once this was removed from group consciousness, the "isolated soul" was free to roam around and latch on to anything that gave it some positive feeling. It is this "free-thinking," attitude that has resulted in the country having over 27,000 variations of Protestantism and a general decline in organized religion. As Belloc put it, the isolated soul will "breed attempted strange religions, such as witchcraft and necromancy." It is not difficult to understand how this attitude has contributed to the current Church situation with respect to its homosexual priests.

Belloc was foretelling the advent of the New Age religion phenomenon that has literally chased God out of His own house. Modern psychological and psychiatric theories popularized in the mainstream media, has been the driving force behind this gradual eviction. As Belloc stated in his 1933 classic "Essay of a Catholic," when these new religions or this "New Paganism appeared they would not merely be insufficient, as were the Gods of Greece and Rome but they would positively be evil." Likoudis spares no word in calling this a decline into "Satanism."

"The New American" editor, William Grigg underscored the extent that the "long march through the culture" has been directed at the Catholic Church. In their June 3, 2002 edition, he wrote "following the blueprint created by Marxist theoretician Antonio Gramsci, those carrying on the assault on the Catholic Church are trying to win a 'war of position' by occupying strategically critical posts, particularly in the seminary system." Michael Rose effectively described this strategy and its successes in his provocative book, "Goodbye! Good Men." Rose interviewed several orthodox candidates for the Catholic priesthood, including some who were unable to get past the homosexual gatekeepers that have put seminary formation in grave peril in some sectors of the country.

Likoudis underscores Rose's thesis with his information that two seminary gatekeepers in Seattle, Sister Fran Ferder and Father John Heagle, co-directors of Therapy and Renewal Associates, have ridiculed the Church's traditional teachings on sex and purity, saying that they were evidence of the Vatican's fixations at an adolescent psychological level. Lifelong Catholic, Joseph Mowbray, concurred when he wrote, in 2002 "Teenage boys are the natural objects of sexual desire among immature the homosexual who has become enveloped in the homosexual subculture in the seminary."

For a greater exposition on this network, one should look no further than the reign of late Cardinal Bernardin of Chicago. Likoudis contends that this homosexual network thrived during the reign of Cardinal Bernardin. The Cardinal's liberal spin on most issues created the atmosphere where a homosexual network could grow and prosper more easily. The record shows that the Cardinal was also a tireless promoter of homosexuality as an acceptable lifestyle and looked the other way when his priests were accused of child molestation. According to Likoudis, under Bernardin's influence, the national Catholic bureaucracy became "honeycombed with homosexuals and radical feminists." Likoudis says that we will probably be debating the legacy of Cardinal Bernardin for centuries, so devastating has his impact on the Church been, especially in his role as creator of the National Conference of Catholic Bishops and United States Catholic Conference.

The Cardinal was also an inveterate bishop-maker who, working with former Archbishop Jean Jardot, gave the American hierarchy a pronounced pro-gay orientation. Shortly after the Cardinal's death in 1996, St. Louis University History Professor James Hitchcock wrote, "He consistently used his influence to promote liberal causes, even attacks on Church teachings and traditions." Hitchcock added that the Cardinal "consistently used his power to build a network of allies within both the hierarchy and the bureaucracy, a network which in effect has controlled the direction of the 'American Church.'"

Two of the Cardinal's most notorious friends were Father Martin Greenlaw and Father Patrick Shea, both of whom served in the Archdiocese's Society for the Propagation of the Faith. In August of 1995, Greenlaw was charged with twenty-two counts involving theft and embezzlement of Church funds. His crimes cost the diocese more than $600,000. His theft came to light after he was found beaten in his residence two years earlier. He reported that thirty-one of his credit cards had been stolen. The police realized that his lifestyle far exceeded his annual salary of $12,000. He admitted to police that he often picked up gay men for sexual liaisons. They also found boxes of gay pornography video films in his house in San Francisco. Two of Bernardin friends died of AIDS, including Fr. John Muthig who died in January 1991 allegedly of "liver cancer." Another was John Willig, who died after he was exposed as the Head of Dignity, the gay support group in Washington, D.C.

Likoudis is unrelenting in exposing the Cardinal's past connection and affinity for some of the most notorious homosexuals in recent Church history. Another close friend from his South Carolina days was Monsignor Frederick Hopwood who had been accused of molesting hundreds of boys dating back to the early 1950's. Hopwood and Bernardin shared a residence at the Cathedral of St. John the Baptist in Charleston, South Carolina where some of the abuse took place. According to Paul Likoudis, Hopwood "was not your ordinary pedophile." It is hard to "imagine Bernardin not being aware of it, since they lived together for such a long time."

Though this could be termed "guilt by association," it is curious that throughout his career Cardinal Bernardin had been surrounded and promoted by so many people of dubious reputation. Bernardin's own rise in the priesthood was sponsored, tutored, and promoted by several people of a dubious character. Archbishop Paul Hallinan of Atlanta, Georgia, who had served in Bernardin's hometown of Charleston, South Carolina, was one of the most prolific promoters of the American Church in history. Another was his other mentor, Archbishop, later Cardinal John Deardon, who would be responsible for the appointment of such notorious pro-homosexual bishops as Detroit Auxiliary Tom Gumbleton, Ken Untener of Saginaw, Joseph Imesch of Joliet and

Springfield's Daniel Ryan. One of his proteges, Bishop Wilton Gregory, has seen his apostolic career rise to new heights amid the darkest scandals the Church has seen in four hundred years. A native of Chicago, the former Bishop of Winona, Illinois, Gregory is also the first black priest to lead the United States Conference of Catholic Bishops.

Stephen Brady, the president of the Roman Catholic Faithful has fully explored the Bernardin legacy. Joseph Bernardin was ordained a priest on April 26, 1952 at St. Joseph's Church in Columbia, South Carolina. In 1954, Bishop John Russell, who had been accused of Satanism, appointed him Chancellor of the Diocese. In the fall of 1957, in Greenville, South Carolina, Fr. Bernardin putatively raped an eleven-year old girl, named "Agnes," as part of a Satanist ritual that involved among others, Bishop Russell. As a young child, her sadistic cousin had molested her. Her abusive father had brought her to the rectory. Agnes "was able to resist Bishop Russell physically out of the knowledge that God had made me good, not bad as I was being told." Bernardin showed kindness and approved of her resistance in order to gain her trust and get her to relax. When she did, he forced himself upon her. The report goes on to say that he followed this with a perverted use of the host, in an attempt to make Agnes swallow the guilt his crime. This same woman took her charges of sexual abuse against Bernardin all the way to the Vatican.

In the fall of 1992, Agnes passed a polygraph examination regarding these events. Two years prior, she had told her story to Father Malachi Martin who dramatized her story in the opening chapter of his frightening novel of ecclesiastical intrigue, "Windswept House." The premise of Fr. Martin's book is that the Catholic hierarchy's tolerance of heresy, liturgical abuse, clerical sexual misconduct and clerical pedophilia had one overarching explanation at root and that was a network of Satanists whose smoke had ascended high into the Church. Her story is overly dramatized in the book, but the essential fact remains, that there was a ritual rape. Thirty-four years later, Agnes went to visit Bishop Russell who was suffering from dementia in a nursing home and he agreed to testify against Bernardin in court. He died before he could fulfill his promise.

The charge of a so-called "black mass" is very pertinent in this context. Leading American Mason, Albert Pike, revised and modernized the ritual of the Black Mass, which is celebrated to emphasize the Luciferian and Satanic victory achieved in the Garden of Eden and over Christ to end his mission on earth. This ceremony included the desecration of a Host consecrated by a Roman Catholic Priest. Lucifer is worshipped as the Giver of True Light. The celebrant introduces a Virgin priestess to the joys of sexual intercourse and makes known to her the mystery of procreation. Brady says the "story of Agnes could blow the lid off the Church's fall from grace." This not universally believed. Some Catholic scholars, such as E. Michael Jones of "Culture War Magazine" are skeptical about the story of Agnes and the conclusions of Father Martin.

A few years before his death, Cardinal Bernardin was accused of the sexual abuse of a man named Steven Cook of Cincinnati, Ohio. Cook filed a $10 million lawsuit against Cincinnati priest Ellis Harsham. The suit accused Harsham of numerous coercive sexual acts against him and then delivering him to Archbishop Bernardin, then the Archbishop of Cincinnati, for the same perverted purpose. Several months later Cook dropped the suit, saying he could not trust his memory. He never retracted his charges, nor did he say that these acts did not happen, contrary to what Likoudis calls "the party line that Bernardin had been exonerated, which persists today." Four months later Cook's suit against Harsham was conveniently settled out of court. Harsham was immediately placed on administrative leave and left the priesthood a few months later. Cardinal Bernardin went on to a very public and documented reconciliation with Cook. While on the surface this reminiscent of Pope John Paul II's reconciliation with his attempted assassin Mohamet Agra, behind the scenes Bernardin's lawyers were hushing up another charge in which seminarians in Winona, Minnesota had accused Bernardin and three other bishops of participating in sexual/satanic rituals in their seminary. Among the facts that their lawyers marshaled were that Steven Cook often accompanied the Cardinal to these orgies. Agnes later came to know Stephen Cook and submitted an affidavit in support of his suit against Cardinal Bernardin. Cook told Agnes before he died that he was writing a book, which differed greatly from his public retraction. To her credit, Agnes proceeded to proceed with her life as a faithful Catholic.

In the two years leading up to his death, even as he orchestrated brutal assaults against clerical abuse victims and their parents in Chicago, one after another of Bernardin's closest clerical friends from the Diocese of Charleston made the headlines, all for charges of pedophilia. Father Eugene Condon, Father Justin Godwin, Father Robert Owens-Howard, and Father Paul Seitz just added to the continuing allegations against Hopwood.

According to Likoudis, Cardinal Bernardin proved himself a showman to the end. He conducted a media campaign that resulted in calls for his canonization. Pro-abortion and pro-gay activists, left their imprint was on virtually everything the Cardinal did. This included everything from the well-publicized deathbed visits from pro-abortionist columnist, Ann Landers, Hillary Clinton and a letter from Bill Clinton. A gay choir sang at his funeral Mass in November of 1996 after his death of pancreatic cancer at the age of sixty-eight.

What have been the effects of the Bernardin legacy? One diocese after another is dying out with no signs of help coming from Rome. It was under the Cardinal's patronage that the homosexual network grew and prospered in Chicago. According to Joe Sobran, Bernardin "discreetly made and quashed appointments and promotions that resulted in the current sodomite strongholds within Amchurch." He also fostered liberal doctrines whose effect was "to soften the church up for subversion." The most outrageous of this was his "seamless garment," teaching which seriously undermined the pro-life impact. Under its thin mantel, pro-choice advocates, many

Catholic politicians, such as Mario Cuomo, could hide their evil intent on abortion and be opposed to the death penalty without instilling the condemnation of the Church. It was a boon to pro-abortionists who "could now claim to be 'pro-life' on balance," even though they favored the taking of innocent human life.

Along with Weakland, Cardinal Archbishop Roger Mahoney, and Bishops Matthew Clark of Rochester, Howard Hubbard of Albany and John Cummings of Oakland are the most daring of those who promote the homosexual agenda within the American Church. Their long-range goal is to eventually eliminate the "heterosexual parishes." They are selling the myth that homosexuals are happy, normal individuals, engaged in "alternate" lifestyles on a moral equivalency with those of heterosexuals.

As designed, a homosexual, effeminate priest empties churches faster than a fire drill. It is no coincidence that the only two dioceses that have withstood many of the liberal incursions into faith are those in Alexandria, Virginia, and Bishop Brueshiwitz's diocese in Lincoln, Nebraska. These are the only two dioceses in the nation without altar girls, and they have the highest growth rate in seminary education in the United States.

Martin wrote of the two Churches that have evolved since Vatican II. They are radically different in character in the minds of bishops, priests, nuns, and lay people. The Conciliar Church lays no claim to exclusive possession of the means of eternal salvation. Other religions can make equal claims. It is obvious that the popes have been special targets in this calculated undermining of the most powerful obstacle to the triumph of modern day liberalism. Besides the memory of Pope Pius XII, the aging and infirm Pope John Paul II has been a target of the cultural Marxists in an effort to fatally weaken the church he has ruled for many years.

Father Martin contends that Pope Paul VI was the choice of the so-called "anti-church." He had the right progressive views and his sociology fit with their plans of leveling the Church. While he was not actually one of them, he felt incapable of thwarting the will of what knowledgeable Churchmen call the "superforce." Pope Paul had alluded to this group when he spoke of the "smoke of

Satan," as having infiltrated the Sanctuary of the Church. This was what Martin called "an oblique reference to the enthronement ceremony by Satanists in the Vatican." The incidence of satanic pedophilia, that is, their rites and practices, was already documented among certain bishops and priests as far spread as Turin, Italy and South Carolina. The cultic acts of satanic pedophilia are considered by professionals to be the culmination of the Fallen Archangel's rites.

The Church's hierarchy is not free from blemish. It has co-conspired with the "pedophilia dodge" so it would not have to admit the great extent that the homosexual movement had penetrated its sacrosanct walls. According to the book "The Homosexual Agenda," published in 2003 by Alan Sears and Craig Osten, it has been documented that a cadre of homosexual priests have caused a large amount—if not virtually all of the abuse. The radical homosexual activists and the media have seized on the opportunity in an attempt to swing the church doors open wide for the practice of homosexual behavior, militant feminism, abortion rights—all of which contradict church teachings.

The real danger to the Church is not the attendant bad publicity, nor the harsh accusations by an nihilist and secular press. No, it is the harm done to the institution of the priesthood itself. God's anointed representatives, his earthly agents, have been vilified and tarnished beyond comprehension. This is part of the larger conspiracy against the Church and the area in which it could be most adversely affected. It is heartening that the Vatican has seen through the bishops' incredulous reasoning and identified it as homosexuality.

Another vehicle for undermining the Catholic Church has been the use of sex education classes, which has generally been based on the lascivious and dubious research of Alfred Kinsey. This can easily be illustrated by the course, entitled, "Sexual Attitude Restructuring," which urges participants to rethink their restrictive attitudes acquired in their religious upbringing and adopt a lifestyle of "free sexual expression." This course is a staple of the San Francisco-based Institute for Advanced Study of Human Sexuality, started nearly thirty years ago by Kinsey's disciples that has directly or indirectly influenced nearly every sex education and therapy program in the nation. Wardell Pomeroy, "the dean of American sexologists," and Kinsey's right-hand man in the 1950's, was one of the Institute's founders. He sought funding from the pornography industry to produce "kiddy porn," according to Judith Reisman in her expose on Kinsey and his cohorts.

In a June, 2000 internet article, Art Moore wrote of Kinsey's disciples making great inroads within the Catholic Church through use of subversive sexual ideas that are promulgated often with the approval of many of the Church's hierarchy. These courses tend to break down the natural reversion from shameful personal acts, destroy sensitivity toward the person of others and destroy the modesty that everyone should show his or her own body. Former Milwaukee Archbishop, Rembert Weakland, offered it to his parishes for ten years. Its sinister purpose is to break down sexual barriers and open people to not being sensitive or ashamed of their aberrant sexual activities. Paul Likoudis estimates that about ninety percent of American parishes have bought its perverted message.

Writing in the "New York Times" in May of 2002, William Keller, a self-proclaimed "collapsed Catholic," assailed John Paul, wondering aloud, "Is the Pope a Catholic?" He irreverently portrayed the Pope as a troglodytic "evildoer," who has "replicated something like the Communist Party in his church." In addition, "he has strengthened the Vatican equivalent of the Party Central Committee, called the Curia, and populated it with reactionaries. He has put the stamp of papal infallibility (sic) on the issue of ordaining women, making it more difficult for a successor to come to terms with the issue. (Sic) He has trained bishops that the path of advancement is 'obsequious obeisance' to his office. Alarmed by priests who showed too much populist sympathy for their parishioners, the pope, according to the Notre Dame historian, R. Scott Appleby, has turned seminaries into "factories of conformity, begetting a generation of inflexible young priests who have no idea how to talk to real-life Catholics (sic)." Were the Pope to follow

Keller's advice, its moral authority would have no greater weight than the local country club. The true aim of the critics from the Left is to weaken the church to the extent that it can no longer be effective in combating the "culture of death," in this country.

One of Father Andrew Greeley's most popular novels was "Fall from Grace," published in 1992. It involved a homosexual priest who wanted to sacrifice a live virgin during a Black Mass. The pedophile had enjoyed an earlier sexual relationship with the husband of the protagonist, an aspiring Ph.D. candidate and mother of three girls. The husband was also a wife-beater, who was being pressured by the pedophilic priest to submit his thirteen-year-old daughter to serve as the "sacrificial lamb," in the satanic mass. The plot was thickened by the fact that the husband's one-time lover was his brother-in-law, who was also a bishop. Father Greeley certainly has a fertile imagination, but given the facts uncovered by Stephen Brady, it is almost as if he had copied his ideas from the sordid pages of Chicago clerical history.

Fifty years ago there were few, if any, whispers of such sexual abuse. Priests had drinking problems then, mostly to loneliness and human weakness. One priest I remember was drunk in the confessional but none of them ever "wrestled" with us spanked, or touched us in any way. This is a new more heinous affliction and it has to do with the homosexual network in the seminaries. Nothing has undercut the Catholic Church more than the revelations of its "pedophilia problem." Of course, anyone with any sense knows that it was a "homosexuality problem." How many of these cases involved little girls? Very few! It was more accurately pederasty, which is a homosexual attraction for little boys. The progressive argument that a heterosexual can be a pedophile/pederast is pure balderdash. Statistics and other empirical data will not back that up. NAMBLA, the notorious "North American Man-boy Love Association," is not a heterosexual organization and there is not one to counter the deviant urges of these sickest of our sick society. "If not sex by eight, it is too late," is their putative battle cry. It was more than strange that the major newspapers never explored this link, since child sex abuser Father Paul Shanley was one of the founding members of the association in Boston and served as their unofficial "chaplain." The only way this would have happened was if the Church had opened its own branch of NAMBLA.

The bottom line of this false guise was the fact that the major media, given its constant gay promotion, did not want to tarnish their progressive advocacy by admitting one of the "unintended consequences," of their advocacy, which was the promotion of sexual abuse of children. Austin Ruse, president of the Catholic Family and Human Rights Institute believes that the homosexual activists concern in not with the Church but with the "overthrowing the church." The whole issue of clergy abuse has been used to defame the saintly legacy of Pope John Paul II." While the church is facing the greatest scandal in its history, its still has millions of believers who rest their faith in the biblical promise that "the gates of Hell shall not prevail against it."

---

*   A short book, "AA-1025: The Memoirs of an Anti-Apostle" lends credence to Bella Dodd's accusations. This fascinating book is the story of a Communist in France who entered the priesthood, along with many others, with the intent to subvert and destroy the Church from within. I have no doubt that it happened here too.

8

God's Footsteps

"There is a power so organized, so subtle, so complete,
so pervasive that they had better not speak above their breath
when they speak in condemnation of it." Woodrow Wilson

Jon Ronson's provocative book, "Them: Adventures with Extremists," raises the question: "Is there really a secret room from which a tiny elite secretly rules the world?" On the surface his book has the depth of a snipe hunt but in the final analysis, after crashing a meeting of the Bilderbergers with "agent provocateur," Jim Tucker at the Caesar Park in Portugal, he seems less than convinced that this shadowy elite does not really exist. His experiences with the Bilderbergers left him with a very large doubt. A dangerous car chase and intimidating bodyguards did more to Ronson's cynicism than a library of Jim Marrs books. In dealing with a secret elite, doubt is about all the reasonable thinker can have. This is true because proof of a conspiracy of elite people in a dark room is so hard to prove. But this problematic supposition does not prove that they do not exist. Ronson's book adds its own conspiracy theory when writer Alex Jones suggested "Maybe they were chased, just so nobody would believe them."

One must deal with the question logically and with an honest understanding of past history and man's undeniable attraction for evil. Take the most powerful leaders, journalists, bankers, politicians and world leaders and put them all together and what do you get? Certainly not a choir assembled to give praise to God or a debate club or even a country club-like social gathering. A rational conclusion is that one gets a consortium, dedicated to cornering as much of the world's power, money and resources as it can. This is precisely what motivates the members of the Council of Foreign Relation, the Bilderbergers, and the Trilateral Commission. Their members rank among the movers and shakers who can affect the fate of the world as well as its direction for the next three hundred years. They can put into practice the means, the money and the armies that will forge a NWO, more akin to Machiavelli than Thomas More can.

Fear of or skepticism of the Great Conspiracy of the NWO is just another sign that the American population has lost sight of history. History, especially that of Western Civilization, is replete with intrigues, plots, cabals, collusion and connivance. Why then can we not believe there is a group intent on using the emerging technologies of cyberspace and international communications to control and dominate the world for its own benefit? It is not as preposterous as it may seem. This is not science fiction but the continuation of an impulse that has existed since the first men grouped themselves into the first family and tribe. To deny that these things did and do happen is to run the risk of seeing life through the eyes of a Pollyanna.

The idea of a conspiracy is intimately connected with the concept of the NWO. Over the centuries there have been a number of works that have described ideal worlds since Plato's Republic and St. Thomas More's Utopia. The first proposal for a world order or world government appeared about seven centuries ago. Norman lawyer Pierre Dubois in 1306 was the first, followed by King George Podebrad of Bohemia in 1460 and French scholar Emeric Cruce in 1623. In the seventeenth century, Emeric Cruce opposed King Louis XIV's plan to make France the dominant power in Europe. In his "New Cyneas," he suggested a permanent Congress of Nations that would anticipate world disorders and solve them before they got out of hand. The thought of men going freely from one place to another without thought of country gave him great pleasure. This was the essence of the idea of the "world citizen," later echoed by firebrand, Thomas Paine who boast that he was, "a citizen of the world . . ." He added that his religion "is to do good," which has become a centerpiece in liberal thought. It has been this liberal impulse that has necessitated some form of world government that would eliminate the independence of nations and enforce global harmony, whether people wanted it or not.

One of the most influential books of the late nineteenth century was Ernest Haeckel's "The Riddle of the Universe." It proclaimed that modern civilization, with its great advances in technology and science, had acquired an entirely new evolutionary character. While its technology was advancing at record speed, its moral concepts and social principles had made absolutely no progress. He alleged it was due to the age old traditions of religious repression and superstition that had held Western civilization back. The root of this unease was the anthropocentric belief that man is somehow special and separate from the rest of nature. This is the essential effect that Christianity has had on western civilization. Haeckel is saying that it was wrong altogether. He attacked the fundamental feature of nearly two thousand years of history. Haeckel's understanding of man was one with nature or the "ecology," a term he invented. Haeckel turned Darwin on his head. While Darwin believed that evolution was a function of natural selection, Haeckel believed the exact opposite. To him natural selection was a life and death struggle for dominance and power. It eventually became a function of evolution, or a single system of growth permeating all of nature. He called this "monism," a strongly deterministic vitalism, in which all forces move toward a single totality, including the human community. This is illustrative the NWO.

While the idea of the New World Order or a One World Government first took the international stage during the administration of Woodrow Wilson, the idea did not receive its first favorable reviews with the foundation of the United Nations in San Francisco in 1945. With future convicted perjurer and identified Communist spy Alger Hiss acting as its first Secretary-General, it is not surprising that the U. N. is nothing more than a socialistic cheerleader. In effect, the U. N. is a Trojan Horse that has carried the enemy into our very midst. It has undermined many of our fundamental institutions and values with a utopian promise of a democratic world free from war.

When President George Bush spoke of a NWO during Desert Storm in 1990, no one thought to question just what he meant by his statement. The NWO is the elephant in the room that no one wants to talk about. The quest for power is an ancient one. The concept of a NWO, author Gary North reminds us in his "Conspiracy: A Biblical View," entailed a new partnership of nations. North writes that the NWO is "freer from terror, stronger in the pursuit of justice." He also believes that many of us "will live in one place for most of our lives and take pride in the local region." What was a passion for the large nation-state will dwindle to the level of a mere local attachment. "A new spirit of global citizenship will evolve in its place, and with it the ascendancy of global governance."

The NWO is primarily an economic and political idea. The social elements are only obstacles that must be cleared like so many little land mines. The key ingredient in the idea of a NWO is what has become the modern mantra, a "democracy," bound together through the glue of global interdependence. This is a nice-sounding idea that is reminiscent of the philosophy of Henry Clay, who lost three presidential elections in the nineteenth century. As a member of the Whig party, the forerunner of the Republican Party, Clay promoted what he called the "American System." This later became basis the for Abraham Lincoln's political philosophy.

The American System was an idea for national unity that was based on the interdependence of the three sections of the American nation. In the 1840's, the Northeast, the seedbed of Whig thinking, was the most powerful section. The North was where all the factories and pillars of finance were located. The system was designed to rely on the South for its raw materials. Cotton and fibers would go to the factories so they could be manufactured into textiles. The West was to be the breadbasket of the nation that would provide the food in return for the finished products, which the East would produce. The linchpin to the complex system and the real fly in the ointment was the protective tariff. It was to be levied on foreign textiles and other goods that had been imported into the South. The money collected was earmarked for additional road construction and waterways. These "internal improvements," were designed to tie the country closer together. On the surface it appeared as an ideal system, one of fairness and balance. In reality, the tariff penalized the other two sections, more specifically the South, which now had to pay more for its textiles. The South hated the tariff and it nearly became the cause for an early rebellion.

Abraham Lincoln was the greatest promoter of Clay's system. He recognized it as one that could lead to national greatness. Author Thomas J. DiLorenzo underscores this idea in his biography, "The Real Lincoln." He writes that the real meaning of Lincoln's presidency was that the Civil War was not primarily a fight for the natural and civil rights of slaves. Lincoln's "real agenda," revolved around his dedication to the Whig ideas of his mentor, Henry Clay. Slavery was only an issue that was used to secure divine blessing for the more mundane goals of economic imperialism.

The American System was a mercantile idea that combined capital favoritism for certain preferred "business partners" with the reigning political powers. If taxes must be raised to pay for these allocations, then the price of capital welfare can be passed along to the taxpayer. Taken at its face value, this system resembles the fascism that permeated Italy in the 1920s. Like other mercantilists of his time, Lincoln ignored the case for free trade that Adam Smith, David Ricardo and Frederic Bastiat had made in his day. It was the protective tariff of Hamilton and Clay that started the Civil War, not slavery. Lincoln was a protectionist and he was not going to allow the South to ignore this. According to DiLorenzo, "lobbying, patronage, and political corruption were the American System." As Ohio Senator John Sherman said, "all private interests, all local interests, all banking interests, the interests of individuals, everything, should be subordinate now to the interests of government." It was a precursor to twentieth century collectivism where individual rights became subservient to the "national will."

Today the term goes by the name of "corporate welfare." Under this system, the government in power would dispense special subsidies and monopolistic privileges to their well-connected friends within the business community. It required a strong central government that could subsidize economic development by doling out subsidies to private corporations. The Civil War made certain of the strong central government.

Clay's system resonated well with the spirit of "Manifest Destiny," that had captured the nation's consciousness. This was an idea that thrived in the major idea centers in the Northeast. Coined by John O'Sullivan, the publisher of the "National Review," in 1845, those who fell under the sway of "manifest destiny" nearly succumbed to America's newfound imperial fever. This idea, expressed with true messianic zeal, promoted the jingoistic sentiment America had a "divine imperative," that America was destined to stretch from ocean to ocean, including Canada and Mexico.

This spirit still thrives in the United States. Americans on the surface have to satisfy their religious and psychological side that they are always on the side of right. Americans must never stoop to acquire land and the natural resources of others. It is the spirit of cognitive dissonance that runs through our veins and motivates our foreign policy. Like Tony Soprano, America is the good but misunderstood giant who has to use its power relentlessly and without remorse to effect its national goals. Manifest Destiny and its implied divine approval has filled this bill since the 1840's, inspiring the nation, while it lusts to be the hegemon of the world.

In the early twentieth century, Senator Albert Beveridge illustrated this fact when he said on the Senate floor: "God has not been preparing the English-speaking and Tectonic peoples for a thousand years for nothing but vain and idle self-admiration. No! He has made us the master organizers of the world to establish system where chaos reigns . . . He has made us adepts in government that we may administer government among savages and senile peoples . . ." Beveridge was part of the Boston Brahmin circle that included the descendants of the Adams family, the Lodges, Lowells and even Harvard's Theodore Roosevelt. The spirit still lives on today.

The above raises the question of just who are these people? In 1909 Walter Rathenau of General Electric in Germany said that there were three hundred European men who directed and controlled the economic destiny of Europe. They all knew each other and drew from their own to replace the members. Researcher John Coleman claims a "Committee of 300" does exist and controls a "secret, upper-level parallel government that runs Britain and the United States." The remaining six billion of the world's mortals are just demographic statistics who can serve to enhance their bottom like of dollars and control. Many of these "insiders" have no use for doctrinaire communism, socialism or even capitalism for that matter. Ideologues serve merely as useful instruments, or what Lenin called his "useful idiots," in corralling the vast majority of wealth and power that exists in actuality and in theory throughout the world.

John McManus contends those tightly knit and powerful groups, his so-called, "Insiders," has run America "far longer than any president has." No matter who the president has been, his administration from Eisenhower through George W. Bush has been staffed and run mostly from Council of Foreign Relations members. Membership in this club is almost a prerequisite for government service on a high level.

The Council on Foreign Relations is the American counterpart to Cecil Rhodes' Round Table. It is an extension of the Old World imperialistic British oligarchy. It is little known because the media wants to control what you know. It has advocated policies, which favor the growth of the super-state, a gradual surrender of the United States' sovereignty to the UN, and a steady retreat in the face of Communist aggression. The CFR was founded specifically for the purpose of conditioning the American people to accept and even want world government. Everywhere Americans are being conditioned to accept the idea of a global order as the natural outcome of historical forces beyond their control. It is pure propaganda that has permeated the nation's conscious in encouraging Americans to abandon the one trait that distinguishes them from people around most of the world and that is their freedom.

This powerful yet enigmatic organization has numbered among its membership virtually every cabinet member, several presidents, and Supreme Court judges to high offices, but is not widely known. Because of the Council's propensity for debating and deliberating on foreign policy and its vision for the future of the world, it has served as a virtual clearinghouse for most political appointments, dating back to the Eisenhower administration. The Council's membership lists over the years has read like a "Who's Who" in government, journalism, diplomacy, economics and business.

The definitive book on the CFR is "The Shadows of Power," by James Perloff. He describes it as a front for J. P. Morgan and Company. By 1945, its members had infiltrated the corridors of power, especially in the State Department, giving it virtual control over the country's foreign policy regardless of who was in the White House. Echoing the words of the late Supreme Court Justice, Felix Frankfurter, Perloff makes an excellent case that the real rulers in Washington are "invisible, and exercise power from behind the scenes." Professor Carroll Quigley studied this organization for twenty years and for two years was allowed in its inner sanctum, studying its papers and its historical documents. Quigley believed the CFR's role in history is significant enough to be known. His only complaint was that the CFR has remained hidden. Quigley was naive to think he could report the secrets of the elite with impunity. His publisher stopped selling his magnum opus, "Tragedy and Hope," in 1968 and even destroyed the plates. They would never reprint it again. The publisher told anyone who wanted his book that it was out of print. It essentially became a banned book, available today only because it was reprinted in violation of the copyright.

The CFR's origins date back to the conclusion of World War I. After the failure of the United States to ratify the Versailles Treaty with its world body, the feckless League of Nations, Colonel Edward Mandel House called another meeting which met at Paris's Majestic

Hotel on May 30, 1919 and resolved to form an "Institute of International Affairs." He had gathered about 100 influential men to discuss the postwar war world. They were known as the "Inquiry," and they laid the basis for what was later called Woodrow Wilson's "14 Points." They were all globalists who wanted equality of trade conditions, free markets and the removal of all economic barriers.

While House described himself as a Marxist, he was more akin to the Fabian socialists of England. He wanted to establish an American counterpart to the Round Table of England. The United States branch was incorporated on July 21, 1921 as the Council on Foreign Relations. It was built upon an existing but lackluster New York dinner club of the same name, which had been created in 1918 by New York bankers and lawyers for discussions on trade and international finance. Since 1945 it has been headquartered at the elegant Harold Pratt House in New York City. The Pratt family donated the house. Its painted French doors, elegant tapestries and fireplaces have made it resemble more like a club than a consortium of power brokers and world leaders.

One of the self-appointed tasks of the CFR was to ensure that there was a world body to carry out the goals of the brain trust. The House cartel had hoped the League of Nations would serve as that introductory vehicle. But the obstinacy of both Europe's leaders and the Republican Senate, led by Henry Cabot Lodge Sr. forced the globalists to wait. When the League started to fail, they conceived of a more powerful world mechanism, which would serve as the transition from national interest to global interest. It was the late Arkansas Senator, William Fulbright, who introduced the resolution in Congress that led to the groundwork for the UN in 1943. In 1949, Alan Cranston, now the late Chairman of the Board of the Gorbachev Foundation, pushed through the California legislature a resolution memorializing Congress to call for a national convention to "expedite and insure the participation of the United States government in a federal world government."

The CFR illustrates how the merger of business and government really works. This quasi-fraternal society served as a conduit for insider policy in and out of the Federal Reserve System.

The CFR was the nexus for all ideas of free trade and global geopolitics. The members would pass along ideas on Insider policy to those who fronted for the Establishment. Virtually every key man in the Federal Reserve System has been a member of the Morgan/Rockefeller CFR. David Rockefeller, the former CEO of the Chase Manhattan Bank, was longtime president of the CFR.

The CFR is at its core a secret society. According to Article II of the by-laws, formal meetings have to remain secret. Anyone who releases the contents of these meetings will be subjected to dismissal. In addition to House, its members have included such luminaries as John Foster Dulles, his brother, Allan and Walter Lippmann. The foundation money came from J.P. Morgan, John D. Rockefeller, Paul Warburg, Otto Kahn and Jacob Schiff. Writing in the "Washington Post" Richard Harwood called the CFR and its members "the nearest thing we have to a ruling establishment in the United States." Other members are many in the news media, such as Dan Rather, columnists George Will, Charles Krauthammer and Jim Hoagland. In a 1958 "Harper's Magazine" article, Joseph Kraft stated that the CFR "plays a special part in helping to bridge the gap between the two parties, affording unofficially a measure of continuity when the guard changes in Washington." They have been publishing since 1959 an influential magazine, "Foreign Affairs," which outlines their global goals through several position papers solicited from government leaders and officials who share and support their global goals. If one wanted to read what the future agenda of the country is, all that person would have to do is read the magazine. It is an "open conspiracy." In theory the Council comes close to being an organ of what C. Wright Mills has called the "Power Elite," that is, a group of men, similar in interest and outlook, shaping events from invulnerable positions behind the scenes.

The destruction of American national sovereignty is at the heart of the CFR's agenda. The CFR prepared a memo to the State Department in 1944 that led the United States down the road of losing its sovereignty. The sovereignty fetish is still so strong in the public mind that there would appear to be little chance of winning popular assent to American membership in anything approaching a superstate organization. Much will depend on the kind of approach, which is used in further popular education. In Study No. 7, which appeared in the November 25, 1959 issue of "Foreign Affairs," the CFR detailed the exact purpose of building a new international paradigm was to create a one-world socialist system with the United States as a necessary part of it.

This is the same idea that appeared in the book, "Wise Men," written by Walter Isaacson and Evan Thomas in 1986. These globalists had a vision that had the equivalent of a religious fervor. John J. McCloy, Chip Bolen, George Kennan, Dean Acheson, and Paul Cravath made up the heart of these "Insiders." The CFR is where they established a geo-political balance of power that provided stability but one with one eye open. The constant strain of having a powerful enemy kept their subjects in a heightened sense of fear that they were often able to do what they wanted to establish their economic positions without too much vocal opposition. The "Wise Men" desired to create their New World Order without the intervention of God. It would be one that would elevate the lordship of man and would be regulated by economic progress beneath human skies. The New World Order, founded on purely human principles can lead only to a world of depravity and despair, a veritable dystopia of human suffering.

John McCloy had a career in world finance, business and politics that spanned seven decades. At his ninetieth birthday Henry Kissinger called him, "the first Citizen of the Council of Foreign relations." He added "I believe that John McCloy heard the footsteps of God, . . . and those of us who were not humble enough or who were not sharp enough had the privilege of knowing that if we followed his footsteps, we were in the path of doing God's work." These globalists realized that anything that would upset the tripod balance of trade, finance and physical security was considered as a threat to the world as a whole and to each nation as a part of that whole. "Everyone must co-operate or everyone will suffer," so wrote Father Malachi Martin. This partially explains the attack on the fundamentalists and terrorists of the world and even Iraq, which has been out of step with the global movement for over a decade.

Another of this global axis of evil is the Bilderbergers. They represent another undercover group of world multinational global elitists who own and control the public press and disclose to the citizens of each country that which they desire us to know and little else. The Bilderbergers are more opportunists than they are ideologues. They are bottom-line Machiavellians. Participants in their meetings make decisions that impact the lives of every American and people all over the world. They are not concerned about the little things, such as national interest, the U.S. Constitution, or the needs of the individual American citizen.

The Bilderbergers have no formal name but have been christened by those who first discovered their secret 1954 meeting at the Bilderberg Hotel in Osterbeek, Holland. Prince Bernhard, the husband of wealthy Ex-Queen Juliana of the Netherlands, who abdicated in favor of her daughter, Beatrix in 1980, initiated the Bilderberg meetings, a half century ago. They meet once or twice a year at some plush resort around the world. The meetings are usually attended by leading industrialists, educators, government, and labor leaders. Luminaries, such as the Rockefellers, Gerald Ford, Henry Kissinger, and Father Theodore Hesburg, the former president of Notre Dame University. Writer John McBeth described the Bilderbergers as "an international who's who of the wealthy, influential and the powerful." He reported that once a year, the 120 men and women credited with putting Bill Clinton in office and ousting Lady Margaret Thatcher from No. 10 Downing Street, "meet to discuss world events" and manipulate them. Journalist Robert W. Lee concluded that the Bilderbergers were "founded in response to McCarthyism in the fifties." He based his assumption on the conclusions reached by Yale alumnus and early "National Review" contributor Medford Evans that the "essence of McCarthyism is patriotism while the essence of Bilderbergerism is internationalism." To them anything that fosters love of country is a bad thing. Evans wrote that the Bilderbergers' conferences were "instituted to carry on the work of dismantling American sovereignty which McCarthy had interrupted." This puts them in step with the CFR with relation to national sovereignty.

The Trilateralists provide the third leg on the imperial stool. The purpose of the Trilateral Commission is to engineer an enduring partnership among the ruling classes of North America, Western Europe and Japan. The members come from international business, banking, government, academia and the mass media. What the Trilateralists truly intend is the creation of a worldwide economic power superior to the political governments of the nation-states involved. They seek an age of post-nationalism when devoid of ethnic culture and history, the social, economic and political values esteemed by these Trilateral members will be transformed into universal values. Their values include an universal economy, government, which would be appointed and not elected, and universal religious belief. They believe every effective international organization needs a custodian. They reserve that role for themselves. Holly Sklar wrote in her book, "Trilateralism," "these men make the most important foreign, economic and domestic policy decisions of the U.S. government today. They set the goals and directions for the administration." Through its organ, the International Monetary Fund, they can control the currency and with it the economy of every country in the world. This is world economic management at its most dangerous. In his book "With No Apologies," Senator Barry Goldwater warned the country and explained "what the Trilaterals truly intend is the creation of a worldwide economic power superior to the political government of the nation states involved. As managers and creators of the system they will rule the world."

John McManus traces the roots of the Trilaterals to President Jimmy Carter's national security adviser, Zbigniew Brzezinski's 1970 book, "Between Two Ages." McManus found a quote that closely paralleled the thinking of Colonel Edward Mandel House. "Marxism is simultaneously a victory of the external active man over the inner, passive man and a victory of reason over belief." "Marxism," Brzezinski also wrote, "disseminated on the popular level in the form of Communism, represented a major advance in man's ability to conceptualize his world." Brzezinski praised Marxism as a system because it appealed for central planning. He recommended the formation of a "community of the developed nations . . . claiming that America was becoming obsolete, appealed for central planning, and recommended the formation of a "community of the developed nations . . . through a variety of indirect ties and already developing limitations on national sovereignty." He also called openly for "the goal of world government." This amounts to a universal assault on the idea of national independence.

Brzezinski fashions himself a world citizen. The NWO was inevitable. It had to be a gradual process because growing doubts, which plagued the country at the end of the Cold War ideological struggle, had not "ushered in a New World Order." He urged that the United States gradually expand "the range of democratic cooperation as well as the range of personal and national security . . . step by step, stone by stone . . . of existing narrow zone of stability."

What Brzezinski had in mind was a regionalization of preliminary steps that would gradually break down national sentiments and undercut the power and hegemony of one state as opposed to another. In the same book, he called for this gradual convergence of the West with the East, analogous to that done on the American System. This would ultimately culminate in "world government." David Rockefeller's Polish protégé aptly proclaimed "National sovereignty is no longer a viable concept." He praised Marxism and Communism as major advances in man's ability to conceptualize his relationship with the world and the maturation of his universal vision.

With Brzezinski at his side, Trilateral Commission Founder David Rockefeller enlisted 300 members for this new commission whose goal, paralleling those of the CFR, called for nations to merge into a world government. The Trilateralists were in a position where they can implement policy recommendations, putting them in the strategic position as some sort of "shadow government." The extent of their power is just another elephant in the parlor that no one wants to talk about for fear of being labeled a conspiracy wacko.

It is amazing who keeps coming to the surface in this issue of globalism. Mikhail Gorbachev, who still thinks in Marxist terms, has become a world leader once again. This time, instead of fronting for the Soviet powers, he is fronting for the global economists who wish to establish this NWO. He has appeared since his fall from power in 1989 at global conferences all over the world, lecturing and promoting the new way to look at things. His ideas resonate well in the land of CFR, Trilateralism, the Club of Rome, and the Bilderbergers. In 1987, while still the President of Russia, Gorbachev, "called for giving the UN expanded authority to regulate military conflicts, economic relations, environmental protection and . . . for enhancing the powers of the afflicted International Court of Justice to decide international disputes." These sentiments came from a man who reminded the world in a November 1987speech that October of 1917 marked the time that "we parted with the Old World, rejecting it once and for all. We are moving toward a New World of Communism. We shall never turn off that road . . . Perestroika is a continuation of the October Revolution." In his book, "Perestroika," Gorbachev wrote "according to Lenin, socialism and democracy are indivisible . . . and the essence of Perestroika lies in the fact that it unites socialism with democracy and revives the Leninist concept of social construction both in theory and practice." To effect this Herculean global task, Gorbachev proposed the establishment of a global "Brain Trust," to "focus on the present an future of our civilization."

This is reminiscent of Franklin Roosevelt's group of closet advisers during World War II, which included the likes of Raymond Moley, Adolph Berle, and Rexford Tugwell. The very notion of a "brain trust" reeks of a Pandora's Box of elitism, social engineering, and social manipulation. The former Soviet premier's brain trust would include a magnificent collection of "selfless billionaires, statesmen, academic double-domes, Nobel laureates and spiritual mahatmas in the service of humanity and planetary survival." Gorbachev has being playing this theme up for years, calling for "non-governmental commissions of "wise men" and "Councils of Elders," to solve the world's "intractable problems." The above clearly illustrates that convergence is at the apex of his worldview.

It was in his newly assumed role as an "Elder" that Gorbachev offered the world a brief glimpse of his vision for the future. "Civilization will shift to new values and new ways of life will be needed to find real solutions to the problems of our environment, a way out of the ecological crisis." Then came his catch. "Gradually we will have to achieve a change of emphasis in the archetypal dilemma: to have or to be . . . ." It is simple as the fact, he states, "that we must change the nature of our consumption." This bastardization of Shakespeare demonstrated the root problem and deep challenge of that entire wish to thwart this play of super power government. They tell us that we must choose between surviving on this planet and giving up our rich standard of living. It is a false choice that they have been promoting for a decade to result in the downsizing of the American power.

The idea of a unified Europe under a centralized control is not new. It is reported to have been the goal of the fourteenth century Knights Templar and now seems on the road to becoming a reality. There are several international agencies that have been created to affect the elimination of national sovereignty, especially that of the United States. There is already in place a conglomeration of alphabetical regional economic alliances that will serve as the basis for the transnational superstructure that the financial elite envisions. It now stretches from the European Community, the Americas and the Pacific Rim, the Caribbean and even the former Soviet Union.

The three-legged plan to control the world's economy was devised at the Bretton Woods Conference after World War II. Financed largely by the United States taxpayer, the World Banks and the International Monetary Fund got off to a running start. But it was the resistance to the global trade leg, then called the International Trade Organization, that was initially thwarted by Harry Truman and the Congress who correctly realized that it would conflict with the country's sovereignty and interfere with domestic law. The potential effects on American labor were also at the root of this bipartisan opposition. Times have changed since then. The WTO has virtually turned control of the U.S. economy to a coterie of foreign bureaucrats in Geneva who would be accountable to no one. The WTO now effectively controls the nation's trade, investment and technology, making vital decisions about the country's jobs, production, labor standards, environment and national security.

Like North American Foreign Trade Agreement, the WTO agreement bypasses the requirement in the United States Constitution that requires a two-thirds majority in the Senate. It is designed to function as the global trade pillar of a triumvirate that will plan and control the world's economy. When linked with the other two pillars, the World Bank, which loans capital to developing nations, and the International Monetary Fund, which supervises the flow of money around the globe, one can easily see the potential for global power and control. Over the years nations have become increasingly dependent on these organizations, allowing them the nascent start of involvement in internal affairs. This is a surefire formula for loss of sovereignty and the eventual disappearance of national identity.

In April of 1997, a hundred and twenty global makers and shakers, including a few women, such as Katherine Graham, the late publisher of the "Washington Post" met in Atlanta, Georgia. The swarm of Bilderbergers included Umberto Agnelli of Fiat Corporation, Paul Allaire of Xerox, Robert Bartley of the "Wall Street Journal," Lloyd Bentsen, former Texas Senator and Secretary of the Treasury, John Browne from British Petroleum Corp., Louis Gesture of IBM, Henry Kissinger, David Rockefeller, James Wolfensohn, the President of the World Bank and current Secretary of State Colin Powell. This hive of power brokers had an agenda of six goals for the coming millennium which included, according to Texe Marrs included "the draining of billions of tax payer dollars to third world countries and the former Soviet Union through the International Monetary Fund." This also included repaying "debts" that the United States owes to the U. N.

Where is this all leading the nation? The answer might be to the establishment of "Corporate Governance," which will eventually strip away national sovereignty and end the control of multinational corporations by the US and other nation-states. It is all about world government, the culmination of a century of work from the spirit of the Knights Templar, the Free Masons, the Illuminati and their nineteenth and twentieth century intellectual heirs, the Marxists, both economic and cultural, Cecil Rhodes and his ideology. A proposed multination investment treaty will bring all the earth's corporations under a single global order, ending national sovereignty and terminating local controls by nation-states over their own corporations. The giants of finance, the AT&T's, Microsoft, Boeing, IBM, Sony, Toshiba etc. will be able to entirely avoid and snub the laws and dictates of national governments. According to Marrs, a new global Fascism will gradually emerge with the new millennium approaches.

The organization that has from the start served to promote the ideology behind the New World Order has always been the United Nations. The UN has stymied the advancement of United States national interests, since its inception at the Dumbarton Oaks Conference. Its first military undertaking, the so-called "police action," in Korea introduced the concept of the stalemate or the "no-win" war, which has literally dominated our fighting philosophy ever since. As the years went on, the UN has served as a focal point for Soviet espionage and a platform from which the Russians could ably contradict and counteract the goals and values of American foreign policy. To make matters worse, the extravagant lifestyle of the UN bureaucrats and employees was largely funded by the US taxpayer. Many of the Third World nations used the UN as a cash cow to dig deeply into the American coffers to support their often-oppressive regimes, which had often killed off their opposition back home.

On the humanitarian front, the UN has blatantly failed to live up to its utopian promises. The extravagant lifestyle of UN bureaucrats and employees and their tax-free salaries are mostly funded by the American taxpayers. Its conniving politicians from tiny Third World countries have used the American public trough, much like our own politicians, to bleed the organization's finances dry. Most humanitarian aid never reaches its intended targets, winding up rather in the coffers of the ruling clique of murders who have killed off their opposition in countries, like Somalia and Haiti.

The UN has continued to push for a Convention of Rights of the child that would authorize a UN bureaucracy to supervise parental relations with their children in America, under the guise of protecting the rights of these children. This blatant attempt to undermine the traditional family is completely in line with Gramascian thinking. The UN continually lobbies for the universal rights of women for reproductive choice, trying to limit families through improper education, the condom philosophy and all other sorts of cultural misgivings that undermine the integrity of the family. In 1995, President Clinton signed this convention, which the Children's Defense Fund, formerly chaired by his wife, Hillary Clinton, supported. This treaty is a broadside attack on the rights of all Americans and could hasten the eventual breakdown of the family. It effectively elevates children to the level of adults without any concomitant responsibilities.

To alleviate this dire financial situation, UN Secretary General Boutrous Boutrous-Ghalis had a plan to raise taxes on the world to finance his global dream of the so-called New World Order. Taxation is a sovereign prerogative. Regardless of how it was implemented, it would establish the UN as a superior entity. Once the UN has the power to levy taxes on the world community, even if only on business and travelers, it would, in effect, function as a world government agency. As the late Supreme Court Chief Justice John Marshall wrote, the power to tax involves the power to destroy. Global taxation would establish an international system of entitlement, like the welfare system that now exists in the United States.

The idea of a global tax dates back to James Tobin, a 1981 Nobel Prize winner in Economics, who has called for a tax on spot transactions in foreign exchange. UN officials are ecstatic at Tobin's prediction that the revenue potential is over $1.5 trillion a year. The Independent Commission on Population and Quality of Life has issued a report that lists dozens of innovative global devices to tax people, corporations and international business activities. The so-called Tobin Tax would include taxes on aviation, traffic and freight, ocean freight and cruises, communication satellites, international postal items and trade in goods and services.

The Tobin Tax has taken a more concrete form in the so-called Independent Commission on Population and Quality of Life, which has issued a report in 1995 that listed dozens of innovative global devices that would tax individual citizens worldwide, their corporations and international business. These new ideas include taxes on aviation travel and freight, ocean freight and cruises, aviation fuel, telecommunications frequencies, satellites, international mail and trade in goods and services. The UN publicly launched this system in 1995 at its World Summit for Social Development, held in Copenhagen, Denmark. James G. Speth, Clinton's-appointed of the UN Development Program called for these taxes on international stock speculation, the consumption of non-renewable energy, environmental permits and arms trade. This financial windfall could enable the UN to finance its global operations, independent the United States and most likely fund the international police force that many of its proponents are saying is the only solution to world conflicts.

Once the basic rule of global taxation to support the UN is firmly established, no matter how remote or minimal the idea sounds, it will deeply embed itself in the world consciousness and will just become another cost of doing business. All this comes at a time when the United States has admirably been attempting to maintain and secure its economic house which has been on a roller-coaster ride of huge profits, computer meltdown fears, terrorist attacks, economic decline, business failures, and accounting fraud. The idea of a world tax can have the same limitations and destabilizing effects overtaxation has wreaked on this country and maybe even worse, because it will more heavily fall on the shoulders of the emerging nations.

The UN plan called for a World Conference on Global Governance in 1998 for the purpose of submitting to the world the necessary treaties and agreements for ratification by the year 2000. This 410-page report, published by Oxford University, entitled "Our Global Neighborhood," categorically states that global governance does not imply world governance or world federalism but then spends 400 pages describing in minute detail just that: world governance. Global governance amounts to an international socialism, resulting in a loss of national sovereignty, private property rights and all hopes of achieving individual prosperity.

The Commission's recommendation rested on the erroneous belief that the world was ready to accept a global civic virtue based on a set of core values that would unite people of all cultural, political, religious or philosophical backgrounds. In truth, the world is more diverse and disparate than ever before. World events have served to illustrate the chasms and distinctions between the various racial and ethnic groups rather than uncover any solid common ground. These new values also revolve around a new earth ethic, which is counter to American sovereignty and property rights. As the report clearly indicated, the impulse to possess territory is a powerful one for all species: yet it is this territorial imperative the people must overcome for global governance to succeed. On a similar note, there is an egalitarian principle that underscores this document that would have serious consequences for the American way of life if something were not done to dispel or defeat it.

The Commission also holds as true the fallacy that the world is ready to accept the proposition that there can be no justice without equity. This notion of economic leveling has already permeated our society, making the country ripe for seduction into the New World Order. As the report says, although people are born into widely unequal economic and social circumstances, great disparities in their condition or life chances are an affront to the human sense of justice. The Commission intends for the United Nations to level the inequities in the world by taking wealth from the rich and giving it to the poor. This new earth ethic ignores the fundamental values upon which this nation was founded, that is, free enterprise, individualism and meritocracy.

The vision of these international social planners has great ramifications for every human being on this planet. It wants to assume trusteeship over the global commons which its defines as the atmosphere, outer space, the oceans and the related environment and life support systems that contribute to the support of human life. This definition embraces virtually all biodiversity on the earth and places it under control of the UN. The utopian goal of the world under the dominion of the UN evokes visions of empire that has inspired megalomaniacs from the time of Alexander the Great through the fascist and communist exigencies of Hitler, Mussolini, and Stalin. The mechanisms have already been set up in over 300 treaties that the UN already administers. These are treaties that can overrule American laws. It is becoming apparent that the UN plans to use the upcoming millennium to effectively organize, control and rule the world. Any nation or country that refuses to comply will be forced to get in line or suffer invasion or ostracism from the global community.

The UN funded Commission on Global Governance has completed its three-year study and has now announced publicly its plans to implement world governance by the year 2000. That has not happened but these forces have not given up. American citizens should have no fear of a foreign invasion. There will be no black helicopters hovering over the Pentagon. They have run interference in the Halls of Congress, while their intellectual and financial mentors in the Council of Foreign Relations, employed its influential through its members in business, the media, the schools and the State Department. All this has worked to condition the American people to think of themselves as global citizens and not Americans. With the ensuing collapse of the pillars of American civilization, it should not be too difficult for the proponents of the New World Order to achieve their ultimate aims. Writer Gary North believes that historians writing about this era, will look at "regional blocs as mere stepping stones toward the world as a trading bloc . . . It will be just a matter of time before these blocs merge into a whole." The World Trade Organization was an important step in reminds us that H.G. Wells's "Open Conspiracy" is still operating today to extend this New World Order.

One of the chief proponents of the NWO is Bill Clinton's former roommate at Oxford and later his Ambassador to the UN, Strobe Talbot. A writer for "Time Magazine" for twenty-two years, he penned an essay for his publication in 1992 that revealed his predictions for the future. Entitled, "The Birth of the Global Nation," Talbot sanguinely predicted that in the twenty-first century, "Nationhood as we know it will be obsolete, all the states will recognize a single, global authority." Talbot believes that "great minds agree that this is the proverbial wave of the future." If something is not done soon, Talbot wrote "we will all be citizens of the world whether we like it or not." According to author William Knoke's book, "Bold New World," world government is not only coming, "it is essentially here!" He warns that businessmen "had better learn the discipline of 'global citizenship'." He goes on to say that in the 21ˢᵗ century, "will each "retain our 'indigenous' cultures, our unique blend of tribal affiliations" setting up this scenario, which he describes as a "limited world government with sovereignty over world trade."

The Clinton Administration seriously advanced this agenda by engaging the United States in a number of different foreign wars, as a means of turning the UN into an international establishment that will someday field its own army. Under the guise of "peacekeeping," the United States military has been turned into a league of armed social workers. The president's secret executive order—Presidential Decision Directive #25—had in effect turned United States military authority over to the UN. This has been a gradual process, dating back to the Korean War that took a quantum leap forward during the "Hundred Hours War" of Desert Storm. When several American soldiers were killed an a helicopter crash in Iraq, Vice-President Al Gore had the effrontery to tell their surviving family members that they could be proud because their loved ones had "died in the service of the United Nations." This can be construed as an attempt to develop a standing global army that can be used in the future to put any local insurrections of groups that will naturally oppose the intransigence of the UN model.

The case of U.S. Army Specialist E-4 Michael G. New, a medic in the third Infantry Division illustrates the rudimentary beginnings of an unconstitutional shift in the nation's military structure. New was court-martialed in 1994 for disobeying an order to "appear in a United Nations uniform." He rebelled at being ordered to wear the ubiquitous UN blue beret because he said his oath was to his country and the international body. He was to have been a UN peacekeeper in Macedonia under the command of a Finnish general.

Not everyone has been cowed into accepting the NWO as the logical consequence of two hundred years of "American progress." Phyllis Schlafly had it right when she said, "world government would require the repeal of both history and human nature." One needs only listen to their rhetoric and easily determine that is what they are attempting, both the repeal of history and human nature. It is the essential goal of global liberalism to "change people," whether they want to change or not. It is the "notion that the world can live in democracy and stability under some international bureaucracy is an impossible pipe dream." Any attempt to join with third world nations can only level America's economic impact and jeopardize its unique system of laws and government to the detriment of the entire world.

In a February 25, 1998 article in the "Conservative Chronicles," Pat Buchanan opined "The Conservative Congress has shown its independence by thwarting presidential attempts to foster the advance of a globalization of the American interests." Congress refused to honor President Clinton's demands that they increase allocations to the International Monetary Fund, pay a billion in dues to the UN and amend our trade treaties to include fast track approval of this international deal. On February 11, the "Washington Post" and the "New York Times," published a two-page letter with this naked ultimatum, signed by two ex-presidents, two ex-chairmen of the Federal Reserve, four ex-secretaries of state, four ex-national security advisors, four former treasury secretaries, and a host of other former cabinet officers. According to Buchanan, the signatures that carried the most weight included the global corporate elite of one hundred of America's money power. This included the chairmen and CEO's of Fortune 500 Companies, such as AT&T, General Electric, GM, IBM, ITT, Exxon, Chase

Manhattan, BankAmerica and the media giants Time Warner and Times Mirror. They wanted eighteen billion dollars for the Asian bailout, which has already hit the cash registers for one hundred and seventeen billion dollars they wanted fast track and one billion dollars for the UN. Buchanan believes that Congress is being ordered not only to embrace globalism but also to abandon conservative principles. This would, in effect, emasculate the Constitution and to surrender powers specifically given to it by the founding fathers.

In his book, "The Great Betrayal," Buchanan warned "These business elite picture themselves as the citizens of the world, in true fidelity to Woodrow Wilson's own visionary political/ economics." This transnational elite yearns to be free of the nations to which they once gave allegiance. They see the state as a dragging encumbrance that limits their ability to control world markets. They dream of a day when the nation-state is as obsolete as the feudal castle. "The expansion of our consciousness to the global level offers mankind perhaps the last real chance to build a world order that is less coercive than that offered by the nation-state" wrote A.W. Clausen, the former president of BankAmerica Corporation. William I. Spencer, former president of the First National City Corporation declared the political boundaries of nation-states are too narrow and constricted to define the scope and sweep of modern business. Author Peter Drucker added, "We must defang that nationalist monster!"

As the Buchanan book stressed, "the winners in a world of free trade and floating exchange rates are regimes whose central bankers manipulate currency values for national benefit and global corporate elite that can shift production from one country to another. Losers are the rooted people." The conservative traditionalists are bound to their country by the cultural ties of family, memory, neighborhood, to one community and one country. Buchanan went on to say, that the "shibboleth, free trade is an invention of early 19th century English thinkers, utopians who accepted this new gospel of salvation." The success or failure of the NWO revolves around the concept of free trade. Buchanan called it "gangster capitalism." He used to be for free trade but realized its evil during a 1990 visit to New Hampshire. Businesses and factories were shutting down, having been sacrificed on the altars of free trade and anti-Americanism.

Henry Fairbairn became free trade's first great enthusiast. In 1836, he wrote, "Nations will become united in the golden bands of peace." He believed that eventually "science and liberty and abundance will reign among the inhabitants of the earth . . . and even now the eye can reach to the age when one language, one religion and one nation alone will be existing in the world." Free trade had its greatest proponent in Richard Cobden, a nineteenth century economist, and statesman, for whom it was "the way, the truth, and the light." He and his disciples were one world advocates, that is anti-traditionalists, anti-conservatives and basically heretics because at the essence of their doctrine was the belief that free trade held the promise of an earthly paradise. It is also deeply un-American. This is the opposite of what Jefferson declared to be the aim of the American Revolution—the cutting of our political bands to England.

The man behind free trade in this country was Congressman Cordell Hull, the father of the sixteenth amendment, the man who gave us the Marxist graduated income tax. He replaced the protective tariff with this dreaded amendment. This came after England's bitter experiment with free trade. The results were dire and fatal. Ireland was ruined. Millions starved and British agriculture collapsed. They became so dependent on Continental grain that they were on the brink of national starvation in 1918.

Free trade has had a hypnotic effect on business elite who equated it with the Christian gospel and the borderless economy with the kingdom of heaven. Roosevelt and his Secretary of State Cordell Hull intensified the American fascination with free trade. Thirty-years of free trade have spawned a new elite. Unencumbered by any national allegiance, it roams a Darwinian world of the borderless economy, where sentiment is folly and the fittest alone survive. In the eyes of this rootless transnational elite, men and women are not family, friends, neighbors etc but consumers and factors of production. Social critic David Morris, who like Marx considers free trade the "Great Destroyer," writes "the emphasis on globalism rearranges our loyalties and loosens our neighborly ties . . ." We are now all assets.

The more practical minded business leaders realized that the greatest enemy their success had was competition. John D. Rockefeller once said "competition is a sin." He and his business associates, the so-called, "Robber Barons," were convinced that under the rules of free markets or laissez faire economics, they would never be able to reap the return on their investments that they wanted, which is under the impartial rules of the free-enterprise system. So they vowed to capture the capitalistic system from within by winning or buying the favors of the politicians who would dream up volume upon volume of regulation, with certain viable exceptions, that would serve to limit the competition and open the doors for mergers and acquisitions. That is what has happened to the NWO.

The men in the "secret rooms" of power are just another example of the natural conspiracy revealing itself through the machinations of elite groups that have world conquest as their goal. They work at parallel purposes with the myriad of other groups in the natural brotherhood of evil design.

PART III
Sly Whispers

9

The Ninth Circle

"Treason doth never prosper . . . For if it prospers, none
dare call it treason." Sir John Harrington (1561-1612)

An old adage exhorts, "with friends, like this, who needs
enemies." It is as true today as it was generations ago. Spies and
enemy agents can be expected during the course of any event. But
what is of grave serious concern is the appearance of enemies within
your own gates. These traitors are sometimes unaware of their
disloyalty, answering more to what Lenin called "useful idiots," as
illustrated by the so-called "fellow travelers" of the McCarthy Era.
This group pretends to be "patriotic," but because of a "higher
calling" or dissatisfaction with the direction society has taken or
because of lucrative inducements, has literally sold out their own
people. Dante Alighieri reserved his Ninth Circle, the lowest place
in Hell for such traitors who would betray their own people. It
was Sinon the Greek who tricked the Trojans into accepting the
wooden horse. As the fictional Henry Wadsworth Longfellow said
in Matthew Pearl's novel, "The Dante Club," "the traitors against
Nation undermine the good of one's people." The same can be
said of conservatives who betray the essence of the traditional way
of thinking. Their punishment in Dante's Hell was to be buried in
ice. The accumulating the frost made it appear that they were
buried in glass and not water up to their necks.

There has been a decided shift in conservative thinking the
last generation. It has not gone unnoticed by traditional

conservatives, such as Howard Phillips' Constitution Party, the John Birch Society and a number of evangelical groups who have seen through the obvious trend to the Left that has characterized the Conservative Movement of the late Russell Kirk, Robert Taft and Barry Goldwater.

A new term has entered the political parlance. It is "neoconservatism," and it means that Conservative philosophy has moved to the center and maybe even a little to the left of center. Neoconservatives, also known as "neocons," were classical liberals who, according to their "Godfather," Irving Kristol, were "mugged by reality." Kristol was just one of many disillusioned left-leaning intellectuals of the 1930's and 1940's. This articulate but relatively small group grew more "conservative," as the conflict with the Soviets intensified. They were basically seeking a "conservative welfare state."

Kristol described this new ideological amalgamation in his lengthy book, entitled "Neoconservatism: The Autobiography of an Idea," written in 1995. He defined the movement as one that "accepted the New Deal in principle and had little affection for the kind of isolationism that had permeated traditional American Conservatism." A Neoconservative is one who unequivocally accepted New Deal socialism and the idea of what the French used to call being the "gendarme of the world," even to the extent of sacrificing American sovereignty on the altar of internationalism. Neocons tend to be very soft on social issues, such as abortion, and stem cell research. They are the ones who gave America David Souter on the United States Supreme Court.

In May 1991, Kristol helped alter the core of Republicanism by sponsoring a conference for several dozen GOP leaders. Kristol reported in a "Wall Street Journal" article that these Republicans had arrived as conservatives, by the end of the meeting, "a significant reversal had occurred." According to Sam Tanenhaus in the July 2003 issue of "Vanity Fair," while "most traditional conservatives lean toward isolation or Realpolitik, neocons inhabit a political shadow land where idealism mingles with ideology." The neocons are derisively called "kosher conservatives," because of the preponderance of Jews within their number.

Author Max Boot, describes a neocon as "someone a liberal wouldn't be embarrassed to have over for cocktails." This is an accurate description because neocons have a common ideological bond with liberals, which overrides all their superficial distinctions. It is analogous to the two party system in American politics. Both the Republicans and Democrats have been slowly melding into one indistinguishable entity. In foreign policy they tend toward "hard Wilsonians." They want to use American might to effect Wilson's ideals of a "world safe for democracy." War often is the chosen vehicle of their agenda. Now that the threat of nuclear devastation has lifted, war can be swift, decisive and a proper extension of diplomacy. Pat Buchanan warns that the "conservative movement has been hijacked and turned into a globalist, interventionist, open borders ideology," which he says is a far cry from the traditional conservative movement he knew as a child.

Neocons have some things in common with traditional conservatives, mostly their hatred of Communism. But neocon hatred was reserved for Stalin. They never really opposed Trotskyism or doctrinaire Marxism. Many neocons were and still are advocates of the idealized form of Communism, advocated by Leon Trotsky, one of the founding members of the Soviet revolution in 1917. This was the so-called "god that failed," or the "revolution that was betrayed," by Stalin and his butchers. Their affection was for Leon Trotsky who had broken with Stalin's purges, show trials, gulags and the gradually expansion of Marxist socialism.

Leon Trotsky was born Lev Davidovich Bronstein in 1879. He was the son of a prosperous Jewish farmer. He became a Marxist at an early age. In 1898, he was arrested and exiled to Siberia. Four years later he escaped and reached England by means of a forged passport, which had used the name "Trotsky," that of an Odessa prison guard. In was in London that Trotsky met Lenin. They collaborated on a revolutionary newspaper, "Iskra," that is, "The Spark." Like Lenin, he spent some years in jail in Siberian exile plotting revolution abroad. Trotsky was a fluent writer and a mesmerizing orator. His main contribution to the communist cause was his idea of "permanent revolution," which appeared in his book, "Results and Prospects," written while in jail in 1906. He envisioned an unending civil war "unfolding the world over."

With the outbreak of World War I, Trotsky moved to Zurich and then to Germany where he was imprisoned for opposing the war. He returned to Russia in 1917 with the help of the United States. Trotsky had been detained in Toronto and it was only through the intervention of Woodrow Wilson that he was allowed to continue to St. Petersburg. When he returned to Russia, he found out that the Hamburg banker, Max Warburg, had granted him funds in a Finnish bank. From there Trotsky successfully led the Red Army during the October Revolution. It was after Lenin's death in 1924 that Trotsky's real problems began in earnest. Stalin believed in socialism for one country. After two years of exile, Trotsky was expelled from Russia. Trotsky was put on trial and was condemned to death in absentia for his refusal to defer to Stalin's reversal of doctrinaire Marxism. Stalin had turned the revolution into a "bureaucratic dictatorship." For the remaining years of his life, Trotsky continued to be a thorn in Stalin's side and a threat to topple him from power. Trotsky believed that true art did not reflect like a mirror but was more like a hammer that shaped reality. Stalin finally caught up with Trotsky in Mexico City, where he had been the guest of painter Diego Rivera and his wife Frieda Kahlo. Spanish Communist, Ramon Mercader, buried an alpine ax into Trotsky's skull on August 20, 1940.

Under neoconservativism, Trotsky's idea of "permanent revolution" has morphed into "perpetual war for perpetual peace." The neoconservatives believe that the real revolution has been betrayed. Kristol once extolled the fact that he was "lucky to have been a young Trotskyite."

Today's neoconservatives are nearly unanimous in calling for police state powers at home and an international coalition under the aegis of the UN to combat terrorism abroad. The soul of neo-conservatism today resides in the Jewish-dominated publication, "The Weekly Standard." While purporting to be the voice of modern conservatism, this neocon organ has a definite liberal slant. It is this magazine that has been mainly responsible for labeling George Bush as a "conservative," and marginalizing or silencing dissent from the right. It has made its goal a defense and an advancement of virtually every policy Israel has concocted in the past ten years. Along with its allies at "Commentary Magazine," it had been the most vocal in calling and even demanding a war with Iraq. Seen in the context of Middle Eastern geopolitics, it seems apparent that it can only be interpreted as a desire to level the Arab resistance in the Middle East and open the doors to the New World Order with Israeli hegemony in the region. These predominant Jewish publications have joined forces with other journals, such as "The Public Interest," to serve as the gatekeepers for those authorized to speak for Conservatism. Traditional conservative columnist Craig Roberts holds the unpopular view that the neoconservatives are "infused with the spirit of 18th century French Jacobins who want to impose American 'exceptionalism' on the rest of the world." Roberts also infers that neocon "foreign policy advisers who believe that the primary aim of U.S. foreign policy is to make the Middle East safe for Israel."

There is another vital and maybe even more important source of neoconservative philosophy. Many neoconservatives are a group of authors, academics, media moguls and public officials who trace their intellectual lineage to the teachings of a German émigré named Leo Strauss, who died in 1973. He said the relativism of political thought since Machiavelli has prevented value judgments that distinguish between good and evil. Strauss was a child of middle class Orthodox Jews. He became a Zionist in his teens, attended Martin Heidegger's lectures at the University of Freiburg, and eventually crossed paths with some of the premier intellectuals in Europe's prewar period, such as Walter Benjamin, Alenandre Kojeve, and Hans Georg Gadamer. In 1934, after having moved to England, he wrote "The Political Philosophy of Thomas Hobbes." He later wrote "Thoughts on Machiavelli."

To understand the neoconservatives, it is important to understand the thinking of Leo Strauss. Like Cecil Rhodes' mentor at Oxford, John Ruskin, Leo Strauss had an affectionate understanding of Plato. The Greek writer shaped much of his thinking. Born in Germany in 1899, Strauss immigrated to the United States in 1938. After teaching at the New School for Social Research, he began teaching at the University of Chicago in 1949, where he influenced many of the nation's future political strategists. In her 1997 book on Strauss, "Leo Strauss and the American Right," Shadia Drury of the University of Calgary elaborates on Strauss' contributions to the Neoconservative Movement. She writes, "What is disturbing about the new conservatism, or neoconservativism, is not so much that it is elitist, but that it cultivates . . . an elite that deludes itself into thinking that it is a natural aristocracy . . . and that it has no obligation to the have-nots of society." She adds that Strauss has contributed a great deal to "the development of an elite that is intoxicated with its own self-admiration." They refer to themselves self-mockingly, but with alarming accuracy as "the Cabal."

Strauss admired the Greek City State of Sparta and its militaristic approach to might making right. He wrote that to "make the world safe for Western democracies, one must make the whole globe democratic, each country in itself as well as the society of nations. Strauss also believed in Plato's idea of the "noble lie," suggesting that those in the know often must deceive the masses for their own good.

The 2002 election was a victory for neoconservativism. It further solidified their hold on the Republican organs of power. Never again will conservatives be able to garner enough support to effect a return to the days of constitutional republican government. Accommodation and progress are the catchwords for their future. Neocons talk of prescription drugs for the elderly, NAFTA, and the United Nations, just like their liberal allies across the aisle. Abortion, euthanasia, and limited government have been relegated to the back of the bus, only to be marched out front during the biennial elections cycle when the traditional basis must be mobilized

One of the leading spokesmen for traditional conservatism over the years has been William F. Buckley, the founding and reigning intellectual force behind the biweekly magazine, "The National Review." To most conservatives he is and has been an oracle of the best policies for God-fearing conservatives to take. A new biography of Buckley, written by John McManus calls him "The Pied Piper for the Establishment." Even coming from McManus, a former president of the John Birch Society, this would on the surface appear as nothing more than a hapless attempt to defame the true leader of Conservative philosophy in this country. But on closer inspection, much of what McManus charges is very convincing. To McManus, Buckley, or someone like him in the conservative, media was needed from within the conservative leadership to serve as a mole to undercut Conservative thinking in light of the major events of the day. According to McManus, "Buckley had become the Establishment's invaluable house conservative, positioned to diminish or silence critics of those who were leading the nation into socialism and world government." In a 1980 column, William F. Buckley even went so far as to defend Jimmy Carter and his fellow Trilateralists in his administration, especially Zbigniew Brzezinski.

In the 1960's, many Americans did believe that a conspiracy was at work and had succeeded in achieving great influence within our government, the mass media, and other segments of our society. The big question always came down to "were our leaders just incompetent do-gooders or evil conspirators handling our foreign policy?" This could relate to the FBI and CIA today. Those who believe that there are "evildoers" in the world will do whatever they can to stop the spread and those that believe in bumbling do-gooders will merely shrug their shoulders and say "that's life."

McManus says that while Buckley commands no army nor has never held public office, he has played an important role in diverting mainstream conservatives away from constitutional principles, limited government and moral discipline. Buckley seems too quick to accept more a larger government and more internationalism. Buckley also served as the point man in the unceasing attacks on Robert Welch and his John Birch Society as early as 1963. In an article in "The National Review," entitled, "Quiet Conspiracy at Work," Buckley stated his purpose was to counter "Mr. Welch's fascination with the conspiracy as the operative agent in our decline and fall."

William F. Buckley was the "Judas goat," who has led traditional Republicans into the ranks of the neocons. In a hypothetical question asked by magazine, "Lingua Franca," in an 2001 interview, Buckley opined that if he were graduating from college in 2000, he would have been "a socialist, "A Michael Harrington socialist . . . 'I'd even say a communist." Buckley has as much right to the title of "godfather of neoconservativism," as does Irving Kristol. He continues to use his "National Review" as a vehicle for transporting the nascent movement away from traditionalists to a new international group that enthusiastically welcomed a burgeoning moral and social imperialism as the true wave of the future.

Buckley has also deliberately sought to advance the cause of homosexuals in this country. He has allowed his magazine to become a forum for homosexual agitprop, as evidenced by the departure of old friend and fellow activist, Marvin Liebman. Liebman expressed his wish to Buckley that he would promote the homosexual lifestyle as "mainstream." Letters from gays and as well as a series of homosexual agitprop started appearing in the magazine. In one article, written under a false name, John Woolman stated that "the first theory we must reject is the traditional view that the purpose of sex is procreation." Woolman warned Buckley's readers "The persecution of homosexuals is deeply rooted in the Judeo-Christian tradition." Joseph Sobran answered the letter in his inimitable style, and in the process ran afoul of the changing attitudes of the magazine. He was writing on borrowed time at that point and managed to get fired not too long after that. A fact that may surprise even the most devoted of Buckley fans relates that even as early as 1952 "Mr. Conservatism," was advocating a more powerful government to combat the Communist menace.

Contrary to true Conservatism, Buckley is in favor of the UN, wants to legalize drugs, prostitution and has a knee-jerk bias in favor of Israel or anything Jewish. His publication has been staffed openly with great numbers of former Communists, or "neocons." The magazine fired Sobran and the wildly acerbic Anne Coulter for their deviations from the party line on culture and Israel. Buckley supports a "mandatory volunteerism," that would draft young citizens for two years of involuntary servitude. Where is his concern for America's freedom and its moral traditions? According to McManus, Buckley had not really defended McCarthy in his book, "McCarthy and his Enemies," written with his brother-in-law, Brent Bozell. The truth about McCarthy was that he took on the establishment and it had to stop his investigation of Communist subversion in our government because it was to their benefit to allow this to happen.

Buckley's past keeps raising all these flags that, in effect, make one doubt the legitimacy of his early conservative predilections that he proclaimed loudly from his masthead at "the National Review." Buckley adopted the moral relativist argument with relation to abortion and many other subjects. "Theology teaches that the conscience is supreme," he stated. "If abortion is objectively wrong, a society may nevertheless wish to abide by the woman's right to pursue her own conscience and proceed to abort.'" Patricia Bozell, Buckley's own sister, blamed the change in moral attitudes to a large degree on "the likes of Mrs. Luce and her Catholic friends at 'National Review' who play the democratic game, the secular game and the pluralistic game in violation of their faith."

Buckley's policies, columns and ideas resonate better with the progressive elite who actually run this country. Buckley is a conservative enigma. He professes a personal Catholicism, which he frequently touts at will. Yet he has written numerous articles for "Playboy Magazine," or what he defensively calls "the magazine within the magazine."

Buckley is a former member of the CIA and in 1977 and was asked to join the Council of Foreign Relations. Given this group's role in the trashing of American history and culture and its ardent push for world government, one might wonder what Buckley was doing in their ranks. Even though he is a journalist, he has consistently refused to explain or expound on what they do behind closed doors. McManus is convinced Buckley is fronting for America's internal enemies. He calls him one of the country's "slyest deceivers," a clever but supremely duplicitous frontman for a behind-the scenes cabal whose operatives have been laboring for generations to steer America into their contrived "New World Order." The late Murray Rothbard, a conservative economist, called Buckley "the prince of excommunication, the self-appointed pope of the conservative movement." Howard Phillips, the 2000 Constitution Party Presidential nominee pointed out that, "Buckley just isn't with us anymore."

Few people are aware of Buckley's neoconservative roots. His mentor at Yale was Willmoore Kendall, an unabashed Trotskyite socialist who served in the Office of Strategic Services, the forerunner of the Central Intelligence Agency. Buckley's father was involved with the Rockefeller oil interests when he was a young man. Buckley has enjoyed a close relationship with the typical Rockefeller "organization man," Henry Kissinger, who was the point man for the liberal infiltration of the Nixon presidency. Yet Buckley is still considered the polar opposite of the anti-conservative Rockefeller Republican, typified by Kissinger. Buckley is a member of the Council of Foreign Relations. What is he doing with this crowd? If his attendance at the Pratt House is not damning enough, what should have tipped off his Conservative readers is his membership in Yale's Skull and Bones Society. It is the select secret society that has been the launching pad for many government leaders and three presidents.

The Skull and Bones Society is a key institution in the gradual march to the NWO. It is this bastion of White Anglo Saxon Protestantism that has driven fears and ambitions for over a century. It dates back to December of 1776, when students at William and Mary College founded a secret society, Phi Beta Kappa. A second chapter was formed at Yale four years later. By the 1820's the anti-Masonic groups that existed in the major cities heavily criticized these groups. The Skull and Bones Society grew out of this sister group.

General William Huntington Russell and Alphonso Taft officially established it at Yale University in New Haven, Connecticut in 1832. His son, William Howard Taft, would eventually become president. It is the oldest and most famous of the school's seven secret societies. These "fraternities," served as a recruiting ground for young men who wanted to have a career in government service. Its critics say that since its founding, it has taken on more of the occult and ritualistic trappings of the majority of Europe's Freemason and Illuminati secret societies. William Huntington Russell, Samuel's cousin, studied in Germany in the early 1830's.

Germany was the hotbed of the new way of thinking and a European ferment that was strongly brewing. The "scientific method," was being applied to several fields outside of pure science. The leading German thinker was Friedrich Hegel. According to him, the individual "has a supreme duty to be a member of the state." Both fascism and communism have their historical roots in Hegel's thinking. Dr. James Wardner establishes in his book, "Unholy Alliances," that Yale's elite secret society, the Skull and Bones Society, has its roots in the Bavarian Illuminati. Anthony Sutton called the infamous society, "America's branch of the Illuminati," in his book, "America's Secret Establishment."

The Skull & Bones Society was incorporated, as the Russell Trust in 1856. It has controlled many important parts of Yale ever since, including its finances and the college press. Many of the country's future leaders, three presidents and wealthy captains of industry, all cut their teeth as Bonesmen. Their membership roster reads like a "Who's Who In American Politics and Business." Both Presidents Bush, the Harriman family, Henry Stimson, the Whitneys and Thomas Cochran, a key factor in the J.P. Morgan banking firm, were all Bonesmen. If Democratic Senator, John Kerry of Massachusetts were to get the 2004 presidential nomination, the election would pit two Bonesmen against each other.

It was a Bonesmen, James Wadsworth, who founded the Peace Research Institute. Billionaire and Russophile, Armand Hammer helped finance the activities of Samuel Rubin, an elite member of the Communist Party. The Rubin Foundation funded the Peace Research Institute, which became the Marxist-Communist Institute for Policy Studies. The Rubin Foundation is a prominent client of Winston Law's law firm. Lord was the chairman of the Council of

Foreign Relations, and a prominent Bonesmen himself. He has been an establishment figure in both Republican and Democratic politics. The "New York Times" is another one of his special clients.

The Skulls have been deeply into the occult. Their "lodge room," the infamous "Room 322," was broken into in 1876 and it was later revealed that there were four human skulls, a fools cap, bells, mathematical instruments, a beggar's scrip and bizarre sayings and writings. Among the "values" taught to its adepts are ambiguity and secrecy. According to tradition, their ritual has many sexual allusions and the group has a room of Nazi paraphernalia. Their rites of passage help them accept the idea of WASP supremacy and the pseudo-religion notion that they must "bear the white man's burden." It is the idea of "noblesse oblige" that permeated the Progressive period at the turn of the nineteenth century. As part of their Spartan mode, they have the ability to steer the country into war and successful prosecute that war.

To the Bonesmen, the use of military might is natural and an essential corollary to political power. They are taught that, although their ideas have their place, to truly transform history, military force is almost always required. This comes straight from the chronicles of the Roman Empire, especially the empire during its decline and eventual collapse. Alphonso Taft was President of the Unitarian Association at the time. He later became Secretary of War under President Grant. He was the first of many "Bonesmen," to run the War Department in the nineteenth century. This is important because the War Department was a critical government position in time of war and has been always a way for the self-sustaining elite to control populations.

The romantic mystique of the purgative powers of combat is key to understanding the political philosophy of the Skulls. There is no better example of than Henry Stimson. A profession politician who served seven presidents during his long life, Stimson was a Bonesman since 1888. He was responsible for creating the economic plan that eventually led to Japan's attack on Pearl Harbor. George the Elder regarded him as hero. He read a biography of Stimson just before engaging in the Gulf War in 1990. Stimson felt that it was good to have a little bloodletting every generation to keep the military sharp in order that they might fulfill their duty of protecting what would become the New World Order. It was a spiritual cleansing operation that would allow a nation to rally around a cause and overcome its weaknesses and shortcoming in one great burst of energy.

According to Alexandra Robbins book "Secret of the Tombs," the legend of the Skull and Bones talks of "curling its tentacles into every corner of American society." This tiny club has set up networks that have thrust three men into the most powerful position in the world. One historian says the secret society is an "international Mafia . . . unregulated and all but unknown." In its quest to create a New World Order that restricts personal freedoms and places political and economic power in the hands of an oligarchy of wealthy prominent families, Bonesmen have already succeeded in infiltrating nearly every financial, research, policy, media and government institution in the Country. According to her telling of the legend, the Skull and Bones have been running this country for generations. They are taught that they get out in the world they are to strive to attain positions of power and influence so that they can elevate the positions of their fellow Bonesmen. This legend seems to mix the fraternal elements of Freemasonry with the secret aspects of Rhodes.

Like anything with a long and mysterious history, the Skull and Bones' legend is a rich mixture of fact and fiction. Nazi artifacts, Geronimo's skull may or may not be accurate renditions of their history but their search for power can be no accidental of history. It is the network that is most important. They stand together "brothers under the skin." Robbin's narrative of the many stories and tales, told to her by a cadre of Bonesmen, does not give lie to the legend. She says that disingenuously the members themselves had made up the legend, so as to keep the "quintessential mystery alive." She did not seem to consider that they have used her book to throw off the scent of what they have been historically attempting to achieve. By taking the shroud off the Bones, she may inadvertently be attempting to shield their secrets for world power and influence from the rest of their countrymen. She says that the society does not dictate a worldview to them. But the Ivy League culture is a worldview. It is a vast monolithic left-wing bent that has its "worker" bees buzzing around its liberal honey.

Others have picked up the baton that Buckley laid down a few years ago because of age limitations. Rush Limbaugh has served ably as the new standard bearer to promote the new "party line," as emanating from the Buckley flagship. He has been more than willing to pick up the Buckley mantel of "turncoat conservatism." At every opportunity, Limbaugh unabashedly demonstrates his profound respect, and near fawning adulation, for Buckley. Every time Buckley publishes a new book, Limbaugh breaks his once rigid ban on "guests," to have him on his program. Limbaugh was once quoted as having said, "If I am ever reincarnated, I hope to be given William Buckley's brain." In my book, "Liberalism: Fatal Consequences," I alluded to the fact that Limbaugh was not much more than a moderate Republican. He has not been the conservative of the Burkean or Kirkean mold. In essence, Limbaugh has fallen victim the lure of neoconservative seduction. He has already repeated the mantra from the left that criticism from the "far right" of the Neoconservative Movement was just an extremist code word for "Anti-Semitic" racism.

There are reasons that explain Rush. Long ago, he realized he could have a dramatic impact on the course of political events in the country's history. Commerce and entertainment slowly evolved into power and influence. Limbaugh has a strong political gene in his make-up. His experience has taught him that power is far more seductive, far more satisfying than money or fame. However, Rush's weakness is that he thrives on popularity. His wide audience and great numbers have let him inside the boardrooms of power. He counts as friends, such political luminaries as George W. Bush, Jack Kemp, Newt Gingrich, Bill Bennett, and Clarence Thomas. The chubby boy from Southeast Missouri was now rubbing elbows and trading quips and stories with some of the most influential and powerful people in the country, if not the world. Understandably he does not want to do anything to upset them or risk their censure. As a cultural warrior, Rush Limbaugh is part of the power game that is changing the internal debate and possibly the course of American history.

While occasionally he does pay lip service in favor of small government and the American way, Limbaugh can not help but be seduced by the "big boys," such as Buckley, who control his numbers and influence his thinking. There is no telling how much of his audience, "mind-numbed robots," have bought his erroneous belief that George W. Bush does actually represent the true conservative way of thinking. Rush cannot afford to give even the slightest nod of assent to any group that is not acceptable in the mainstream of Republican and Neonconservative thought. This would make it impossible for Rush to be a true disciple of democracy and would seriously limit his relentless search for the truth.

John McManus has also explored Rush and his propensity for being nothing more than a shill for Republican imperial policies, under the pretense that they are actually "conservative" principles. There are very few subjects Rush will not broach. One such subject he angrily shies away from is the notion of the conspiracy theory. Rush, who can wax intellectually at times, has a knee-jerk dismissal for all conspiracy theories. To him they were the demented produce of "kooks and wackos." His bout with addictive prescription drugs will limit his future role in promoting the unique philosophy of Bush and the neocons.

The closer to the truth writers and commentators get, they are ostracized from the mainstream. One by one, the old conservatives, so-called "Paleo-conservatives," to quote Pat Buchanan's phrase, have been pushed to the "extreme" right. They have been marginalized and virtually run out of the mainstream of "conservative" thought. Big government neocons, such as the Kristols, Irving and Bill, Bill Bennett, Jack Kemp, Norman Podhoretz, both George the Elder and George the Younger Bush, Dan Quayle and others have changed the rules and re-invented the definition of "conservatism." They have done this to the extent that it is hard to fathom just what a conservative is.

Look what happened to those magnificent conservative writers when Joseph Sobran and Samuel Francis criticized the mainstream views? Rush Limbaugh searches for truth every day until it starts cutting into his ratings and his ad revenue. He is as in the mainstream as the New York Times on many issues.

Sobran, a brilliant essayist and Shakespearean scholar, was ostracized for a series of articles criticizing the Israeli Government and the leftist proclivities of the American Jewish community. For what he admits amounted to "an act of insubordination," he was summarily fired from his job at the "National Review," after twenty-two years. Midge Decker, Norman Podhoretz's wife, savagely castigated him, writing he was "little more than a crude and naked anti-Semite." Her charges were disseminated to several papers that ran his column with the hope of ruining his career.

Since then Sobran, who probably is the most insightful and articulate writers in America, has seen his reservoir of writing opportunities dry up to just a few and some of them in marginal publications with little circulation. Decter treated Russell Kirk, the "Father of American Conservatism" after he had remarked in an American Heritage speech in 1988 that some conservatives have "mistook Tel Aviv for the capital of the United States." For this wisecrack about the "Amen Corner" among the neocons, she denounced him predictably as "an anti-Semite." "Commentary Magazine" weighs in periodically with an attack on some traditional conservative with the same tired charge of "anti-Semitism."

Sam Francis is another critic who disdains neoconservatism. Like Sobran and Buchanan, Francis has been ostracized and nearly eliminated from the political arena. His views on Southern history and culture, immigration and economics do not resonate well with the leftward trend of the neoconservatives. He chides conservatives for allowing a dilettante like Buckley to define it for them. There have been many others who have been labeled conservatives who bear no resemblance to traditional Conservatives. Newt Gingrich, Bob Dole, Bill Bennett, George Will and the like all pay mild lip service to the natural law, limited government and pro-American agenda that flourished under traditional conservatism.

One tactic the neoconservatives use is to raise the bloody shirt of anti-Semitism. They spare no effort in their attempts to link traditional conservatives to the notorious "Protocols of the Council of Elders." A version of these protocols first appeared in 1864 in

France in a book entitled, "Dialogue in Hell between Machiavelli and Montesquieu or the Politics of Machiavelli in the Nineteenth Century by a Contemporary." It was written anonymously by a French lawyer named Maurice Joly. It has been purportedly to be a diatribe against the dictatorial policies of the regime of Napoleon III. Joly was reputed to have been a friend of writer Victor Hugo. Both men were putative members of the Rose-Croix or Rosicrucians. After Joly's authorship was exposed, he went to prison for fifteen months for anti-government activities.

In the mid-1890's the book was resurrected and given an anti-Semitic theme by members of Czar Nicolas II's secret police. The forgery was the work of a writer named Sergei Nilus. It was published in order to undermine the founding of the Zionist movement, which had just begun in Basel, Switzerland in 1897. The main objective was to relieve the Czar of any responsibility for the plight of the Russian peasantry. All of their problems could be attributed to a Jewish conspiracy with the Freemasons in control of the world. The "Protocols" still chills its readers with prophetic descriptions of the methodology for tyranny by a coterie of evil conspirators. It does resonate well with the elitist outlook of men like Rhodes and the Rothschilds. As the Protocols state "We are the chosen, we are the only true men. Our minds give off the true power of the spirit."

The Protocols go on to explain that the goal of world domination will be accomplished by controlling how the public thinks and hears and "by creating new conflicts or restoring old orders, by spreading hunger, destitution and plagues, by seducing and distracting the youth." They would disparage heroism. They will equate it with political crime and brand it with the same contempt reserved for murder, thievery and filthy crime. Protocol #20 dealt with taxation. It proposed the lawful confiscation of all sums for the regulation of their circulation in the State. This would be followed by a progressive tax on property. Then a graduated income tax, sales taxes and every tax imaginable in the early twentieth century. They believed that no one would figure out what was happening. There seems to be a great deal of similarity between these Protocols and the teachings of the Cultural Marxists.

Despite their dubious origins, both Kaiser Wilhelm II and Czar Nicholas II took the Protocols quite seriously, as did American industrialist Henry Ford who used them to argue against President Woodrow Wilson's League of Nations. Aspiring young Socialist Adolph Hitler, also saw them as real, despite the evidence to the contrary. In "Mein Kampf" he wrote, "They are supposed to be a 'forgery' the "Frankfurt Zeitung moans and cries out to the world once a week. . . . But the best criticism applied to them is reality. He who examines the historical development of the past hundred years . . . will immediately understand the clamor of the Jewish press."

The Protocols still remain a textbook for world domination. They could easily serve as the ruling philosophy of a natural hierarchy. The spirit of the Protocols therefore contains historical truth, though all the facts put forward are forgeries," wrote anti-Nazi Konrad Heiden. Some see the remarkable resemblance between the Protocols and eighteenth century Illuminati strategy. Considering the numerous Masonic references in it, it could well have been developed from Adam Weishaupt's philosophy as well. There also could have been a deeper conspiracy at work—one that employed anti-Semitism to further divide the world and get the West at each other's throat.

In a September 2002 article for his "Culture Wars," magazine, E. Michael Jones writes of how the "defenders of the Jewish race," such as columnist Charles Krauthammer and polemic author Jonah Goldhagen have mounted a full-scale attack on outspoken Jews, such as Norman Finklestein and Ruth Birn. They have successfully used verbal scare tactic to silence the critics of Israel, Jewish bankers, businessmen and writers. According to Jones, they wield the anti-Semitism card "precisely because they want to deflect attention away from the behavior that is causing the criticism onto the supposed prejudices of the critic as the real source of the problem."

Norman Finklestein is a Jew who has paid a heavy price for writing the truth. Even though his parents were Nazi concentration camp survivors, he critiqued the shakedown activities so prevalent in his book, "The Holocaust Industry," about the politicization of the Holocaust and its attendant issues. For his honest endeavors, he has been condemned and castigated by his own people as being an anti-Semite and "a self-hating disgrace to his people." His critics have said he was "irreversibly tainted" because of his anti-Zionism, which "disqualified" him from commenting on the Holocaust. This criticism had gone way "beyond the pale." Who determines what the pale is? Well, self-appointed gatekeepers of the Zionist tradition, such as Abraham Foxman and author Goldhagen, the author of "Hitler's Willing Executioners," a deeply flawed study that attempted to blame the Holocaust on all Germans.

Zionism is instrumental in this moral conundrum. Donn de Grand Pre, in his book, "Barbarians: Inside the Gates," states that "Zionism was established as a world political force in 1897. Its aims since then have been centered on setting up a one-world government with Zionism in control of worldwide finance . . ." According to Edward Gibbon's "Decline and Fall of the Roman Empire," the enslavement of man "usually begins in the economic sphere." In 1881, in a business proposal to the Rothschild family, Dr. Theodor Herzl, the father of Zionism, wrote, "when we rise there rises also our terrible power of the purse." He called it a "chain of destiny," the unbroken link between the twin banners of the New World Order, Fabian Socialism and International Zionism.

It does not matter whether there is any analogous truth to the Protocols. It is important that in the culture war too many Jewish people have allied themselves with the secular forces of pornography, abortion, and homosexual rights. Too many have adopted the philosophy of the French revolution and all of the fatal consequences that have emanated from those beliefs. Does this make the idea of a conspiracy a Jewish phenomenon? Of course not! But it does alert unsuspecting and overly guilt-ridden Christians from not joining the welkin clamor for castigating anyone who might point out the abject evil of some of their positions. And then should they be allowed to condemn as intolerant and anti-Semitic, anyone who would dare to do so? It seems that so many of the Jewish people in this country call themselves liberals and thusly have adopted the pro-choice philosophy. This paints traditional conservatives in the proverbial corner. If they attacked those who are pro-choice, the "anti-Semite" epitaph can be used effectively to stifle their right of free speech and even lawful assembly. It is just an unpalatable fact of life that many Jews hold opposite of the Christian moral system and its attending moral suasions. This tactic has been an old one, especially on tradition and even some neoconservatives. Writers like Michael Lind attack people such as Pat Robertson for talking about secret societies and international bankers in his book, "New World Order." To Lind this is a veiled attempt to attack Jews. He cavalierly dismisses Robertson's laudatory references to Jews and Israel and slanders him with a vicious assault in his own book "Up from Conservatism: Why Conservatism is Wrong for America."

Another group that has been marginalized by its own people has been the John Birch Society. This society was named after an American Army lieutenant, John Birch, who was executed by the Chinese Communists in 1945. Candy manufacturer, Robert Welch, founded the Birch Society in 1966. Its main purpose is to oppose and stop America's historic march toward world government. To Birchers, their namesake was arguably the first victim in the Cold War. It essentially picked up the pieces after the demise of Joseph McCarthy.

Former Birch president, John McManus, states that the main reason the left was able to virtually destroy Welch and his movement was that his grass roots support was not organized and dissipated after his demise. For decades their goals have been to "spread the word of the Conspiracy." To them the conspiracy is the international bankers who pull the strings. They are the ones who really control the rise and fall of Communism and the United States government, as well as its economy. They do this through extraneous groups such as the CFR, the Trilaterals, the Bilderbergers, and the Federal Reserve System. Their key objective is to create a world government under the auspices of the U. N., ostensibly for the "good" of all mankind but in reality for the manipulation of the world's natural resources, populations, currencies etc, so that they may truly dominate the world.

Robert Welch attacked Communists and pro forma Communist agitprop for many years. He was a freedom-loving patriot who did not like the decisions coming out of Washington. He did not like the subtle and direct attacks on the basic sovereignty of his country. He complained about President Eisenhower and many of his minions who seemed to be taking America down a road that was contradictory to the ideals and principles of the country's founding fathers. For attacking the nation's "beloved," president, Welch ran into a firestorm of criticism that attempted to drive him from the ranks of conservatism. He has been attacked, vilified and marginalized to the outer fringes of society as a fanatical wacko.

Robert Welch was born in 1899 on a farm in Chowan County, North Carolina. The America of his youth was vastly different from what we have today. Self-reliance was the rule and not the exception. Good manners, moral uprightness, respect for hard work and personal integrity all meant something. He started out as a candy manufacturer but answered a larger calling in life in 1957. He was a "fanatic for the truth." He knew what the word "is," meant.

His "problems" began with the publication of lengthy letters about President Dwight Eisenhower, later published as a book, entitled "The Politician." The impression most people had of President Eisenhower was that he had been a great general and a kind President. He presided over the dull and unexciting days of the 1950s. He was painted as a man who seemed more at home on the golf course than in the Oval Office. Welch saw him in more of a sinister light. In "The Politician," his portrayal of Ike bears little resemblance to the grandfather figure, who "fooled," a majority of the people for eight years.

Welch begins by emphasizing how rapid was Ike's rise within the military ranks. It seems that he knew how to play the politician's game very well, even while in uniform. In 1941, he was a Light Colonel in the Army. Three years later he became the Supreme Allied Commander. Welch discovered that Eisenhower, unlike General Douglas McArthur, was no military genius. His mercurial rise bears no connection to his ability to lead men on the battlefield.

His military ascendancy was more for his ability to be a "fixer," than his innate ability to get along with our allies, and assuage any difference between. This was contradictory to the image that was cultivated by the liberal media. Ike was more the wily politician. Mediocrity could have been his middle name.

His political and strategic decisions during and after the war did not receive the scrutiny they warranted. Welch makes it apparent that Eisenhower did his level best to aid the Russians throughout the war. He did every thing in his power to assure that the Red Army would take possession of as much of Europe as it could. He ordered the American armies to stop their advance thus assuring that the Russians would enter Berlin first, where they took out their bloody revenge on the German civilian population. Ike's overt vengeance on the German people in his support for the Morgenthau Plan and his role in "Operation Keelhaul," that is the repatriation of thousands of Russian subjects after the war, did not fit his kindly postwar image.

Welch painted a picture of an American general with many contacts on the far left in American politics and academia. As president of Columbia University, Ike took great pains to protect university professors with communist sympathies. He underscored the fact that Communist Joseph Fels Barnes ghostwrote his autobiography, "Crusade in Europe." Welch was visibly upset with Eisenhower for hijacking the Republican Party from its voice and conscience, Senator Robert Taft. Welch believed that Ike was "one of the most vigorous and vicious anti-anti-Communists in American public life." He did everything in his power to thwart the work of Joe McCarthy and other who were pursuing Communists in the 1950's. Welch faulted him for undermining our allies in the Suez crisis and turning his back on "Der Alte," German Prime Minister Konrad Adenauer. Ike was most responsible for beginning the fissure in the Republican Party that has carried through today. He assailed Ike for his callous treatment of the Hungarian patriots who were encouraged to rebel against their Communist rulers.

In a footnote, Welch quoted Frank Kirkpatrick who pointed out one of the great paradoxes of the last half-century. Many of those "who believe Roosevelt and Truman protected the Reds, close their eyes and their minds to both the suggestion and the overwhelming evidence that the communists have been given as much or greater protection and encouragement by Eisenhower." Welch could not conclude whether Ike was an ideological convert to the Communist philosophy that racked American government in the 1950's or merely an opportunist who played his cards well and advanced from virtual military obscurity in 1941 to the highest office in the land. For this Welch and his Birch Society have been ostracized and virtually eliminated from the respectable corridors of political respectability.

Welch's critique of Boris Pasternak's book, "Doctor Zhivago," also brought him the undying wrath of the establishment right wing. He said Pasternak was wrong for merely labeling Stalinism and its abuses as the only evil in the system. Pasternak erroneously contended that communism was a noble idea whose only failure was that its goals had been highjacked by the Stalinist thugs. One of his characters has the temerity to say, "Marxism arose, it uncovered the root of evil and it offered the remedy, it became the great force of the century."

Given their philosophy, one could easily think that any patriotic conservative would find a haven in its confines. This is apparently not true. The members of this new conservative elite signaled the John Birch Society for extinction. The Birch Society has served as the catch phrase for anyone, right or left, who wished to discredit the arguments of any individual. He died in January of 1985.

Buckley wanted to destroy the John Birch Society because of its isolationist stance. Isolationment militated against the inherent logic of his Trotskyite leanings. One of Buckley's minions, Tom Bethel, thoroughly denounced the Birch Society, more specifically its founder Robert Welch, because of his attacks on Eisenhower and his lack of success in the face of World Communism in 1959. Much of what Ike did or did not do may have, unwittingly aided the communist movement, but to say he was a card-carrying Communist is silly nonsense. Too often Welch confused the so-called fellow traveler with hardened and conscious agents of the communist conspiracy. The same is true with the accusations the right has made against members of the intellectual community, which was filled with thousands of smart, logical people who have adopted the ideology of the Communist philosophy. Too often their predisposition to liberal causes prompted them to misread the utopian promises of Lenin, Stalin and Marx. For this they are to be censured. But to say that they are part of a conspiracy does great harm to fighting the negative and erroneous messages they promote about this country.

Buckley also expelled one of the leading opponents to Roosevelt's New Deal, John T. Flynn. He totally marginalized him from the movement for his anti-socialist and anti-internationalist ideas. In his 1944 book, "As We Go Marching," Flynn predicted that the nation was being prepared for the emergence of gigantic bureaucracy, government take-over of business, welfare schemes, deficit spending and meddling internationalism. He claimed all this would be done under war or the threat of war. A constant threat of war was necessary to condition the American people that their government knew best and was doing everything available for their protection. The same case may have also been made about George W. Bush and His "never-ending war on terrorism."

Neoconservatives have found a ready made ally in the pages of the "World Street Journal." which has a vested interest in free trade and the growing trend towards world government. Irving Kristol once wrote, "One of the most important agents in this transformation has been the WSJ." Kristol developed a close relationship with Robert Bartley who became its editorial page editor. Kristol became a frequent contributor. This provided him with a new audience to spread his neoconservative ideas. The WSJ has become a repository of and a sounding board for pushing the country closer to Israel. Neoconservatives appeared almost daily, to lead the clarion call for greater allegiance with and protection for Israel. As the power in America has shifted from the White Anglo-Saxon Protestant minority to the Jewish interests, anyone who refused to dance to the rhythms of what Pat Buchanan called "the Amen corner," risked losing his seat at the table where the stakes were power, money and global hegemony.

Another port of entry into the heart of American traditional belief has been the tax-exempt foundations. Not only have they allowed large fortunes to be squired away, safe from the Marxist confiscatory tax code, but also they have allowed the liberal mindset to use the public largesse to undercut the Judeo-Christian principles that gave birth to the America. Conspiracy was and is a key goal of the various foundations, especially the Ford Foundation. Author James Wardner believes that foundations have historically supported a conscious distortion of history, propagandized blindly for the United Nations as the hope of the world. Their approach has been consistently leftist in leaning. As a result of this leaning, they serve to undermine the very foundations upon which this nation has been based. Foundations, such as Carnegie, Rockefeller and Ford functioned as quasi government bureaus in attacking whatever group they did not favor. The foundations have historically served as a fifth column of deceit, destruction, and devastation.

In 1953 Representative B. Carroll Reece, a Republican from Tennessee, convened a House Committee to investigate the role these tax-exempt foundations played in undermining the nation's democratic institutions. Reece sent his research director, Norman Dodd to interview Ford Foundation President, H. Rowan Gaither. In a burst of candor, Gaither coolly admitted he was attacking under directives "issued by the White House" and that we should make every effort "to alter life in the United States as to make possible a comfortable merger with the Soviet Union." From the Committee's final report to Congress in 1953, it concluded "Those foundations which are concerned with internationalism along political lines appear to center their activities around projects which support the Government policy of participation in United Nations activities."

Chairman Reece remarked that there should be further investigation into these foundations because "tax-exempt funds in very large amounts are spent without public accountability or official supervision of any sort, and that admittedly, considerable questionable expenditures have been made." The Committee further stated that foundations give "enormous power to a relatively small group of individuals, having at their virtual command, huge sums in public trust funds." The committee felt that the whole system was "antithetical to American principles."

In 1954 Representative Carroll Jones noted that these hearings remained a historical curiosity because of the media campaign waged against them by their media allies, all who seemed to be alumni of the Office of Strategic Services. Reece was vilified with the smear tactics the denizens of the liberal left had applied to Senator McCarthy because he had attacked the Rockefeller Foundation for its support of Kinsey's homosexuality.

Dr. James Wardner states in his book, "Unholy Alliances," that Richard Arens, staff director of the house Committee on Un-American Activities, testified during these hearings about Communist activity in the religious field. "Thus far the leadership of the National Council of Churches of Christ in America, we have found 100 persons of leadership capacity with either Communist-front records or records of service to Communist causes. The aggregate affiliations of the leadership . . . is now in the thousands, and we have basis of authoritative sources of this committee that the statement. To say that there is infiltration of fellow travelers in our churches and educational institutions is a complete understatement."

The teaching profession has unwittingly signed on to the culture undermining that has plagued American pedagogy for forty years. Bella Dodd wrote eloquently in her book, "School of Darkness," how the teachers' union of New York City has been infiltrated and overrun by communists and their sympathizers to eliminate God, clear thinking, and moral formation from the public school curriculum. Using the rubric of "separation of church and state," throughout the last sixty years, Americans have seen God, and His commandments ignored and vilified. The results are apparent on police blotters, morgues, divorce courts and abortion clinics. The irony of the true facts regarding the term "separation of church and state," should not be lost on the true American. It is a citation from a 1802 letter from President Thomas Jefferson to a group of Connecticut ministers that assured them that they would not have to worry about government intervention in church affairs. In an Orwellian twist, it is now government that is being protected from the moral intrusions of religious principles and moral standards.

Whittaker Chambers once said that the great failing of the conservatives was that "they do not retrieve their wounded." I believe that the same can be said of the Buckleys and the Limbaughs and other so-called conservatives. They are pragmatists that realize that change is the unstoppable flow of history. To be heroic and oppose this tidal wave would be professional suicide. None of them has the courage to oppose this wave of history. It is part of the weakness of human nature that the best way in life is to go along to get along. And it can be argued that change is not necessarily a bad idea because so much of our knowledge is imperfect and subjectivity is an indelible sign of the human condition, even for Popes and world leaders. What it does mean is that the die may have already been cast and we are being driven inexorably to a new watershed in human history that may have severe consequences for the moral traditionalists and the religious orthodox. But if history can be any guide, it is likely that this ferment within traditional political and moral thinking will take its toll on the character and moral dedication of future generations of American children.

10

The Silence of the Skylarks

"Government, like fire, is a good servant but a fearful master." George Washington

In a culture war with global stakes, it is not surprising that violent death and what has been called the "politics of personal destruction" have been employed as a special weapon. As in a nuclear war, "winning is the only thing." How you play the game counts for little in the "city of man." Most people would be shocked if they thought that their government really would do deliberate harm to them. There were few tears shed for a few separatists in Idaho, religious nuts in Texas and of course, Timothy McVeigh, who killed 168 American civilians in Oklahoma City. Hitler murdered, and so did our ally, Stalin. Mao Zedung, Fidel Castro, Pot Pol, Ho Chi Minh, Saddam Hussein, all the evil dictators of history killed. Even in a democracy, government is all about power and control. It is hard for the average American to imagine that Franklin Roosevelt or Winston Churchill could ever be included in this list.

Historical investigation proves it is not beyond the pale of possibility that government could kill or allow its own people to die. In fact, government kills its own citizens and has been doing so since humans formed the first government. It is simply the nature of the beast. The secret is limiting the opportunities that government has to exterminate an individual's life. Many people believe that President Roosevelt deliberately sacrificed over 2,402 American lives to get America into a "good war." In his 1999 book, "Day of Deceit," author Robert Stinnett made the solid case that President Roosevelt had advance warning of this attack and had even encouraged Japan to fire the first shot. Despite this case, Stinnett justified the "sacrifice," on the grounds that war was necessary because of the sacredness of the American crusade against Hitler and the Japanese.

The British sacrificed hundreds of Canadians at Dieppe for similar reasons. On November 16, 1940, Nazi bombs shattered a quiet fall evening in Coventry, England to avoid informing the Germans that they had broken their "Ultra" code. Churchill allowed 900 townspeople to perish to protect that secret knowledge. This illustrates the fact that even "good governments," will sacrifice innocent civilians and military personnel to effect their political goals. A paraphrase of Churchill is apropos. "Never have so few been sacrificed for the good of so many."

It is important to remember these men run governments and many of them adhere to the basic Machiavellian principle that "the ends justify the means." These are men who have to sleep nights and often it is the case where some people have to die for a greater good, a greater benefit to that society. And those deaths have to be covered up, less the reigning government lose face, the next election or suffer a serious crisis in confidence.

Waco is a case in point where everything is not as it appears. Part of the problem is with government and its intricate and philosophical union with business and their mutual mouthpiece, the media. In their book, "No More Wacos," David B. Kopel and Paul H. Blackman revealed how the gas used was not your typical tear gas but a dangerously potent mixture that was known as CS gas. CS gas is metabolized in the body to form cyanide. The toxicity of hydrogen cyanide is increased in the presence of carbon dioxide. It has some common properties with the cyanide gas, Zyklon B, which was the gas used on the Jews, gypsies and others in the Nazi death camps. As William Grigg wrote in "The New American

Review" in an article entitled "No More Wacos," the fate of the children of Mount Carmel "was not dissimilar to that of the children at Auschwitz, followed by cremation."

The attack on February 28, 1993 was originally nothing more than a publicity stunt designed to warrant the Bureau of Alcohol, Tobacco, and Firearms more government appropriations. The ATF agents could have taken the cult leader, David Koresch, prisoner any time they wanted. He even offered them the right of inspection of his firearms but they refused. They thought a high-profiled assault on Koresch, who was a sexually disreputable megalomaniac, would resonate well in the media with a generous reward from the public treasury. The script for "ShowTime," the code name given to this blundered assault, called for the heroic AFT agents to lead a paramilitary assault upon an armed cult seizing its arsenal, neutralizing the grave threat it supposedly posed for the surrounding community. ATF agents never considered a peaceful rendering of the situation. They had only trained for a "dynamic entry" that resulted in several deaths, including four of their own men.

To cover the assault, the ATF also trumped a "drug war" charge. This allowed them to sidestep the nation's Posse Commitas laws, which prohibit the government from enlisting the support of the military, or the National Guard on American civilians. There never was any hint of drugs being used or manufactured by the Davidians. This was clearly a deception employed to allow the government greater latitude in ending the siege. BAFT officials reportedly used flash-bang grenades, but pointedly neglected to ask for specialized assistance to deal with the incendiary aftermath of the use of this type of weapons. After the attack they gave up any pretense of looking for drugs.

The 1993 Treasury Department investigative report concluded that they might have minimized the risk of death or injury to the innocent civilians, especially the children involved. It became apparent that the ATF agents planned to leave no survivors. They never considered any other options than an armed raid.

Because the ATF agents needed to include the press, the element of surprise was lost. The Davidians could have slaughtered all of the initial force as they drove up in the cattle cars but they were not interested in ambushing them as the agents later claimed. Their ATF informer, Robert Rodriguez was allowed to go free. As the authors opined, "If Koresch had wanted to massacre the ATF agents, he could have held Robert Rodriquez hostage and perhaps prevented the ATF from learning that the raid had been compromised." Koresch let them come and even opened the door to the agents, only to have them shoot first and ask questions later.

The authors concluded that the FBI employed tanks, partly to destroy the incriminating evidence of the initial raid and the incineration of the seventy-eight men, women and children that followed. The Texas Rangers were prevented by FBI agents from examining the scene of the probable execution style slaying of Davidian Mike Schroeder, who was shot outside the compound. The Rangers signed over $50,000 in cash, plus platinum and gold that had survived the inferno in a safe. It never showed up on the FBI's evidence list and remains missing.

Probably the most damning piece of evidence on this siege was the video, nominated for an Academy Award for documentaries, entitled, "Waco: The Rules of Engagement" by two liberal filmmakers, Dan and Amy Gifford. This masterful piece of video journalism exposes many of the lies the ATF and FBI told at various committee hearings following the loss of life. As film critic Roger Ebert noted, "You could look in the eyes of the people in this film and tell you is telling the truth and who isn't." He also noted, "if you are looking for people who are the unbalanced zealots, you don't find them among the Davidians, you find them among the FBI and the Alcohol, Tobacco and Firearms. Those are the people that need to be feared." They were the ones who were boasting about their eagerness and willingness to kill the Davidians on camera.

The FBI's informational blackout during the siege constituted a terrifying precedent by imposing wartime news controls on a domestic law enforcement exercise. The FBI seized and confiscated film from independent journalists and prevailed upon the FCC to revoke the broadcast license of radio station KRLD whose coverage of this disaster was sympathetic to the Davidians. It also refused to allow the media to broadcast the video made by Koresch and his followers. "Rules" used excerpts from these tapes as well as a store of other information that had been suppressed by the federal authorities during the climatic assault. A new technology, FLIR, or "Forward Looking Infrared," utilized during the April 19th deadly assault, provides the most damning footage. Analysis of the heat signatures contained on the FLIR footage strongly suggests that FBI troops, armed with automatic weapons, systematically thwarted escape efforts by the Davidians, and then cut down those who attempted to escape from their church.

This material had been available to CBS News program, 60 Minutes, which spiked it. Governmental power is like a loaded gun. It is not the power that is scary but the people holding the power. What this demonstrates is the fact that those who get on the outside of the mainstream of cultural thought and habit can be violently reined back in or neutralized in the process. This can be done peacefully or with fatal consequences. Government can and often does kill its own citizens. This raid sent a message to other dissident groups as to what would happen if they got out of line. Waco should serve as a warning to every American who is critical of the U.S. Government.

The assassination of government leaders, whether elected by the ballot or the bullet, has been an historical constant for millennia. A quick survey of the last 150 years has witnessed widespread political and military assassinations throughout the world. The United States has seen only two presidents die by an assassin bullet since the turn of the century. But there have been attempts, as in the case of the 1981 shooting of Ronald Reagan which came within an inch of ending the president's life. In the case of John Kennedy's mysterious death in Dallas in 1963, it has been shrouded in a mysterious web of deceit, confusion and direct obstruction for over forty years. The violent deaths of witnesses, the assassin himself and several other peripheral players have created a cottage industry of trying to explain, just what happened in Dallas and why.

We may never know the real cause of the Kennedy murder but it is very clear that the prosecution's case rested solely on the theory of the so-called "magic bullet" provided by the chief prosecutor, Arlen Specter. Without this unblemished bullet that putatively passed through thirteen human bones, there is no way that Lee Harvey Oswald could be construed as the lone assassin. It is obvious that the Warren Committee whitewashed the complex plot against him for national security reasons. Only a simpleton would believe Oswald acted alone in the President's brutal death.

There have been other celebrated mysterious deaths since the Cold War began. Frank Murphy, a Supreme Court Justice since 1938 told the Chairman of the House Committee on Un-American Activities Committee, Martin Dies: "We are doomed! The United States is doomed. The Communists have control completely. They've got control of Roosevelt and his wife as well." In 1949, Murphy died in a Detroit hospital, days before he was to be released from the hospital. Dies was convinced he was murdered.

James Forrestal, who became the first Secretary of Defense in1947, was another possibly fatality in this internal struggle. He was virtually hounded from office in 1949 for complaining how the United States had surrendered its interests to the Communists. He lamented this fact when he said; "Those men are not incompetent or stupid. They are crafty and brilliant. Consistency has never been a mark of stupidity. If they were merely stupid, they would occasionally make a mistake in our favor."

Forrestal had dedicated himself to destruction of Communism after the war. He was alarmed by Roosevelt's paternalistic trust in Stalin and believed that capitalism was under siege all over the world. President Truman asked for his resignation. The Secretary had files of those under Communist influence. Because of his "paranoia," Truman had him sent to the Neuropsychiatry Department at the U.S. Naval Hospital at Bethesda, Maryland to see Dr. George N. Raines. If he were no longer a government employee, what right did Truman have to send Forrestal to Bethesda? Forrestal had fifteen loose-leaf binders, totaling 3,000 pages. They were removed from his office and taken to the White House where they remained for one year. This is reminiscent of the secret raid on Vince Foster's office, just hours after his body had been found in the park.

Before he left for the hospital, Forrestal told friends that he had been followed, watched and his phone had been tapped.

Noticeably upset by this exercise in government sanitation, Forrestal boldly predicted that American soldiers would be dying within one year. Dr. Raines said he was all right but would not allow his priest nor his brother to visit him in the hospital. Monsignor Maurice Sheehy had tried six separate times. Henry Forrestal decided to take his brother into the country to recuperate on May 22, 1949. Only hours before they were due to board their train, his brother received a call telling him that his brother had jumped sixteen floors to his death. The cord of his bathrobe was tied securely around his neck. It was theorized that on the night of May 22nd, he got out of bed, and tied one end of the cord to the radiator and the other around his neck. The official record states that Secretary Forrestal jumped in an attempt to hang himself. Grave suspicions still hang over Forrestal's death because he was not critically ill or even sufficiently depressed and was about to be discharged said Raines. There was not one shred of the cord on the radiator, which seems to indicate that it had never been there. The ex-Navy man had it tied tightly around his neck but not around the radiator. The medical inquiry found, not for suicide, but simply that he had "died as a result of injuries, multiple, extreme, received incident to fall." Forrestal had planned to start a new career as a journalist and write a book. The Pentagon and the White House gutted his fifteen volumes of diaries, according to Cornell Simpson's book, "The Death of James Forrestal."

Mysterious circumstances surrounded the strange death of Vince Foster and a host of others who surrounded the sordid, and quite possibly criminal, career of former President Bill Clinton. A cloud of putrid smoke has followed Clinton from his ascendancy to the White House and beyond from the tiny obscurity of a drug-infested governor's mansion. On the same day that David Hale of the Whitewater scandal was indicted by an Arkansas Grand Jury, the President's personal attorney took his own life in a strange park. To complicate the case, he appeared in a coffin like posture with little blood around him, carpet fibers on his clothes, including his underwear, no dirt on his shoes, a strange weapon found without any bullet or suicide note. The Clinton administration sent the

Parks Department to answer these questions instead of the FBI. The drug-induced stupor of a Edgar Allen Poe could not create a scenario more bizarre that this. There is a favorite truism among members of the world spy network. "Anyone can commit a murder but only an artist can commit a suicide."

Another egregious example of a timely death that surrounded the affairs of Bill Clinton was the demise of Commerce Secretary Ron Brown's whose plane went down in Bosnia in 1996. There are as many similar unanswered questions in his mysterious death three days before his possible indictment, just as there were with Foster's "suicide." Nicholas A. Guarino, the editor of "The Wall Street Underground" has written a booklet, entitled, "Murder in the First Degree: An Interim Report on the Death of Commerce Secretary Ron Brown and 34 Other United States Citizens." It describes an elaborate, yet not totally verifiable report on a conspiracy of government operatives who caused the crash of Ron Brown's Boeing T-43A plane with its entourage of industrial wheeler-dealers. The key to the crash near the Cilipi Airport was the activity of Maintenance Chief Niko Jerkuic who allegedly turned off his NDR (Nondirectional Radio) beacon, the only eyes that IFOR-21 had in landing that afternoon. At precisely that same instance, unidentified operatives turned on a similar beacon in front of Sveti Ivan (St. John's Hill), one of the highest mountains in the area at 2,400 feet. This caused the pilots to veer an astonishing eleven degrees off-course.

Jerkuic committed suicide a few days later, a fact verified in the "New York Times." The accident's only living witness, Sergeant Shelly Kelly, died en route to safety in a Medvac helicopter. Witnesses reported that she walked to the helicopter under her own power. However her autopsy revealed that she died of a three-inch incision over her femoral artery, apparently administered three hours after the cuts and bruises she suffered in the crash.

In his 2004 book, "Ron Brown's Body," investigative reporter, Jack Cashill agrees with a great many of Guarino's suppositions. However Cashill punches huge holes in the untimely demise of Sergeant Kelly. He states that her autopsy proved that she died from a broken back and that no helicopter was able to reach the "survivors." He does imply that delay tactics were implemented that might have hasten the death of any survivor.

Several mysteries revolve around the timely deaths of former presidential business partner, James McDougal, who purportedly knew where all the Whitewater bodies were buried. He died abruptly, a broken, crazy man in solitary confinement in Federal prison while his ex-business partner has more political lives than a black cat. Along similar lines is author Richard Odom's captivating book, "Circle of Death: Clinton's Climb to the Presidency." Based solely on circumstantial evidence and realistic inference, Odom details all the bodies that have been found over the state of Arkansas that bore any connection to Governor Clinton. The term "Arkanicides" has become an accurate part of the Clinton mystique and a valid part of his legacy. From drug dealer and later FBI informant Barry Seal of the Mena drug cartel to Jerry Parks, Clinton's former bodyguard who had kept a file on the Governor's extensive sexual liaisons, several unsolved murders continue to haunt the Clintons.

Much of the rationale for this deadly part of the Clinton legacy can be found in the Zeitgeist of the Clinton era. Its origins trace back to the heresy known as Antinomianism. This is the false belief which contends that Christians are exempt from socially established moral standards by virtue of the state of grace conferred by one's faith in their belief system. The mark of the elect, is that of "conspicuous compassion." I feel your pain would serve as a verbal identification of this belief system. The true antinomian replaces traditional morality with the false pieties of the consecrated belief system.

But actual killing is not the only method governments and their allies have used to maintain their power and control. Poet Khalil Gibran once wrote "you can muffle the drum, and you can loosen the strings of the lyre, but who shall command the skylark not to sing." Slander is the twin sister of murder in the Machiavellian course of doing global business. The cultural left has employed a willful strategy of slandering their opposition's reputations so that they are thoroughly discredited in the eyes of an often unforgiving and bloodthirsty public. The goal of tyrants is to effectively silence their opponents, destroying their credibility in the process and allowing the left to run free and easy with its pernicious agenda. People who criticized President Clinton or his wife, were opposed to affirmative action were branded with the vicious canard that they hated the Clintons and all black people. This strategy immediately puts the target on the defensive. It is virtually impossible to prove a negative. In general, the left's tactics has devolved into what may be called the "politics of hate." It is an approach they use to silence their critics by soiling the reputations of those who would expose the nefarious deeds that they wish to keep hidden from the public consciousness. It is an alarming wrinkle in the social fabric that strikes at the very nature of a civilized society. It renders null and void the unwritten gentleman's agreement present in most debates so opponents can agree to disagree on an issue without demonizing the motivation of an opponent. It is a dangerous weapon that may effectively limit the nation's most critical political and social discussions. It is also a mark of the anti-intellectualism that clouds public understanding.

In November of 1996, Bill Clinton compared his critics to a cancer and vowed to cut them out of politics. Slander and blackmail would be the de rigueur to protect his administration. His aides called this tactic the "Ellen Rometsch Strategy." Ellen Rometsch was an East German spy and one of John F. Kennedy's paramours in Washington D. C. His father realized that his son's blatant lack of personal discretion could negatively impact his plans for John's political career. He pressured the Navy to send him overseas. Former Clinton insider George Stephanopoulous unabashedly revealed this on ABC TV. He described how the Clinton White House intended to use the nine hundred purloined FBI files to blackmail and intimidate anyone who might chose to pursue them on these matters. Former Clinton aid, Dick Morris, alleged in the "New York Post" that Clinton had a virtual secret police whose goal was to dig up embarrassing information to silence or intimidate witnesses against the president.

This approach has degenerated into the use of hate as a political weapon. The charge of hate is another method that government and its allies in academia, the press and other self-proclaimed groups can employ to undercut and eventually destroy its enemies. I have noticed an interesting phenomenon that has recently entered the public forum. It can be called "playing the hate card," and it is practiced mostly by denizens of the left. Today it is not enough to disagree with someone on the basis of personal prejudice, opinion, moral, ethnic or religious background. This new technique charged those who disagree with or question the conventional wisdom with hate, which was an abstraction designed to silent criticism by its toxic vagueness. This is a tactical response that is based on the fallacy: "he disagrees with me, therefore he must hate me and my group." It is a sophomoric approach that effectively lowers the tone of political and moral debates. Psychology 101 warns of people caught within the neurotic web of projecting their own hatred onto those who disagree with them.

These proponents of hate have taken the rule of law to a new depth by attempting to criminalize "hate" into a series of offenses that would seriously limit the ability of anyone to denounce any of their views or behaviors. Were the public to accept this tactic, the country would be faced with the specter of the "thought crime." It would no longer be necessary for someone to actually commit a crime against another person. Rather, one could be prosecuted for merely "thinking" or speaking critical thoughts about Jews, blacks, gays or abortionists. They reason that this would create an atmosphere of hate that could lead others to commit violence against individuals in this group. It is an idea adapted from the pages of George Orwell. No free society can sustain such an unmitigated assault on its basic foundations and survive for too long. Society as we know it now hangs in the balance.

To run afoul of the cultural and political gatekeepers is to risk losing one's social position and livelihood. It is a form of cultural syphilis as Parker Yockey called it in his book, "Imperium." In the hands of a damning liberal press, the three most frightening words are "unholy trio" of ant-Semitism, homophobia, or racist. The left uses them as an "axis of evil," which serve as code words to end all possible debate. They provide a cultural sanctuary for themselves and isolate anyone foolhardy enough to run afoul of their policies. The first of these is Anti-Semitism. It is one of those meaningless words that bear more bite than bark. It is meaningless because most Arabs are also Semitic peoples. Anyone who hated Arabs, Jews and any other of the inhabitants of the Middle East would be technically an "anti-Semite." Ironically, many Jews migrated from Russia to Israel. They are not Semitic people and to hate them would not be real anti-Semitism. In political discourse today, the term has a potent and devastating impact that is applied indiscriminately to anyone who not only hates the Jewish people in this country and abroad, but merely disagrees with the policies, violent as they often are, of the Israeli government. This term has served as an effective protective screen that has covered up many of the controversial and anti-West policies of the Israeli Government.

In his book "The New World Order," evangelist Pat Robertson made allusions to international bankers, such as the Rothschilds, who were Jewish. He was immediately labeled anti-Semitism. In such cases, I believe it is a false argument and an aversion to dealing with the merits of the charge. Since not all bankers in Robertson's charge were named "Rothschild," it is clear that he never meant to level his charge solely against the Jews. Writers like Michael Lind and Daniel Pipes belief talk of secret societies and international bankers as a veiled attempt to attack Jews. Pipes' book, "Conspiracy," is obsessed with linking all conspiracies to attacks on Jews, or at least downplaying conspiracies which were linked to Jews, to the point that they seem silly and childish. He says that this inordinate fear about conspiracies, secret societies and Jews started with the Catholic Crusades, which were a "detestable disgrace." Criticism such as this emanated from years of bigotry against the Catholic Church. Conservative Senators Rick Santorum of Pennsylvania, and Sam Brownback from Kansas had to recall legislation that would have denied federal aid to colleges and universities that allowed free speech and academic freedom to include criticism of Israel or support for Palestine. The fact that the bill was even presented represents how deeply embedded Jewish support of Israel is in Congress.

Racism or "racist," is another term that has been skillfully employed to discredit, humiliate and silence those who would criticize the shakedown policies of many black activists in this country. In 1965, future Senator Patrick Moynhan pointed how the very high rate of illegitimacy within the black community was negatively impacting its chances for self-improvement and economic and educational advancement. His facts and statistics were accurate and they honestly portrayed the ravages that the sex revolution had already inflicted on the black community. For merely pointing out the truth, he was called a racist.

Homophobia is the word that covers a multitude of sins within the gay community. Homophobia is defined by the homosexual network in the Catholic Church, as "the irrational hatred, fear and disgust of lesbian and gay persons based on heterosexism. The Catholic Church sees homosexuality as deviant and abnormal and labels homosexual behavior as crime or a sin. The is fear is not an irrational phobia. What frightens straight people is the belief that homosexuals will seduce their young children, especially their sons, into a harmful and tragic lifestyle. A 3/26/92 editorial in the "San Francisco Sentinel," proclaims that love between men and boys is the foundation of homosexuality. A 5/1989 survey from Focus on the Family revealed that seventy-nine percent of homosexuals had a relationship with a person under the age of nineteen.

The Gay-Rights movement also adopted a slanderous defensive strategy to hide its real agenda. Their movement is dedicated to, not just legalizing homosexual behaviors but more importantly, it legitimates the gay lifestyle in all of its sordid expressions. As F. LeGard Smith wrote in his book "Sodom's Second Coming: What You Need to Know about the Deadly Homosexual Assault," we must be aware that "unrestrained and aggressively promoted, homosexual behavior can easily become the sex of choice for an entire society." Senator Rick Santorum felt the full brunt of the homosexual lobby with his faith-based comments on a Texas sodomy law in April of 2003. Not only was he savaged, but his words were distorted by fallen-away liberal Catholic, Bill Keller who called him a "Republican theocrat," in his "New York Times" column.

Traditional standard bearers in health and religion regard homophobia as a deviancy which is a neurosis that necessitates psychological and spiritual counseling. In 1973, homosexual intimidation forced the American Psychiatric Society into removing homosexuality from its "Diagnostic and Statistical Manual of Psychiatric Disorders." Psychiatrists were pressured into changing their sexual perversion to sexual orientation. This raises the question: Will pedophilia and incest and even polygamy someday be regarded as orientations also? And if so, will there be any recourse against child molesters? This was precisely the argument that Santorum made. The Homosexual Lobby plans to establish their homosexual lifestyle as an attractive choice by further confusing young men and women about their own nascent sexual roles and feelings. Their assault on general consciousness will also condition the average American into thinking that gay behavior is healthy and morally proper. The new standard will be that being gay is just a different lifestyle that is no more harmful than being left-handed or a bird watcher.

Just how far will the left push to defame and slander and slandering opponents? As Pat Buchanan revealed in his book, "The Death of the West," "political correctness" will often label its opponents insane, so as to marginalize them from the informal public square. He quoted Peter Hitchens' book, "The Abolition of Britain," which talks about the new regime imitating the methods of the Soviet Union's Serbsky Institute. They used to classify political dissidents such as Natan Sharansky as insane before locking them up in a psychiatric hospital. Hitchens says it is "the most intolerant system of thought to dominate the British Isles since the Reformation." This is tantamount to what is being done to people who oppose homosexuality. These traditionalists suffer the rancor of the Left. They are portrayed as the sick ones when it is homosexuals who engage in such perverse behaviors as "rimming," "fisting" and "bare backing."

The political ramifications of hate and slander are deftly treated in Ann Coulter's best seller, "Slander." She tells one anecdote after another of Democratic bias in their febrile attempt to undercut the power of George Bush and the many Republicans in Congress. Reports of Republican faux pas, such as those of former Vice President Dan Quail and President George W. Bush fill the two hundred-page book with alarming frequency and partisan intensity. Coulter shows how the term "the religious right" has been used to denigrate and tarnished about twenty percent of the American people. The Left's constant abuse of fundamental Christians has made many of them shy away from reminding the American people of the pathological evils that liberals have been foisting on American society. She nails down their persistent and predictable game plan or what Hitler's propagandist, Dr. Joseph Goebbels, used to call the "Big Lie."

A more sophisticated use of the politics of hate revolved around the nomination of Judge Robert Bork to the United States Supreme Court in 1987. The eponymous term "borking" refers to the attacks made on Justice Bork who was nominated to the Supreme Court by President Reagan in 1989. Due to his conservative philosophy and his belief in the "original intent" of the Constitution, Judge Bork was singled out for the most atrocious character assignation in recent political debate. Democratic Senators Joe Biden and Ted Kennedy were pimping for the abortion lobby because it feared the repeal of the infamous Roe v. Wade decision, which had legalized abortion nationally in 1973. They raked Judge Bork over the proverbial coals with a vile and indecorous rhetoric that exposed their demagogic predisposition.

The vitriol that Senator Edward Kennedy used on Judge Bork fathomed the evil machinations that the denizens of the left will go to in order thwart the will of a conservative judge from getting on the Supreme Court. Kennedy took great pains to describe "Robert Bork's America." According to Kennedy, Bork's "perverted vision" saw "a land in which women would be forced into back-alley abortions, blacks would sit at segregated lunch counters." If Bork became a Supreme Court Justice, Kennedy predicted a return to an America where "rogue police could break down citizens' doors in midnight raids, schoolchildren could not be taught about evolution, writers and artists would be censored at the whim or (sic) government, and the doors of the Federal courts would be shut on the fingers of millions of citizens for whom the judiciary is often the only protector of the individual rights that are the heart of democracy." This was pure slander but the public bought Kennedy's "Big Lie." Had not Kennedy's two brothers been sacrificed on the altar of tyranny and racial injustice? America could never look back in its past because these things might certainly happen again.

With Bork's defeat, slander became a very successful stratagem. When George H.W. Bush nominated Clarence Thomas some years later for a similar position on the Court, it was hoped that his race would help him pass muster. Presumably, the only thing that could trump a black man was a black woman. According to Conservative turncoat, David Brock, whose homosexual proclivities caused him to renounce his book on Anita Hill, it was Democratic staffers who recruited Hill, a professor at the University of Oklahoma Law School and a former government associate of Thomas. She was told she would be doing a service to women's rights if she would accuse him of sexual harassment. The Democrats, given their patronizing attitudes toward American blacks, believed that Thomas would slink away into the dark night of oblivion after hearing the charges. The Committee assured Hill that they would keep her testimony anonymous. Given their belief in the inherent inferiority of black people, the Democrats did not expect that Thomas had the guts and the temerity to fight his public "lynching." The Democrats threw Hill to the media dogs, forcing her to defend herself in the public forum. Most Americans believed Thomas' testimony over her incredulous claims of "pubic hairs" on coke cans and "Debbie Does Dallas" porno movies. A year later after the media blitz was put into effect, the tide had turned and more people believed Anti Hill's apparent fabrications. Fortunately for Thomas it was too late to derail his seating on the Court. On a similar note many of George W. Bush's federal court nominees have had to runs the same kind of nefarious gauntlet, especially John Ashcroft who had to grovel before the Senate before being confirmed in 2001.

There are other salient examples of slander being used to subvert legitimate opposition. Martin Dies was the House Chairman of the Dies Committee, which investigated the Communist scandals. He was one of the first to bear the sting of the Communist propaganda onslaught and it nearly ruined his health. The Dies Committee was formed to investigate all the major ideologies that threatened the West. "I regard Communism and Nazism and Fascism as having one underlying principle," he said and that "dictatorship—the theory that government should have the right to control the lives, the fortunes, the happiness, the beliefs . . . of the human being." What Dies noticed near the end of his fight was the fact that of the three, only Communism had the undying support of millions of Americans who would stop at anything to thwart his obligations to get at the truth. He felt it strange that liberals like Walter Lippmann and Drew Pearson never seemed to express quite the same vehemence or antipathy toward Stalin and his admirers that they did toward Hitler and Mussolini. In 1944, with his health in decline and a tough re-election campaign at hand, Dies quietly retired from the political battles.

John T. Flynn, an ardent opponent of FDR's New Deal was fired as financial editor of the "New Republic" for joining a non-interventionist group, known as "America First." John Chamberlain pointed out in the 1930's "any author who attacked communism could count on similar smear treatment." The intellectuals of the left had succeeded in poisoning the intellectual atmosphere against legitimate dissident. Other critics of the party line, such as Whittaker Chambers and Bella Dodd, who labored against Communist teacher unions in New York, were dismissed as "red baiters and reactionaries."

The pre-Bork paradigm for this approach of vicious character assassination and career ruination dates back to the days Wisconsin Senator Joseph McCarthy. His name serves as the symbol of slanderous assaults on an opponent's character and personal life. In an illuminating article written for "The New American" in 1987 and reprinted in 1996, James J. Drummey answered all the objections the left has ever had about Joseph McCarthy and the opprobrious "ism" that bears his name. He not only clarified the verbal obfuscation and immoral distortion the left had done to McCarthy and his record, but he raised several questions about the indefensible behaviors of President Harry S Truman and many Democratic Congressional leaders of the 1950's.

As a Roman Catholic it was natural for Joseph McCarthy to be an ardent anti-Communist. Communism as a political issue appeared in his campaign against Howard McMurray in the 1946 senatorial election. McMurray had been endorsed by the Communist "Daily Worker," and McCarthy told the "Madison Capital Times," that his top priority was to "stop the spread of Communism."

At an Ohio County Women's Republican Club on February 9, 1950, McCarthy let it be known that the nation was in a Herculean struggle, which he defined as an "all-out battle between communistic atheism and Christianity." He blamed the fall of China and of Eastern Europe on the previous six years of "traitorous actions," of the State Department's "best and brightest" luminaries such as John S. Service, Gustavo Duran, Mary Jane Keeney, Julian Wadleigh, Dr. Harlow Shapely, Hiss, and Dean Acheson.

During the 1952 election campaign for the Senate, McCarthy dated his own dedication to this issue to the night of May 22, 1949 when James Forrestal was found dead on the grounds of Bethesda Naval Hospital. McCarthy was convinced that the Communists, whom Forrestal hated very much, had hounded him to his death. McCarthy went on to say that he was much more deeply affected "when I heard of the Communist celebration when they heard of Forrestal's murder."

McCarthy believed that Communist infiltration of the State Department began in the 1930's. On September 2, 1939 government witness, Whittaker Chambers, provided Assistant Secretary of State Adolph Berle with the names of two dozen spies in the government, including Alger Hiss. Berle brought the information to President Roosevelt who laughed in his face. This is not surprising since Hiss, who is clearly identified in the Venona Papers, moved quickly up the ladder in the State Department. He was an influential adviser to Roosevelt at the disastrous Yalta Conference that laid the basis for the Communist acquisition of all of Eastern Europe. Hiss also served as acting Secretary-General at the founding meeting of the United Nations. As historical events unfolded in the 1950's, it is increasingly more apparent that McCarthy was more victim than villain.

McCarthy's troubles began when he started getting too close to the truth. The left realized that he was becoming an irritating factor who was developing a strong bastion of support, especially among American Catholics. He had to be neutralized. Instead of killing him, the left decided on character assassination. The left enlisted all of its heavy guns in the media and in Congress to subvert, demonize and castigate McCarthy in an assault that is still ongoing. McCarthy was highly critical of General George Marshall while he was Secretary of State. His distrust of General Marshall dated back to 1947, starting with Executive Order #9835, which established a federal loyalty program that prohibited the employment of loyalty risks on June 10, 1947.

McCarthy sent this report to Marshall, who promptly ignored it. McCarthy was presented with an FBI report that indicated a strong Communist subversion in the United States and penetration of the State Department. It detailed the operations of spy networks in the State Department and other places. McCarthy later charged that Roosevelt and Stalin had planned the Korean War and Indochina Wars at the Yalta Conference in 1945.

It was on the Senate floor, where McCarthy delivered a speech that exposed his deep-set fears about the Communist menace. His speech, which later became a book, "America's Retreat from Victory," drew from sources almost totally friendly to Marshall. McCarthy explained his alarm at several of the General's policies toward Asia that, in the context of the Cold War, had been inconsistent with American interests in the Pacific. As he said, "I do not intend to go into his motives . . . Unless one has all the tangled and often complicated circumstances contributing to a man's decision, an inquiry into his motives is often fruitless . . . I shall leave that subject to subtler analysts of human personality."

To his credit, McCarthy refused to blame it on a conscious effort of Marshall to subvert American foreign policy. McCarthy said that he was disturbed by at the U. S. 's international decline that could only have come "from a great conspiracy on a scale so immense as to dwarf any previous venture in the history of man." This conspiracy was "so black that when, if it is finally exposed, its principals shall forever deserving of the maledictions of all honest men." While this statement was controversial in 1951, given our failure in China, the stalemates in Korea and the defeat in Vietnam, it stands out for its prescience and alarming accuracy.

McCarthy's enemies spared no quarter in attacking him for his timely exposure of the country's Communist influence. Writer Richard Rovere made a career out of vilifying McCarthy. I heard him speak at an Asian Conference at Harvard University in April of 1965. The grave did not stop Rovere's incessant politics of personal destruction. He was relentless in his personal assault on McCarthy even eight years after his death in 1957. McCarthy would have no peace as long as there was breath in Rovere's body. He once wrote that the people who supported McCarthy were low class and low intelligence "zanies and zombies and compulsive haters." These were the same crazies who had followed earlier demagogues, such as Huey Long and Father Coughlin. This bears a rhetorical resemblance to Vice President Al Gore's salacious characterization of those who opposed abortion as being comparable to retarded victims of "missing a chromosome."

For Lillian Hellman McCarthy's short period of notoriety, was nothing less than "scoundrel time." For blacklisted Hollywood writer, Dalton Trumbo, it was "the time of the toads." Arthur Miller's play, "The Crucible" opened in 1953 to critical acclaim. Miller compared McCarthy to the group of self-righteous Puritans who burned witches at the stake in the seventeenth century. His analogous play is still being performed on the stage today, reinforcing the false notion that anyone with religious principles who attempts to influence society is engaging in a "witch hunt," which is repulsive to a free and democratic society. This is part of the negative legacy that anti-McCarthyism has left to our society. Richard Condon displayed his own version of the McCarthy period in his book "The Manchurian Candidate," in which a former army sergeant is brainwashed into being an assassin for the politics aspirations of two of his family members. The "evil stepfather," who is just waiting in the wings to ascend to the presidency is a perfect caricature of the stereotype the media and rival politicians created of McCarthy in the 1950's. He babbles like an incoherent idiot repeating, as if some trance, his contention that there were first 57, then 205, and finally 79 communists in the State Department, while waiving his tattered list like a red flag. This is an historical allusion to McCarthy's Wheeling, West Virginia speech on February 20, 1950. In the speech, McCarthy referred to a letter from Secretary of State James Byrnes, sent to Congressman Adolph Sabath in 1946. In that letter Byrnes said the State Department security investigators had declared 284 persons unfit to hold jobs in the Department because of Communist affiliation and possible homosexual behavior. Only 79 had been discharged, leaving 205 still on the payroll. McCarthy told the audience that while he did not have the entire list, he did have the names of 57 who were either members or fellow travelers of the Communist party. He later said he had a list of 81 names, which included the 57, plus 24 of lesser importance and about whom the evidence was less damaging. The numbers worked! McCarthy's dedicated enemies juggled the numbers, so as to make him appear like the bumbler in the Condon book. To his credit, McCarthy did not relate the names on this list because he felt it might discredit them and ruin their reputations if it turned out that they were innocent. This is precisely one of the accusations attached to the "evils" of McCarthyism.

To get at the bottom of McCarthy's accusations, the Senate set up the Tydings Committee, a subcommittee of the Senate Foreign Relations. Ostensibly this committee was established to weed out the Communist influence in the State Department. It was to give "a full and complete study and investigation as to whether persons who are disloyal to the United States are, or have ever been employed by the Department of State." Senator Millard Tydings, a Democrat from Maryland, ignored his constitutional duty and turned the committee's powerful guns on McCarthy himself. Aided by his Democratic colleagues, Brien McMahon and Theodore Green, Tydings attacked, vilified, heckled and irterrupted McCarthy so that he was never able to make his case. One can only speculate why Tydings did this. Like the Senate vote during President Clinton's impeachment trial in 1999, it seems clearly obvious that partisan politics won out over integrity and honesty.

After 31 days of "anti-McCarthy" hearings, Tydings labeled his colleague's charges a "fraud," and a "hoax." After little attention, the committee concluded that the individuals on McCarthy's list were neither Communist nor even pro-Communist. In essence the Tydings Committee failed dismally to carry out its Senate mandate. It was a cover-up worthy of severe historical condemnation.

While McCarthy was getting the rail from his colleagues, the real subjects of investigations, like Philip Jessup, were treated like heroes. The "Venona Papers" later vindicated McCarthy. The very fact that of the 110 names he turned in to Tydings, the State Department employed sixty-two of them at the time of the hearings. While Tydings' Committee was busy exonerating these security threats, the State Department started dismissal proceedings against forty-nine of them.

After McCarthy implicated the United States Army for its laxity toward communist infiltration, McCarthy's enemies went for his jugular. The "politics of personal destruction," had taken their toll on the Senator from Wisconsin. His drinking had become more severe and he could not stand up under the repeated personal attacks. McCarthy suffered the great indignity of being censured by his peers in the Senate. Republican President Dwight Eisenhower had tired of McCarthy's constant probing. He had become an embarrassment to the president who apparently tended to reign without any regard to political principle and concern for the integrity of the nation's security. Ike literally threw McCarthy to the partisan wolves. He entered Bethesda Naval Hospital, the same place Forrestal "committed suicide," suffering from infectious hepatitis.

McCarthy died of acute hepatic failure on May 2, 1957. In a book "The Assassination of Joe McCarthy," by Dr. Medford Evans, the author states that toxic hepatitis can be induced by any of several poisons, including chloroform, mercury, carbon tetrachloride. McCarthy had been placed in an oxygen tent and it is theoretically possible that something could have been administered to him while he slept. Since no autopsy was performed, we will never know.

Louis Budenz, former member of the Communist party said at Senator McCarthy's funeral that "The destruction of Joe McCarthy leaves the way open to intimidate any person of consequence who moves against the Conspiracy. The Communists made him their chief target because they wanted to make him a symbol to remind political leaders in America not to harm the Conspiracy or its world conquest designs." Evans says that it was really the American establishment who was gunning for him. The very establishment who should have joined him in his fight finally brought him down.

McCarthy did have his supporters, including Joseph Kennedy and his son, John. Others such as Indiana Senator William Jenner, whose Subcommittee investigated Communists in education tried to warn Americans of this "hidden revolution," that was sheltering Communists in the government. When both of these men were ousted from the political arena, the only ones who were brave enough to pick up the mantel, were those already been marginalized to the outer fringes of political debate. By this I mean such writers as John Flynn, and John Stormer, who wrote the best seller, "None Dare Call it Treason," Robert Welch and his "John Birch Society as well as Willis Carto and his "Liberty Lobby." To the Left, these men and their beliefs were more harmful to America today than anything the Communists could have ever done. This is the reigning viewpoint today that dominates the debate. Any collective attack on the liberal viewpoint or liberal conduct evokes the epithet that it is McCarthyism and "automatically implies a paranoid and dysfunctional view of reality."

Catholics especially looked to McCarthy to clean out the secular heresies that had infected American society in the 1950's. Protestant opponents, such as Dr. John Mace, moderator of the Presbyterian Church USA, thought McCarthyism was an "American version of the Sixteenth Century Spanish Inquisition." Catholics knew then that the liberals wanted to banish religion to the outer areas of society. Conservatives and Catholics believed that religion was central to their lives. Bishop Fulton J. Sheen, who never mentioned McCarthy or took a stand on political issues, put it a bit differently. "The basic struggle today is not between individualism and collectivism, free enterprise and socialism," but a moral battle over whether "man shall exist for the state or the state for man."

In 1990, London researcher Roger Scruton revisited the McCarthy Era and found, (not surprisingly) that "McCarthy was right!" It was also during the mid-to-late 1940's that Communist sympathizers in the State Department played key roles in the "loss" of Mainland China to the Communists. Massachusetts Congressman John F. Kennedy joined him in his concern over Asia. Kennedy placed a great deal of blame on "a sick Roosevelt, General George Marshall, and our diplomats and their advisers, the Lattimores and the Fairbanks." One just has to read the works of the latter to see the deep affection and high regard they had for the likes of Mao Zedung and other Communist murders.

Later revelations, says McCarthy biographer Arthur Herman, have tended to bear his charges out. What they found in Joe McCarthy was a politician who had the temerity to speak out publicly on issues, which had been ignored for years. Even the "New York Times," mildly concurred in a 1998 article, in which they revisited McCarthy's activities and took his excesses in the context of the times. Jessup, John S. Service and Owen Lattimore were all found within the Venona Intercepts, which were the KGB documents that were published years after the fall of the Berlin Wall. Jessup continued his work for Communist fronts and he was closely associated with the Institute for Pacific Relations, (IPR) which the Senate Internal Security Subcommittee (SISS) described in 1952 "as a vehicle used by the Communists to orientated American Far Eastern Policy toward Communist objectives." The SISS also reported that 46 persons connected with the IPR while Philip Jessup was a leading light who had been named under oath as members of the Communist Party.

Lattimore was one of the key architects of the State Department's pro-Communist foreign policy in the Far East. While he was not a Russian spy as McCarthy erroneously had labeled him in a closed hearing that was later leaked to the press by columnist Drew Pearson, Lattimore had a pro-Soviet predilection that dominated his writings and motivated his activities. The SISS declared in 1952 that Lattimore was "from some time beginning in the 1930s, a conscious articulate instrument of the Soviet conspiracy." In polite terms, he was a very important "useful idiot."

The Venona Intercepts removed all doubt about the American Communist Party 's role as the linchpin of a Russian spy network, which had penetrated the U. S. Government at its highest levels since the 1930s. The intercepts identified Hopkins as more of an agent than a "dupe." Sometimes there was a fine line between a mindless ideologue and someone wholly conscious of what he or she was doing. Robert Oppenheimer was another who had strong leanings toward Communism but seemed to be motivated by his fear that if the United States were the only country to possess the atomic bomb, they would use it more frequently. He attempted to level the playing field by "lending" American secrets to the Soviets. It was Oppenheimer's high-minded treason that led to the loss of 50,000 American soldiers in Korea and the forty-year stalemate of the Cold War.

Willi Schlamm writing in the "National Review," put the McCarthy legacy in its proper perspective. His chief "crime," was the fact that he "had rejected the moral relativism which insisted that a person's moral and political choice scouted for nothing. That relativism had allowed liberalism to sympathize with and protect communism's champions and profess to find moral worth in a system of absolute evil." According to Forrest Davis this was liberalism that "looks evil in the face and pronounces it half-good." Relying heavily on the work of McCarthy expert M. Stanton Evans, conservative firebrand, Ann Coulter goes a long way in her book, "Treason," in rehabilitating McCarthy's memory. She points out how much he was loved by his supporters because he had a "gift for appealing to the great common sense of the American people." To his millions of supporters, Joe McCarthy was a "poet," and even though liberals "may have written the history books," at the time, "the instinctual response of the American people prevailed over the left's theatrics." Many of those who became the "silent majority" still loved him, no matter how much the left scorned him. McCarthy had so badly stigmatized Communism, that "his victory survived him." He sacrificed his life, his reputation, and his good name so that the American people could hear and remember the truth.

Despite the revelations of Venona and the KGB files, the liberal left still clings tenaciously to their fallen icons, just like junkyard dogs, hovering around a piece of rotting meat. They continue to recycle the same old canards that Alger Hiss was framed for perjury by the FBI for forging incriminating documents to make them seem as if they had come from his Woodstock typewriter. They still provide twisted interpretations of the other incriminating evidence, such as the Bokhara rug, the prothonotary warbler, and the famous "Pumpkin Papers." It was probably the first instance of the "vast right-wing conspiracy," to frame the innocent proponents of progressivism and personal freedom. This echoes what would be said about Kenneth Starr in his pursuit of the real truth of the Clinton years. Like Nixon and McCarthy, Starr's investigation warranted the "treatment." The Left's sordid "politics of mass destruction" are always lurking in the wings, ready to pounce like a hungry lion on any high-minded conservative who thinks he can profess the truth with impunity.

11

A Conspiracy of Love

"This soul can only be a conspiracy of individuals."
Pierre Teilhard De Chardin

M any impulses and currents in the Conspiracy Matrix conflated in the religious expression of the New World Order. The proponents of the NWO realize that there has to be religion in the utopian world of the future but one that bears little resemblance to the traditional religions of the past. The New Age religion will be dominated by the existential belief that the individual can do whatever he or she deems right for that person. It also will have several identifiable features. It will be secular, humanistic, with a strong flavoring of the occult. It will naturally include nature worship, a kind of Neo-pantheism. Individuals will think of themselves as possessing a "god within," making each human being, not merely a reflection of God, but nothing less than a god.

According to Christian writer Ted Flynn's book, "The Hope of the Wicked," the term New Age, is really an amalgamation of Babylonian paganism, combined with elements of Hinduism, Buddhism and an assorted mixture of other philosophies and what he calls, "psychobabble." There are no moral hierarchies. One must give equal honor to the Buddhist or the homosexual. All pathways lead to God, and none is better than the other in this theology.

The New Age is eclectic and occultic. It promotes evolution, self-deification and the transformation of individuals and their human nature so as to transform the world into a place where peace and harmony will reign supreme for all time all over the globe. All reality is one. Therefore everyone is God. Man is divine and has unlimited potential. Its only flaw is its ignorance of its own divinity. This is why religions that preach man's depravity or weakness because of original sin have no place in the modern world. They have outlived their usefulness and must be relegated to the ashcan of history. It is the enlightened who can truly understand this New Age. Some offshoots of the New Age and the attainment of the euphoric state of enlightenment include yoga, the martial arts, Therapeutic Touch, iridology, acupuncture and reflexology.

Since it is a given that the planet's resources are limited, population control will hold a huge priority. To assuage the scarcity of new births, New World citizens will have to humor themselves with as much unrestricted sexual behavior they can stand. This promiscuous dystopia will offer "bed and breakfast," in place of the Romans' "bread and circuses."

Sex is an intricate part of the New Age religion. The NWO leadership has chosen to control and program its billions of servants. It is the essence of "Libido Dominandi." Tantra comes from the Sanskrit, which means "woven together." It is a term that is loosely applied to several different and even contradictory schools of Hindu yoga. Archaeologists have discovered artifacts, which give credence to the belief that sex worship in some form, or another is humanity's oldest religion. It is an ancient philosophy that is a cornucopia of sexual techniques as outlined in the Kama Sutra. Tantra asserts that enlightenment can be found in all activities, especially in sexual intimacy. It is an uninhibited sex, free love-cult to some. It has become part of the New Age spiritual sex therapy, part of the California lifestyle.

Tantra is the total surrender, or releasing of all mental, emotional and cultural conditioning so that universal energy may flow through one like a river without any efforts. Though some techniques are used to control ejaculation, Tantra does not teach one to control the sexual urges to reach God. It is the exact opposite. Worshippers use sex to achieve union with divinity. Sex becomes sacred when one approaches it from the heart and body rather than from the mind. When the energy comes from deep within oneself, one's essential self, it then connects to the god or goddess within. The focus is on pleasure and the mind-numbing release of orgasm. It is the magnetic ocean in which human beings are floating. Tantra teaches one to be familiar with his or her mystical nature. Sexual pleasure can cause a release from the quotidian responsibilities and pressures of ordinary life.

New Age sex resembles the warm and fuzzy version of the modern era that will also serve the NWO. The international elite intend to establish a World Ecumenical Initiative so as to unite all the world's religions, including Christianity, Buddhism, Judaism, Islam, Hinduism and Catholicism. The city of Jerusalem, the birthplace of monotheism, will be at the focal point of this plan. Texe Marrs has predicted a religious czar will emerge to rule over this New Age religion. Of course, this czar will be nothing more than a puppet of the real ruling elite. The purpose of the NWO religion is to deconstruct religious truth into the spiritual pabulum, a hazy, undefined idea of God while fundamentalists will be suppressed in unprecedented horrors and tribulations. The Bilderbergers have instructed their minions that Christian and Islamic fundamentalists were the major threat to this New World Order. They are to be demonized and branded as religious fanatics and ostracized as a terrible threat to the tolerance-based, non-judgmental "community of faith" composed of all religions.

The NWO religion traces its origins to the French Revolution, which took upon itself the loftier goal of not merely changing a government but reinventing human nature. Its sordid legacy has threatened the basic system of American liberties and freedoms. The French Jacobins attempted to destroy the basic pillars of French society, the Church, nobility and bourgeois, just as the liberals are doing to American society today. They wanted to remake French culture by erasing its cultural history and redefining the family into new alignments, not unlike what has befallen the American family today. According to their leading spokesman, Jean Jacques Rousseau, "All men are like gods!" Uninhibited by the restrictions of the Church and societal norms, they were free to do whatever they wished. According to Rousseau, human society's basic institutions had been responsible for all the evils in society because men were basically good. By cleansing France's social institutions, they could establish utopia or heaven on earth for all peoples. Jealousy, crime and envy would disappear in a wave of liberty, equality, and fraternity would reign supreme. This new way of thinking promoted egalitarianism as its core belief. Such a system required an intellectual elite to guide ordinary individuals in the attainment of global peace and eternal brotherhood, whether they wanted it or not.

The revolutionary vision of the French Revolution is alive and well in the United States today. The nation's intellectual elite in government, the universities, media and legal profession have their feet planted in the ideological concrete of the French Enlightenment. They dream dreams that visualize a new global society, with new men and new women populating a futuristic realm, devoid of crime, war, evil and maybe even death. Like President Woodrow Wilson, they envision a worldwide democracy dominated by eternal peace. They foresee an international society where differences of race, social status and gender orientation will coalesce to produce harmony and a universal brotherhood. All this will be under the guiding and watchful eye of the elect whose Gnostic sense of order will bring this progressive chimera to fruition.

Religion in this new imperial age is a divisive force that must not be tolerated in the age of planetary conformity. In order to establish the NWO religion, the old order must be totally dismantled or at least neutralized to the extent that it bears little resemblance to its former importance. The naked public square must refuse to tolerate or allow displays of religious fervor and devotion. Under the rubric of the "separation of church and state," organized religions must be marginalized to the private sector. That private sector, through legislation, court decision and media pressure must be continually reduced so that eventually the "old time religion," will be nothing more than what philosopher James Wilson, called the "hobby principle of religious belief." This religious edict applies to the entire world. The Bush mandate to end the threats of Saddam Hussein and the like is a very forceful message to the rest of the dogmatic world: repent or suffer the consequences of the NWO. This New World Religion wants to replace organized religion with a more personal, non-denominational creed that adopts the dogma of certain social crusades, such as AIDS research, the Environment, the Homeless and the Rain Forest.

The question remains on whether this will be accomplished. On the surface it is called "Entertainment Paganism," that is, a freak show that ranges from TV shows about "Buffy the Vampire Slayer," to games like "Dungeons and Dragons," through the Gothic drag look of freaky hair, body piercing, tattoos, body art, black raincoats, studs and chains. Ecology Theology carries it further. This involves free-form sexual morality, "Gaia worship, native spiritual and American Indian rituals to the wide-ranging "New Age Movement." To them humanity is on the cusp of a new dawn, a new phase in evolutionary history. Dark Paganism goes even further. According to this belief, there is no such thing as evil and death and destruction are forms of beauty. The ultimate purpose of the "green religion" is to convince the people of the world to embrace world governance. For a free nation like the United States, this represents a tremendous loss of national sovereignty and personal freedom. This is all for the sake of "Mother Earth," and the environment. It is a lot easier to administer world government if all the people believe it represents their salvation rather than their tyranny.

The vanguard of this movement explains Henry Lamb in the "The Rise of Global Green Religion," with people like James Parks Morton, James Lovelock, Robert Muller, Timothy Wirth and Al Gore. It is environmentalism that has spawned a revival of pagan earth worship in the form of Gaia, a concept first advanced by atmospheric scientist James Lovelock more than twenty years ago. This is the belief that the earth itself is a conscious, living organism. The movement has also attracted followers among feminists who are drawn to the idea of a Mother Earth or Earth goddess. All humans are a mere part of this living organism. As a result they know what is best for the planet. They also know that the only way to protect the planet is to control the people who despoil it. The only way to control them is through the use of big government and its bureaucracy, whose tentacles reach into every corner of life and every aspect of human endeavor around the globe.

The ultimate purpose of "green religion," is to convince the people of the world to embrace world governance—which for a free nation like America are presents a great loss of national sovereignty and personal freedom. The once-hated idea of world government has been renamed "global governance." The concept of national sovereignty is slowing being transformed into the idea of "sovereign equality." The vanguard of this movement is the environmental movement with its green theological roots. The salvation of the planet has replaced the salvation of individual souls in the metaphysics of this new religion. There is no human soul but only the continuation of the Gaia or Mother Earth.

In a February, 1983 issue, of "The Humanist Magazine," a writer proposed the idea that the "classroom must and will become the area of combat between . . . the rotting corpse of Christianity . . . and the new faith of Humanism." Secular religion will eventually converge into a universal religion that bears more resemblance to New Age pantheism than it does Christianity. Victor Gollancz, Marxist millionaire, writer and publisher wrote in 1948, "The ultimate aim should be that Judaism, Christianity and all other religions should vanish and give place to one great ethical world religion, the brotherhood of man." He would call this universal mega-religion "monodeism."

The humanists found a home in the New Age Movement. There are many similarities between the environmentalists and the humanists. Humanists believe that man has emerged as part of the evolutionary process. Both agree that man has a self-sufficiency that will become godlike. In the book, "The End of the Nation State," Jean Marie Guehenna, chided Montesquieu who erroneously predicted 250 years ago that the "historical dynamic started by the Age of Enlightenment does not lead to the death of religions, but to their revival in new, sometimes degraded, forms."

Humanitarian action offers the wealthy the same sensation of a moral experience, individual but shared, that Islam offers to the poor. Islam, says Guehenna, is incapable of fully responding to the changes of the world. Modern humanitarianism remains an act of faith in the unity and fungibility of the human condition. By religion, according to Guehenna, ""one must in fact now understand, not the belief in a transcendence, a God, of principles, but, far more modestly that sum total of rites and what may be called "habits of the heart" that—as Tocqueville said of America—shape our behavior." Guehenna goes on to say that there is no contradiction between "the globalization of the imperial age and the anarchism of religious fragmentation," that is taking place now. The second is "the natural consequence of the first."

New Agers are dabblers who wear their crystal necklaces and copper bracelets for good luck to keep away the evil spirits or bad karma. They attempt to create their own personal reality by chanting their mantras and practicing visualization. New Agers believe in a syncretistic religion that equates all faiths as equal, no matter how contradictory they may be. It has combined Christianity with different eastern religions to provide a new, feel-good amalgamation of religious sentiment. It relies on tenets of Buddhism, Hinduism, a mixture of the Taoism of yin and yang and the Cosmic Christ. There are some Gnostic elements that have found their way into the New Age. The Gnostic Jesus was not a savior but a revealer. He came into the world to communicate his secret gnosis. Man's redemption took place though secret knowledge, freeing them from the prisons of their bodies and reuniting them with the god from which they had originated.

New Age philosophy has permeated virtually every aspect of our culture. A web page search uncovered over four million places to learn about the New Age on the Internet. There are books, movies, records and plays with New Age themes. It has invaded and made itself an integral part of the environmental movement. The monism of the New Agers is easily fused with the need for a global oneness, a unity of all men, underscoring the innate brotherhood of the humanity.

The New Age has a dark side with occultic forces. Constance Cumbey saw the New Ager as a "highly organized satanic conspiracy." It deals in psychic phenomena, re-incarnation and the like. Shirley MacLaine claims to have been "reborn" several times. It relies heavily on astrology. George Lucas and his blockbuster movies, the "Star Wars" series and that of "Indiana Jones" moves are filled with ideas of cosmic spirituality and new Age catch phrases and themes. "The Force be with you," was the battle cry and greeting of many of the figures. It is an occultic energy field that has been created by living beings. Indiana Jones searches for the "Holy Grail," which is a symbolic hunt for the divinity in all of us, according to Lucas. New Age has attracted covens of witches and wiccans who ply their trade with the spiritual intensity of the New World Order.

New Age has led to the neo-paganization of the American culture. It is a matrix of beliefs that the world is sacred, nature is sacred, the body is sacred, sex is sacred, and each individual life, no matter how evil it may be, is sacred. Each individual is a god or goddess. The New Age spreads the collective wisdom of the Orient and its divergent philosophies and religions throughout the world. It spread the wisdom of the ancients which it was convinced that such wisdom provided the answers for man's search for spiritual meaning.

The "Big Lie" of the new Age is that man is God himself, the oldest and first sin. It was the biblical serpent who first seduced Adam and Eve with the plea, "And ye shall be like gods." Man only has to realize this and strive for the God within. Most of this new paradigm seems like the mind-boggling result of too much science fiction. In effect, it does to religion and dogma what the movie "The Invasion of the Body Snatchers," did for physical fitness. It is a true invasion of the Mind-Snatchers. It appears as an effort to rehash the pantheistic thinking of the old pagan order.

One of the keys to understanding the New Age is to examine the writings of Madame Blavatsky, the originator of Theosophy, which is a term derived from two Greek words, "God," and "wisdom." The idea of "divine wisdom" came into vogue when a

Russian born mystic, Helena Petrovna Blavatsky founded the Theosophical Society in New York City. She has been called the "Mother of the New Age." Her writings provided the present pseudo-scientific underpinnings for religion then in decline because of the theories of Charles Darwin. Blavatsky's book, "The Secret Doctrine," is the foundational "sourcebook for New Age belief systems." Her teaching's foreshadowed Lovelock's Gaia hypothesis by characterizing the earth as a living organism."

Theosophy traces its roots back to the hermetic brotherhoods of the eighteenth century, including the Illuminati. Many of her ideas were firmly established in the enlightened philosophy of French writers Diderot and Voltaire. The Masters led Blavatsky to Tibet where she learned the secrets of ancient wisdom. She claimed to be a spiritual tuning fork that vibrated through the same wavelengths as the hidden Masters of the occult Brotherhood.

Two years after founding the Theosophical Society, she published her book "Isis Unveiled," a farrago of mysticism and poorly written pseudo-science that numbered over 1,200 pages. Her writings had a deep-seated anti-Christian and anti-bible tint to them. She said that belief in the Bible was an absurdity and set among her goals the elimination of its influence from public life. She felt that Jesus Christ was a myth and hoped to destroy the Christian worldview and replace it with a new world spiritual order. Given her beliefs, it is not surprising that historical figures with a lust for power such as Adolph Hitler have found her self-empowering philosophy resonated with their visions of world conquest.

Blavatsky effectively forged the European esoteric tradition of Spiritualism and the so-called Oriental Renaissance into a coherent system that approximated a religion. She claimed to have received from the Masters of Wisdom the key to unlocking the mysteries that had long been kept from the masses, echoing the Gnostics of the 2nd century. It was a remarkable and revolutionary concept of life in the universe that gave man a new purpose, aside from that of the Bible, for living in this world, based on the ideas of the Orient and India. It found a receptive audience in the nineteenth century.

Theosophical societies spread all over the world and eventually came to America, bringing serious attention to eastern religions. Essayist Ralph Waldo Emerson and his Transcendentalism effectively laid the foundation blocks for an easy acceptance of some of Madame Blavatsky's teachings. This promotion of Buddhism and Hinduism greatly impacted several religious movements, including liberal Catholicism, the Unity Church and many more Protestant denominations.

On September 15, 1887, Blavatsky unveiled her monthly publication, "The Lucifer," which was designed to bring to light the hidden things of darkness. Under the guidance of Annie Besant, a Fabian Socialist who later became President of the Theosophist Society, its name was wisely changed to "The Theosophist." The magazine continued its linkage to the Lucifer Press, whose Lucis Trust sponsored the Temple of Understanding and Meditation Room located in the U. N. building in New York City. Science fiction author, Kurt Vonnegut, a co-endorser of the Planetary Citizens, a New Age group with United Nations affiliation, said of Blavatsky in 1970, that she "brought wisdom from the East . . . She was a citizen of the world." This veiled association with the vision of Woodrow Wilson is no mere coincidence.

Theosophy also drew much of its inspiration from the same early philosophers venerated by the Illuminati, Freemasons, and the Round Tables, namely Plato, Pythagoras, and the Egyptian Mystic schools. Blavatsky also borrowed from the Cabala and Talmud. As Nesta Webster wrote in 1924, "The Theosophy Society is not a study group but essentially a propagandist society which aims at substituting for the pure and simple teachings of Christianity the amazing compound of Eastern superstition, Cabalism and eigteenth century charlatanism."

It is a common misconception that mere dabbling in Oriental mysticism and New Age spirituality is basically harmless. The truth of the matter is this kind of "spirituality" is very dangerous and can lead to the horrific consequences of the Third Reich. The roots of the World War II can be found in a secret society called the Thule Society in 1919. It was here that Hitler developed his Weltanschauung that led him to the control of the German government. The inner core of the Thule Society consisted of Black Magicians who practiced Satanism. This is a constant thread among many of these secret groups. Trevor Ravenscroft wrote that the Thulists were a "society of Assassins," who "used many of the Communists or other unsolved murder victims of the Weimar period as sacrificial lambs to appease the angry gods in the German galaxy."

The sun plays a great role in Thule philosophy. It had been a sacred symbol of the Aryans. They also practiced Satan worship, including "Black Magic." It was not a working man's group, but the cream of German society that included judges, police chiefs, lawyers, university professors, artisans, leading industrialists, surgeons, scientists as well as a host of rich and influential people, the so-called cultural elite of Germany.

Dietrich Eckart, one of the seven founders of the Nazi Party, was also a charter member of the Thule Society. He was a dedicated Satanist, who was a supreme adept of the arts and rituals of Black Magic. On his deathbed, Eckart said: "Follow Hitler! He will dance, but it is I who have called the tune. I have initiated him into the 'Secret Doctrine,' opened his centers in vision and given him the means to communicate with the Powers. Do not mourn me: I shall have influenced history more than any other German." This secret doctrine was an amalgamation of ideas and philosophies largely stemming from the theosophical works of Madame Blavatsky.

Reichsfuhrer SS Heinrich Himmler appropriated the legend of Thule from Eckart and Karl Haushofer. Haushofer was a professor at the University of Munich. It was here that he terrorized an important segment of the German academic world into perpetuating the myth of German racial superiority. He was also a member of Vril, which was another secret society based on a book by British Rosicrucian Lord Bulward Litton, about the visit of an Aryan super race to earth in the distant past. Haushofer mentored not only Adolph Hitler but also his deputy, Rudolf Hess. Haushofer also developed Hitler's geopolitical policy of "Lebensraum," or more living space for a land-locked Germany. He felt his German's

Workers' Party needed a charismatic leader who could enthrall the people with tales of national greatness once lost but possible to recover. He once described Hitler as a "child of Illuminism." Hitler's intellectual roots included Hegel and his philosophies, ancient history, Eastern religions, Yoga, occultism, hypnotism, Theosophy and astrology.

While in Vienna, Hitler also met Jorg Lanz Von Liebenfels, the publisher of "Ostara," a magazine with occult and erotic themes. Liebenfels was a Cistercian monk who founded the anti-Semitic, Secret Order of the New Templars. With his mentor, Guido Von List, he sought to revive the Medieval Brotherhood of Teutonic Knights, which had used the swastika as its emblem. List was a respected author on pan-German mysticism until he was chased out of Vienna following disclosures that his secret brotherhood had involved sexual perversions and medieval black magic.

It was the philosophy of Liebenfels and List, extolling the glories of pagan occultism and the superiority of the Aryan race that provided the intellectual foundation for the Thule Society. Both Liebenfels and Von List were occultists, who had borrowed heavily from Blavatsky. They sought to show how the ancient Germans had been the keepers of a secret science that would elevate the German people to their rightful status among other nations.

It was their Pan-German "volkisch" movement that gave rise to the Nazi Party. If it did this for Hitler, one could just imagine what havoc this thinking might reek in the United States.

New Age authority, Constance Cumbey also discovered that Hitler believed in the same kind of occultism as the New Age Movement, that is Gnosticism and Mysticism. She says that the "plans of Alice Bailey, which are followed with precision by the New Age Movement, are identical to Nazism." They both resonate well with the same kind of fascination with mysticism and the black arts that have become fashionable today. The New Age elite does not believe in a transcendent God to whom all are accountable. They do not believe in good or evil. There is no heaven or hell. Good Friday, Christmas and Easter were unnecessary appendages on the human calendar. This might explain why Americans have such great fascination with Halloween in America. It is not just human nature that they want to recreate but Western Civilization itself. Futurists, Alvin, and Heidi Toffler said it themselves, in their book, with a forward by Newt Gingrich, "Creating a New Civilization."

This all begs the question of "what has any of this to do with 'conspiracy?'" Marilyn Ferguson in her book, "the Aquarian Conspiracy," shows great insight into exactly how a political-religious conspiracy can take place. She writes of an unseen but powerful network that has broken with the American past. They have coalesced into small groups and live in every hamlet imaginable across the country. She is referring to "Non-governmental Organizations. (NGO's) There are legions of these conspirators. They are in corporations, the universities, hospitals, factories and doctors' offices, and in state and federal agencies. According to Ferguson, the "paradigm of the Aquarian Conspiracy" sees humankind embedded in nature. It promotes the autonomous individual in a decentralized society." These spiritual conspirators are using their outposts of influence to combat the old ideas that have preserved man's traditional concept of love. These dangerous myths and mystiques are presumably the basic essence of the Christian religion, especially those surviving tenets of the Catholic Church. It is called "Aquarian," to stress its benevolent nature in anticipation that after such a dark period the world is entering a "millennium of love and light," or what Jesuit Pierre Teilhard de Chardin called a "conspiracy of love." To him it is a conspiracy of men and women whose "new perspective would trigger a critical contagion of change." The Aquarian Conspiracy is the logical outcome of the concerted attack that Cultural Marxists have unleashed on the traditional concepts of Christian Orthodoxy since the Protestant Revolution in the sixteenth century undermined the very foundations of Western belief.

The New Age is a leaderless but powerful network that is attempting to create a New World spiritual philosophy. It is the spiritual equivalent of Sobran's "hive." Its members have broken away from the traditional way of thinking, praying and believing.

It is an apostasy of love and re-directed faith. According to Ferguson it is a "new mind—the ascendance of a startling worldview that gathers into its framework breakthrough science and insights from earlier recorded thought." Their disciples come from all walks of life. They are schoolteachers, government officials, artists, lawmakers, scientists and homemakers. Believers serve in hospitals, corporations, law offices and on the White House staff. Their thoughts are in all the bookstores that have New Age sections larger than those devoted to Organized Religion.

The Aquarian conspirators have gleaned their doctrines from the alchemists, Gnostics, cabalists and hermetic of the past. Their early secrets now have become "open secrets." They are now spiritually free and the "stewards of our own evolution." The Transcendentalists were some of their early American progenitors, such as Ralph Waldo Emerson, Henry David Thoreau and Bronson Alcott. They felt something was missing from the religious debates of their day. They called it an "Oversoul." They sought understanding from several sources in this country, such as the Inner Light of Quakerism but it was essentially the Orient that provided the strongest influence in this new thinking.

There is a strong scent of Buddhism and Hinduism in the evolution of the New Age Mind. They also looked to Germanic Romantic philosophers and the writings of Swedenborg and the seventeenth century English metaphysicians. Theirs was a search for meaning and transcendence. They looked for God in others and then found God in themselves. Once this happened it did not take a great leap of faith to arrive at the conclusion that the self is God or a form of God.

The teaching profession has been another weapon employed to brainwash and propagandize the general population about the New Age Religion. Just as Bella Dodd and her agents were instrumental in infiltrating and undermining the teacher's unions in the early 1930's, the new thinkers intended to mobilize the teaching skills and enthusiasm of sixteen million teachers nationwide in this Herculean experiment in mind control. One of the prime movers in this has been Stephen Rockefeller. A religion professor at Middlebury College in Vermont and scion of the Rockefeller family, he is the chairman of the Rockefeller Brothers Fund and Earth Charter International Drafting Committee. Their Website declares that these values of the Earth Charter must be "taught, contemplated and internalized." It urges that various communities must "integrate the Charter into the curriculum of schools and universities, and constitute an ongoing process of life-learning."

In his book, "A Religion for the New Age," John Dunphy remarked that he was "convinced that the battle for humankind's future must be waged and won in the public school classroom by teachers who correctly perceive their role as the proselytizers of a new faith." To Dunphy, the New Age was "a religion of humanity that recognizes and respects the spark of what theologians call divinity in every human being." It is here that the "battle between the rotting corpse of Christianity . . . and the new faith will be waged."

The apostles of the New Age religion firmly believe in the Gaia Hypothesis, a grand synthesis that considers the earth one vital, living organism. Gaia was the goddess of earth in Greek mythology. It was British scientist James Lovelock and the late Carl Sagan's ex-wife, Lynn Margulis, who promoted the Gaia ideology that modern man is morally responsible for maintaining Nature's fragile balance. True Gaians understand that the traditional Christian mindset is a threat to their enlightened paradigm because the Mosaic Law prohibits worshiping false gods before Me. This explains the dedicated attack on the Catholic Church. Feminists and other spiritualists, such as witchcraft, goddess worship, eco-feminism, and other pagans have joined in the movement supporting the mystical quasi-religious Gaia. All these groups are interwoven with the visionary and artistic tradition. The ecology movement, feminists and libertarians are all natural parts of the movement. The New Age has something for every one, like a Forrest Gumpian box of chocolates.

Former Vice-President Al Gore shares much in the New Age approach to religious belief. In his book "Earth In the Balance," Gore insisted that Western Civilization was dysfunctional and that those who resisted his radical environmental prescriptions were in denial, were mentally infirm and could not be trusted to exercise their rights honestly. His chapter, "Environmentalism of the Spirit," followed Blavatsky's template of exalting pagan religious systems, such as Native American spiritualism, Hinduism, Ba'hai and goddess worship, while at the same time indicting the theology of human dominion over the earth as the root of our environmental crisis. Gore stressed that monotheism was an outdated model for the world of the future. Empowerment must come from consulting the wisdom distilled by all faiths. Gore believes that the automobile was the greatest threat to the continuation of Western civilization. Gore lamented the fact that the human race having lost its "feeling of connectives to the rest of the nature." He accepted the macro-evolutionary theory without batting a skeptic eyelash and also "posits global climactic changes as essential to human evolution . . ." He pointed out the earth-honoring wisdom of American Indian spirituality, that of the Hindus, the Buddhists and Islam. He accepted at face value the belief of the Gaia hypothesis in pre-historic Europe in which the prevailing spirituality centered on the worship of "a single earth goddess."

The roots of New Age Environmentalism run very deep. Like good Marxists, environmentalists believe that private property and Christianity are threats to the earth. The process of eliminating Christianity from the face of the earth involves more than secularizing Christmas and Easter. This revival of a natural religion opens another front on the war on the middle class and its value structure. Millions of people who fear for their survival and that of the planet will be seduced by this terminology, especially if it clothes itself in the religious language of traditional teachings. Before people know it, they will forget the primary purpose of traditional faith—the avoidance of sin and the salvation of one's soul. There is no commandment against littering or wasting tap water. But there is one prohibiting the worship of false gods, the very nexus of what constitutes religious environmentalism.

While the Environmental Movement began with an emphasis on scientific data, activists have always resorted to terminology, such as ancient cathedral for native forests and the desecration of nature warning that an apocalypse would result from human transgressions against Mother Earth. These sentiments hearken back to a 1967 written article by Lynn White in "Science Magazine" that argued that environmentalism would only succeed when it had a religious foundation. This echoes the belief of John Muir, the founder of the Sierra Club in 1892, who referred to the sound of wind in the trees as "psalm singing." To the New Age environmentalist, the wilderness was a "terrestrial manifestations of God." This reflects Muir's New England Transcendentalism, which held "that nature was the best link between God and humanity." Their Puritan forebears inspired Emerson, Thoreau, and their followers. According to colonial historian Perry Miller, "New England Puritans were obsessed with the theology of nature." In the Puritan theology of the colonial period, "everyday plants and animals of the natural world were like ministers and apostles of God, the vehicle and the way by which we are carried to God."

A New World Religion fits in perfectly with the notion of a one-world government because global unity is essential to the god-flow, which goes through all natural things. Pantheism originated in the ancient Babylon and then spread to all corners of the globe. According to its doctrine, everything has an equal, intrinsic value. Man has no more value than a tree, rock, water, mouse, mosquito, rattlesnake or bubonic plague virus. This is the impetus behind the anti-human bias that propels this radical environmentalism.

This also helps to explain why so many people are prone to accept New Age thinking. It resonates with the Puritan underpinnings of American colonial history. Some might conclude that New Age thought is somehow uniquely American and therefore worth preserving. The fallacy inherent in New Age thinking is that while it make many overtures to religion and the powers of a godhead, that godhead bears no resemblance to the God of the Judeo-Christian roots of American Civilization. At best, their thinking more closely resembles Animism, or the attribution of conscious life to nature or natural objects. At worst, it is Pantheism without the idea of a death with judgment from a personal God.

The New Age's marriage with environmentalism is a sterile planetary union. The New World Order's elites are prolific in stressing the need for strict population controls in the Third Millennium. In 1989 the "Washington Post" published an article by foreign policy expert George Kennan in which he said, "we must prepare instead for . . . an age where the great enemy is not the Soviet Union, but the rapid deterioration of our planet as a supporting structure for civilized life." Lester Brown, director of the Worldwatch Institute wrote in their 1991 annual report entitled "The State of the World," that the battle to save the planet will replace the battle over ideology as the organizing theme of the NWO. The influential Club of Rome, whose membership roster includes Council of Foreign Relations members Jimmy Carter, Claiborne Pell and Sol Linowitz, answers overpopulation with a plan for world government to control birth rates through birth control, abortion and euthanasia if necessary.

In their 1991 book "The First Global Revolution," Pell and Linowitz wrote, "in searching for a new enemy to unite us, we came up with the idea that pollution, the threat of global warming, water shortages, famine, and the like would fit the bill . . . All these dangers are caused by human intervention . . . The real enemy then is humanity itself." Others, who worried about overpopulation, included the late Fabian Socialist, Bertrand Russell. He believed that there would be no stability unless there was a world government that could control the worlds' food supply. If one nation had too many people, the government could withhold their food ration until their population decreased in number. If that failed, he also suggested that a bacterial war could be spread through highly populated areas each generation. The survivors could procreate freely without fear of filling the earth.

Willis Harman's essay, "Our Hopeful Future: Creating a Sustainable Society," near the turn of the last century grappled with the population problem. In the economy-dominated world, as the outspoken anthropologist Margaret Mead once put it bluntly, "The unadorned truth is that we do not need now, and will not need later, much of the marginal labor—the very young, the very old, the very uneducated, and the very stupid." Harman indicated that society can't afford from an environmental standpoint of tearing apart of the social fabric—the economic growth that would be necessary to provide jobs for all in the conventional sense, and the inequities which have come to accompany that growth.

Worldwide availability of abortion figures largely in the environmentalists' plans to limit world population. In the late 1960's, Planned Parenthood revealed its goal of family limitation to one child per family. This is not much different then the repressive and violent policies of the People's Republic of China. Stephen Mosher's articles and books on China describe the harrowing tales of truckloads of late-term pregnant mothers on their way to abortion centers. Planned Parenthood promised that abortion on demand would result in less child abuse, divorce and crime. Illegitimacy and poverty would cease if we just had free, legal and safe abortion. Since Mosher's book in 1990, all of these social pathologies have increased geometrically. While there are approximately 1.3 million annual abortions in the United States, the worldwide figure hovers around 40 million.

A logical consequence of this policy of worldwide abortion under the rubric of population control is to dehumanize human beings. One way to do this is to regard them as no better than lower animal species. In his fascinating book, "The Intellectuals and the Masses," John Carey explored the tendency to dehumanize groups of people by the use of pejorative terms, such as vermin, scum and swarming insects. At the end of the last century, it was commonplace among intellectuals such as Bernard Shaw, H.G. Wells, Virginia Wolf, E.M. Forster and others, such as Adolph Hitler, to use such dehumanizing language in describing the Jews. In the same vein, Green Literature describes humans as a horde of rats, an uncontrolled virus, and an infestation on the planet. The "London Times" in 1989 devoted an issue to "The World Is Dying" with the ominous and threatening subheading, "You Damage the Earth By Living on It."

The last twenty years have witnessed a growing movement to establish legal rights for animals. Throughout the Western world, a plethora of laws have been passed to protect whales, seals, birds of prey, spotted owls and natterjack toads. There is scarcely any animal or insect species which has not found its constituency of human supporters. It seems that every existing species is eternally valuable to the delicate balance of the eco-structure. This movement thoroughly devalues the sanctity of human life as it lowers the latter in a false argument of the egalitarian nature of all life.

At the same time, abortion or "womb cleansing" has become widely accepted as a normal part of Western life styles. Despite the great advances in embryology and fetology, which have established beyond a doubt that the baby in the womb is alive and human from the moment of conception, many Western nations have taken steps to remove legal protection from the unborn. The child in the womb no longer enjoys the most basic of all human rights: the right to life. Abortion has also led to the acceptance of practices so barbaric that they would have been regarded as unthinkable only thirty years ago. These include the trade in human parts from aborted fetuses, the use of living embryos for experimental purposes, the cannibalizing of aborted babies to patch-up adult patients suffering from Parkinson's Disease and the infamous "partial birth abortions." If human beings are really a form of pollution, a sort of cancer on the face of earth, then it makes sense why the Greens advocate using the abortionist's knife to cut the cancer out. This juxtaposition of basic animal life with human life is just another page torn from the writings of George Orwell.

Many people have used environmentalism to fill the spiritual void created by secular humanism. New Agers have tried to superimpose an exalted, ritualistic view of nature that echoes the natural religions of the ancient pagans onto traditional teachings. Matthew Fox, a former Catholic priest and the author of "The Coming of the Cosmic Christ," describes the Earth as a kind of Christ figure. He deems any theology that views Jesus' personhood as a unique revelation as "Christofascism." He urges Christians to move beyond a theology based on sin and redemption toward a spirituality of creation with nature as its primary revelation. Fox has repudiated Christian tradition and replaced it with a utopian naturalism that totally distorts the Christian message. Another clerical luminary in this New World Religion is Father Thomas Berry who has substituted being one with Mother Earth for the traditional biblical relationship with God. His book, "The Dream of the Earth," has fast become a primary Gaian text. It is laced with sermons that stress the urgency of replacing the old above-the-earth religion with an earth-centered enlightenment.

Many liberals assent to the belief that the New World religion is more an absolute faith in mankind. Machiavelli was responsible for transferring religious fervor from eternal spiritual goals to socio-political ends. He held that religion is good only when it serves the State by encouraging civil virtues. While Machiavelli would be right at home with regard to the politicization of environmental problems, it is difficult to believe that he would approve of our civil virtues of aberrant homosexual behavior and unrestricted abortion rights. According to Thomas Molnar, Machiavelli and philosopher Comte de Saint-Simon believed that religion was merely a phase in man's gradual understanding of himself and his world.

Julian Huxley was in full agreement with Machievelli and de Saint-Simon. His religious cynicism prompted him to write that religion was to be equated with "cynicism, stupidity, dishonesty and ignorance." Huxley believed "gods are peripheral phenomena produced by evolution, leaving us to conclude that stupidity, dishonesty and ignorance." Huxley also believed that "all shelters for religious belief are only the peripheral manifestations of an inferior phase in evolution, all of which, except for a few fossilized specimens, will vanish why higher phases have vanished." Once this higher plateau is reached, men will no longer have any use for the "god hypothesis" because they will be intelligent and well educated without any need for a personal god. This sentiment adapts perfectly to the neo-Gnostic sense of elitism that propels much of the environmental movement in the world.

Julian's brother, writer Aldous Huxley, was one of the high priests of this philosophy. They were both grandsons of Thomas Huxley, who was one of the founders of the Rhodes Roundtable. Aldous Huxley was one of the initiates in the "Children of the

Sun," a Dionysian cult comprised of the children of Britain's Roundtable elite. Among the initiates were T. S. Eliot, W.H. Auden, and D. H. Lawrence, who was Aldous Huxley's male lover. Huxley had studied at Oxford where H. G. Wells tutored him. In his book, "Open Conspiracy," he detailed the rationale behind the idea of a conspiracy. To him it was "a conscious organization of intelligent and quite possibly . . . wealthy men, as a movement having distinct social and political aims, ignoring most of the apparatus of political control."

Huxley went to Hollywood in 1937. He and pederast Christopher Isherwood were scriptwriters for MGM, Warner Brothers, and Walt Disney Studios. Here he founded a nest of Isis cults in southern California and later in San Francisco. They read and practiced Zen Buddhism before it became a California fad. Huxley experimented with hallucinogenic drugs, including mescaline. In 1953, he wrote "The Doors of Perception," the first manifesto of the psychedelic drug culture, which claimed that hallucinogenic drugs "expanded consciousness." LSD and peyote followed. Ken Kesey, who wrote "One Flew over the Cuckoo's Nest," became one of the leaders in "flower power."

In 1958, Huxley revealed his vision of what the purpose of government was in his "Brave New World Revisited." He described a society where war had been eliminated and the "first aim of rulers is at all costs to keep their subjects from making trouble." The likely future to him in the completely organized society was to eliminate the free will by "methodical conditioning." This would make their compliance in this servitude by "regular doses of chemically induced happiness. This would be a stylized form of chemical tyranny. (Prozac and Ritalin come to mind too quickly for it to be a coincidence.)

In 1962, Huxley helped found the Esalen Institute in Big Sur, California. This became the mecca for hundreds of Americans to engage in weekends of T-Groups modeled on the behavior studies of B. F. Skinner. They also practiced Zen, Hindu and Buddhist transcendental meditation, and had out of body experiences. Their newsletter described that Esalen was "started in the fall of 1962 as a forum to bring together a wide variety o approached to enhancement of the human potential . . ." They did this with encounter groups, sensory awakening, gestalt awareness training and other related disciplines. Huxley spent the rest of his life living and working with Cultural Marxists, Theodor Adorno and Max Horkheimer. He died on November 22, 1963, the same day President John Kennedy and English philosopher C. S. Lewis died. True to form, his last request was for an injection of LSD.

If this movement were to have a patron saint, it would undoubtedly be French Jesuit, Pierre Teilhard de Chardin. A paleontologist who died in 1955, Father Teilhard made the mistake of mixing religion and philosophy with his science. This mixture has caused him to be badly misunderstood by a generation of readers. As the author of such books as "The Divine Milieu" and "The Phenomenon of Man," Teilhard appealed to many New Agers who erroneously assumed that his attempt to reconcile the religious theory of creation with the scientific theory of evolution supported their neo-pagan view of creation. New Age advocates have interpreted his belief that man was evolving mentally and socially toward a final spiritual unity, to mean that we were all one with the earth. While Fr. Teilhard emphasized the communion of all men, present, past and future, his teaching should not be taken to mean that God is a mere impersonal representation of the unity of all things. Teilhard saw the earth as transformed by Christ, arguing that since God took human form humans should also embrace the world rather than reject it. By acting, human beings cooperate in the Almighty's creative powers. But they must act with their faith rooted in the belief that everything forms a single whole. Philosopher Etienne Gilson has labeled Teilhard's Gnostic interpretations of Divine Revelation as "theology fiction."

Like all utopians, Teilhard was apprehensive about human freedom and insisted on reducing it to a strict planned order, recommending eugenic measures to discipline the human race. When the utopian finds that mankind does not fit in or is an obstacle to his order of things, he abandons the idea of political regimentation and directs his plan to medical intervention. As the world saw during the "Nazi Utopia" total power permitted medical experimentation in view of what is euphemistically called improving the quality of the race. This idea appealed to both Adolph Hitler and Margaret Sanger, the founder of Planned Parenthood. Professor Thomas Molnar argues correctly that it would be an error to separate Teilhard's religious utopianism from "the quixotic manifestations of today's totalitarian ideologies and empires." Teilhard's thinking merely sets the problem of man, as the utopian sees it, on a loftier plane although his terminology—a composite of archaeology, sociology, biology, astronomy and a vulgarized theology—can easily be translated into the language of collectivism and totalitarianism.

Fr. Teilhard creates an artificial separation between two imaginary categories of men. He simply labels people of belief and people of unbelief. His contributions to utopian philosophy are akin to the sprinkling of some holy water in the form of an undeniable and intangible substance which he calls "a passionate longing to grow and to be or consummated human thought." Evolutionary utopians, such as Teilhard or Marx preach, not of freedom, openness or progress but of "a frozen rigidity as to the desirable ideal and the mechanism of adaptations which leads to it."

New Agers agree with many of Teilhard's theories because they revolve around the abolition of war and the establishment of a world government. This is why liberals can regard the enslavement of millions under communist tyranny as merely a temporary misfortune which will ultimately evolve into something good. The very idea of global unity assumes the existence of a new and mature mankind capable of transcending all the evil that used to be mankind. Teilhard's "new man" is derived not from religious conversion, but from political turmoil. Thinkers, like Teilhard, believe that perfection is an attainable goal on this earth and its religious nature is best reflected in an evolutionary pantheism that will lead them to increase their moral substance among brotherhood that will result in what Teilhard called the "divine milieu."

In Christian revelation, the stress is on the salvation of each individual person. Teilhard's theology stresses the progress of the earth leading to his Christ-Omega who bears little resemblance to the biblical Christ. In his prophetic book, "Trojan Horse in the City of God," German philosopher Dietrich Von Hildebrand says that Teilhard is a false prophet more dangerous to Catholic teaching than Voltaire, Renan or Nietzsche because of his apparent devotion to Christian imagery. Von Hildebrand likened Teilhard to one of the many termites who undermines Christian faith with their claim that they are is giving to Christian revelation the interpretation that suits "modern man".

Where Teilhard went wrong is that he identified God with the universe—a standard pantheistic procedure that has found a home among New Age philosophers of the New World Order. The God of Teilhard's system is tied to the evolution of matter for God could not have created life and later man, unless the material preconditions were ready. According to Teilhard, God is not a static Being but grows along with His creation. He is not an Almighty God, but limited in His powers and His relation to mankind. Sooner or later the heretic will associate this kind of god with Hegel's Absolute Spirit of history, secularizing the notion of a personalized God.

The solidification of the New Age Religion, as many other liberals and conspiratorial ideas has looked to the United Nations and its world structure in an effort to provide the vehicle and structure for the new universal religion. Eldon K. Winkler's book "The New Age is Lying to You," has emphasized just how diverse and widespread the New Age Movement has become. The New Age is an umbrella term that connects a weblike structure of people and ideas that fall under the mantle of the "Hive Theory of Liberalism." They have no central organization that directs them, with one human leader but rather a honeycomb of like-minded people who all desire social change and a new spiritual reawakening that will usher in an existential age of self-fulfillment. They believe that all religions are equally true, no matter how contradictory they may be.

Writer William Jasper thoroughly explored this phenomenon in his feature article for the "The New American," in September of 2002, "New World Religion: The U.N. Earth Charter." The charter is actually a diabolical blueprint for world government. Mikhail Gorbachev believes that it "will be a kind of Ten Commandments," a proverbial "Sermon on the Mount," that will serve as a "guide for human behavior toward the environment in the next century and beyond." This coincides with the deliberate policy to subvert and expunge all vestiges of God, religious symbols and traditional religion observations from the public marketplace. We have witnessed the elimination of the Pledge of Allegiance, the posting of the Ten Commandments in schools, Nativity scenes, the use of the greeting "Merry Christmas," the singing of religious hymns and songs at Christmas and even the elimination of the Crucifix in some Catholic institutions of higher learning.

The Earth Charter was formally unveiled at the Earth Summit meeting held in Johannesburg, South Africa, during Earth Summit II in the Summer of 2002. Many feel it will become the Holy Writ of the world's new "global spirituality." Its preamble states: "We are one human family and on Earth community with a common destiny. We must join together to bring forth a sustainable global society founded on respect for nature . . . Towards this end, it is imperative that we, the peoples of Earth, declare our responsibility to one another, to the greater community of life, and to future generations." It also states that humanity must undergo a global change of mind and heart. It plans to recruit America's children to serve as agents for this new consciousness in understanding the plight of the planet and Americans' deep responsibility to protect and cherish it. Professor Steven C. Rockefeller has written that the "Earth Charter is the product of a worldwide, cross-cultural interfaith dialogue of common goals and shared values that has been conducted as a civil society initiative." In actuality, according to Jasper," this is not a grass-roots campaign "but a loosely controlled, top-down operation, masquerading as 'dialogue'"

The Earth Charter is the product of a coalition of non-governmental groups, mainly environmental groups, with a strong admixture of feminist organizations. They work in cooperation with the United Nations and national governments in an attempt to gain juridical status for this document. According to Maurice Strong, the Earth Charter promulgates the "basic principles for the conduct of nations and peoples with respect to the environment and development, to ensure the future viability and integrity of the earth as a hospitable home for humans and other life forms." The notion of sustainable development and its attendant ideas and policies is implicit in this document. This document presents a holistic formula for the governance of the international community. It is important that people realize that this charter is not just an environmental charter. It has serious ramifications for the future of global freedom and humanity. They believe the "Charter," can be used to effect the New World Order.

The charter itself is housed and transported in something they call the "Ark of Hope," a blasphemous mimicry of the Biblical Ark of the Covenant, which held the two tablets, proclaiming the Ten Commandments. In this case, imitation is *not* the highest form of flattery but a vain attempt to devalue and undercut something of the sacred traditions of the Christian religion. Its' followers pay the same respect and solemnity that religious believers would pay to the Ark of the Covenant. It is one of the totems the U. N. uses in its new global eco-religion. This Ark, its Charter and Temenos Books were placed on display at the U. N. Summit.

Before it was taken to the Summit in South Africa, the Charter was carried by foot, car and boat and arrived in New York City, on November 8, 2001 to be greeted by 1960's radical, singer, Pete Seeger. On January 24, 2001 the Ark and the Charter were carried in a procession from the Interfaith Center of New York to the United Nations Church Center Chapel, a distance of fifteen blocks. To these disciples, the earth is a sacred place and all human beings have. It is the responsibilty of the world's people to choose "between the forces of darkness and the forces of light." The old way of doing things, the way of our forebears has been replaced by the "enlightened" way of compassion and concern for the sustainability of the planet. Population controls must be effected and unnecessary people eliminated, by stealth and without any advanced fanfare. A naïve and undereducated global population will not see the signs of their own destruction coming. Children, college students, university professors, journalists and media moguls will invest all their energy to make this Charter appear to be a grass roots movement. It is the inescapable wave of the present.

12

Under Heaven's Banner

"Americans were . . . the Israel of our time." Herman Melville in "White Jacket."

The debate over imperial designs and the New World Order has wreaked havoc with the American people. Much of the debate has brought out into the open what being an America really means. This situation revolves around the idea of "patriotism." The American Flag is a good place to start. Flags are convenient and visible symbols of a nation's heritage. The attacks on the World Trade Center and the Pentagon on September 11, 2001 seemed to have led to an outpouring of patriotic fervor that bordered on a religious happening. The urban landscape seemed buried in a surfeit of American flags. From automobiles, lapel pins, front lawns and window decals to tee shirts, caps and underwear, "Old Glory," displays were ubiquitous. The excess of flag-waving exuberance was overwhelming. Such vulgar exhibitions turned what should have been a reverential showing of true love of country into a gaudy display of self-indulgent "Hey look at me" chauvinism.

The subsequent wars in Afghanistan and Iraq have given further test to both nascent and deep feelings of patriotism. Most Americans were in favor of weeding out both the "evil doers," the infamous al-Qaeda cells and the destruction of the theocratic Taliban in Afghanistan but the invasion of Iraq caused consternation, especially among American Catholics. Pope John Paul II severely condemned the war, evoking the "just war theory."

President George W. Bush tried his best to sell a complex war to the American people with a simple rhetoric that ignored the many nuances of the long-range conflict. He offered a farrago of reasons that included his strongest argument, the elusive "Weapons of Mass Destruction," (WMD) which the President knew were there, but could really never find. Saddam was purportedly to have been linked to Osama bin Laden in some mysterious way. Today they are linked only in their mutual disappearance. For all the American public knows, they both reside in a New Jersey cave with their weapons of mass destruction.

President Bush made overtures to the United Nations but they ended in a frenzied display of stonewalls and biting criticism. As a result, the President had very few members in his "coalition." Most Europeans led by France and Germany, together at last, did everything they could to prevent President Bush's pre-emptive war. After the war was won, U. S. Deputy Defense Secretary, Paul Wolfowitz revealed in a "Vanity Fair" interview that the WMD were more of a "bureaucratic" excuse for the war than any viable threat.

President Bush's deep religious faith has reshaped his life and made him the heir to the Puritan tradition of America's messianic promise. He believes that since he is not only fulfilling America's historical promise but God's divine mission, how could anyone of faith stand against him. It is the nation's Calvinist past that is fueling this push for world domination. If it is America's duty to rid the world of evildoers, then anyone who stands against the president must be evil. That is the twisted logic of the Bush Presidency. If evil is loose in the world, then it is America's job to destroy that evil wherever it may reside. His vision is suspect. Evil lurks in every abortion clinic in America, yet Bush has been uneasy about seeking it out and destroying it. There will be no pre-emptive strike on Planned Parenthood because there is no oil or business interest inherent in its demise.

The war was an especially hard choice for American Catholics. No true Catholic ever wants to be outside of what the Pope teaches. Many others felt uneasy about the idea of another war, which could possibly end in what Samuel Huntington called "A Clash of

Civilizations" and inevitably World War III. The media continually fanned the flames that sparked into a blaze of paralyzing fear that included Islamic jihads, or "holy wars," terrorist bombings of sports arenas, airports, and shopping malls. Fear and anger formed their own potent coalition in these often-heated debates. Fortunately, most debates stopped when the first missiles hit Baghdad because our sons and, regrettably some of our daughters, were in harm's way. George Wiegel, the Pope's official biographer, politely disagreed with his most renowned subject and said that America's pre-emptive strike on Iraq did, in his opinion, pass all of the tests of the just war theory.

Before the war started commentators, such as radio host Rush Limbaugh, tried to rouse their audiences into rage that bordered on war mongering. I had never been exposed to such a raucous clamor for war in my life. It was as if the U. S. S. Maine, Pearl Harbor and the Gulf of Tonkin had all happened at the same time. Then again New York City's Financial Center had been reduced to bloody rubble. The Pentagon had been scorched. When Americans feel violated, someone must pay dearly.

Others such as national conservative Catholic columnist, Joseph Sobran, viewed the war differently. He wrote several columns denouncing the war, defending the Pope and rebuking the President. Others, the so-called Paleolithic conservatives such as former presidential hopeful, Pat Buchanan, were quick to link the war with imperialism, oil and the "Amen corner" of pro-Israel lobbyists, who seemed to project a "dual patriotism," for America and Israel.

Were these writers unpatriotic by arguing against the war? Were they bad Americans because they attempted to warn America of what they perceived as a dangerous course of action? Was this another classic case of "the enemy within?" They certainly were not kin to the bearded pack of unwashed nation-hating hippies left over from the Vietnam War. They wore suits, went to church and paid their taxes. Like most Americans, they never engaged in public protests with hateful placards. Unlike the revolutionary priests of the Vietnam War, the Berrigans, Daniel and Philip, they never vandalized draft records with goat's blood, impeded the war effort in any physical way, nor had they sold military secrets to the Iraqis. They had merely used the power of their keyboards to express opposing ideas about a war that quite possibly could have severe unintended consequences, thus impacting the nation for generations to come.

Many pro-war advocates strongly condemned this kind of thinking. For their efforts in defending the integrity of the nation, traditional conservatives were subjected to a savage flurry of personal attacks that deemed them "un-American," "unpatriotic," and even "treasonous." The crescendo of vitriol reached its pinnacle with Canadian writer David Frum's feature article, "Unpatriotic Conservatives," in the "National Review" for April 7, 2003. David Frum, a former presidential speech writer who gave us such memorable lines as "axis of evil" singled out Sobran, Buchanan, Sam Francis, Bob Novak and others for as being un-American, racist, and anti-Semitic. The latter epithet is the moral equivalent of what "National Conservative Magazine," writer Scott McConnell has called "the nuclear weapon" of personal attacks.

In a more sinister attempt to vilify and silence critics of the war, "NewsMax.com" raised the ante with their production and distribution of a "Deck of Weasels." This nasty deck of cards was a pale imitation of the "Deck of Death" cards the Pentagon had issued to aid in their capture of Saddam Hussein, his sons, high-ranking officials and military executioners. These American "weasels," included members of the Hollywood elite, such as Barbra Streisand, Jane Fonda, Michael Moore, Martin Sheen, Susan Sarandon, Sean Penn and politicos Democratic Senators Ted Kennedy and Robert "KKK" Byrd. The "weasels" deck was promoted as "great fun." I found the cards to be dangerously inflammatory, and unworthy of the high-minded idealism that has been evident in support of the war. These pejorative cards spoke loud volumes about those who supported the bloodshed in Iraq.

Sobran had a warning about "patriotism." To him "A lot of people assume that patriotism means supporting any war your government chooses to get into." Many would agree with that. One of Sobran's readers opined that the government should go to the extreme of "nuking Damascus, Baghdad, Teheran and for good measure, Paris." Sobran is absolutely correct. Love of country does not mean love of one's government. Political leaders come and go. Some have been statesmen, while others have been scoundrels. It was former President Bill Clinton who wrapped the American Flag around his sordid presidency. When the Murrah Building in Oklahoma City was bombed in 1995, he painted his critics, especially radio hosts like Rush Limbaugh, with the broad smears of having contributed to the hateful atmosphere that had given rise to the murder of 168 Americans. Clinton echoed the egregious statement that "You can not love country and hate your government." To him "Love thy president!" was the greatest commandment.

This was strange talk coming from someone like Clinton. He had always defined himself as a "world citizen," a member of the global community which sought to eliminate "artificial national borders," and presumably with that "patriotism." He wanted to lead the United States into a world community where national sovereignty was a muddy relic of the past. What Clinton failed to understand was that his loathsome activities engendered more real patriotism in millions of Americans, who despised him for what he had done to the nation's integrity than a month of July fourth parades. Neoconservatives are not fond of patriotism. Irving Kristol believes that nationalism is much different from patriotism. "Patriotism springs from the love of a nation's part," but he adds "nationalism arises out of hope for the nation's future."

In figuratively besmirching the American Flag and everything it stands for, President Clinton trampled on an internal sentiment that many people still hold dear to their hearts. It was Christian philosopher, C. S. Lewis, who best put this into words. In his wonderful short book, "The Four Loves," Lewis discussed patriotism in terms of "affection." To him "affection is the humblest form of love." It is a form of comfort one feels for a pet, a good friend or a favorite book. It is something personal that has become intimately intertwined with one's own sense of self. It does not matter if someone was born in America or migrated to her shores. It becomes part of what people are and what they are most comfortable around. Hyphenated or split loyalties, such as African-American, or Latino-

American, or ethic prejudice for Italian, Irish or Scottish-Americans, undercut the spirit of what a nation proposes to be. The Bible warns that one cannot "serve two masters."

Abortion has been legal in this country for over thirty years. It is deeply embedded in our legal system, court structure and the minds and hearts of millions of Americans. In what seemed just like moments after 9/11, while the bodies still simmered in the Ground Zero devastation, Planned Parenthood offered free abortions to any pregnant woman whose husband or boyfriend had been lost in the attacks. Similarly, after the bombs stopped falling in Kabul, women's groups, urged on by Senator Hillary Clinton, pushed for abortion rights in Afghanistan. A headline on the Internet, promoted by Planned Parenthood, proclaimed that "Iraqi women need abortions." If free access to "abortion services" was an essential component of the democratic heritage of the American way of life, then the country's leaders should expect a great deal of grass roots opposition for its war efforts.

Does the American Flag stand for abortion rights? Is it part of what America is all about? How does one reconcile what this country has stood for and what it now seems to promote with its basic principles of natural law and justice? These are difficult questions without any set answers. This is one good reason why the government can never be allowed to decide who is a patriot and who is not, no matter how many Patriot Acts they may pass. True patriotism seems to gravitate between the two extremes expressed by English lexicographer, Dr. Samuel Johnson, and Naval Officer, Stephen Decatur. Many years before the Declaration of Independence was signed in 1776, Johnson warned, "Patriotism is the last refuge of scoundrels." Decatur proclaimed a toast at an 1815 dinner in his honor, "Our country! In her intercourse with foreign nations may she always be in the right but our country right or wrong."

Sobran corrected these extreme notions when he wrote: "My country win or lose." Unfortunately this approach does not resonate well in the United States. Too many Americans, especially sports fans, are often fair weathered in their affection for their teams.

They are kindred spirits with the "sunshine patriots," of Thomas Paine who decried them in his 1776 pamphlet "Common Sense." The good test then of patriotism is how loyal one is to one's country when it is challenged, defamed, humiliated and punished, without compromising his basic principles. Until Americans can see patriotism in that light, it will be impossible to fully understand what it means to be a patriotic American.

To accuse Joseph Sobran of being disloyal to his country is to demonstrate just how far the neoconservatives have strayed or fled from the traditional conservatism of the Founding Fathers, Edmund Burke and Russell Kirk. Sobran has been even more critical of George W. Bush than he was of his father, the first President Bush. Sobran does not feel that Bush is smart or principled enough to lead the nation into the troubled waters of the twenty-first century. To him, Bush is a "temporary Caesar," who has initiated a bloody war with true Constitutional justification. Sobran is a true Renaissance Man with a scholar's expertise in not just one subject but three. He knows and writes with passion and insight on the U.S. Constitution, Abraham Lincoln and William Shakespeare. His modern role, unfortunately in American social and political issues, is to play the role of the disabused prophet whose stinging words irritate and generate the scorn of his subjects. As a modern day Joshua, Jeremiah, and Ezekiel, Sobran suffers the indignity of being disrespected in his own land. For his true patriotic fervor, he is scorned and denigrated by the likes of such verbal courtesans as David Frum.

The war in Iraq has thrown a monkey wrench into the equation of the New World Order and the grandiose plans of the Council on Foreign Relations, the Trilaterals and the Bilderbergers. This phenomenon clearly demonstrates that the struggle is not a clash of cultures so much as a clash of utopias. There are two opposing utopian ideologies at work in this dualistic battle of ideas. First is the "world citizen," philosophy of Woodrow Wilson and Bill Clinton as countered by the re-emergence of imperial theories that dominated the thinking of Republicans from William McKinley through the second George Bush.

Clinton, who was an avatar of the Jacobean Revolution, wanted to destroy the "Presidential Monarchy" that is now represented by George W. Bush. In its place he wanted to establish a "New World Order," or a "Universal Republic." The French Revolution served as a blueprint for revolutions of the future. In a very real way, Clinton represents the European approach as contrasted by Bush's the traditional approach.

Robert Kagan has captured the metaphorical symbolism of this dichotomy in his book "Of Paradise and Power." He contrasts Europe's approach and response to world events with that of the United States. His thesis is that strong nations usually view the world in a different way than a weak nation. America has power and is willing to use it as demonstrated in Afghanistan and Iraq. Europe is weak and vulnerable and thusly has a much higher tolerance for terrorism and other international evils. These differences are compounded by their very different historical experiences since the conclusion of World War II. The threat of force and an occasional invasion was crucial in securing America's success in the Cold War. To the United States, when it has a hammer, so many of the world's problems look like nails.

Reviewer Ivo H. Daalder, a senior fellow at the Brookings Institute, says that globalization is a two-edged sword. "It promotes the free flow of goods across borders and thus enhances prosperity and undermines repressive regimes. But porous borders can also be exploited by terrorists, narcotic traffickers and money laundress bent on doing harm." Therefore the consequences of globalization are beyond the powers of any one nation to control, even one as powerful as the United States. The U. S. will have to cooperate with the rest of the world before engaging in a unilateral response to world events. If not, globalization's inevitable gains will be jeopardized.

Kagan also contrasts the different world with the United States being more comfortable in a Hobbesian world of pure power politics and military might, while Europe resides in the more utopian world of Emmanuel Kant, where peace is the ultimate goal and power politics are replaced by negotiations and compromise. It is what Kagan refers to as "Machtpolitik." "Europeans," according to Kant have "stepped out of the Hobbesian world of anarchy into the Kantian world of perpetual peace." Kant had argued that the only solution to the immoral horrors of the Hobbesian world was the creation of a world government. But he also feared that the "state of universal peace," was also fraught with danger and could easily turn into a greater threat to human freedom than the Hobbesian international order, inasmuch as such a government, with its monopoly of power, would become the "most horrible despotism." Kagan adds that the hegemony that America established at the end of the eighteenth century has been a constant part of international politics ever since. The ideas of the American System, coupled with the messianic drive of "Manifest Destiny," have propelled the United States to a position of preeminence in the world today. The U. S. is a "behemoth with a conscience."

George W. Bush is heir to the intellectual largesse of one of the most potent ideas in all of American History, namely that of "Manifest Destiny," or what some called "Anglo-Saxon Destiny." The waters of "Manifest Destiny" run deep within American History and religious culture. It is a characteristic that has dominated American foreign policy since the early nineteenth century. As Benjamin Franklin once pointed out, America's cause "is the cause of mankind." Since the mid-sixteenth century America has been a "city on a hill," the true Christian community that would serve as a beacon to the world.

The President has charted a new course that is more consistent with America's past. "Manifest Destiny," as coined by John L. O'Sullivan in his publication, "the Democratic Review," in the early 1840's, articulates the vision that the United States, so specially blessed by God, has been divinely ordained to spread its boundaries over the entire North American continent and even Mexico. Sullivan believed that expansionism was a natural progression inherent in the American character or what has been called "the American givenness." It is a dynamic combination of messianic puritan zeal and business acumen that has prompted the nation to make the move up the ladder of imperial success. But it is a divergent way of thinking that sees only American fiscal support as the large prop in underscoring the NWO.

This is not the Novus Ordo of the Founding Fathers who saw America as the proverbial," "city on the hill." It is part of the American heritage, mythology if you would, that has underwritten American History throughout the course of its long history. The nation's roots inherent in "Manifest Destiny," belied that patriotic slogan of "all men are created equal," because the nations most in line for American liberation were considered inferior peoples and not able to prosper under the banner of American-inspired democracy. Any way the president shades it, American domination has a built-in aura of superiority that fuels and energizes its expansion.

President Bush also believes that America's bountiful success throughout its history resonate with the country's Puritan heritage that took wealth and prosperity as a providential sign of God's divine favor. It has become an ideological concept that now means the United States has a modern "divine right," not of kings but a "Divine Right of Hegemony," destined to extend the blessings of liberty, democracy, and free trade, to the world, whether they like it or not. This is the notion behind Francis Fukuyama's "The End of History."

The idea of empire is hardly a new one. From Alexander the Great, the Roman Caesars, Mohammed through Napoleon, Adolph Hitler and Josef Stalin, driven men with the vision of world conquest have tried to conquer the world. Often as was the case that behind these well-known men existed a more secretive group that wielded their own subtle but just as ruthless degree of power and influence.

With the rise of the United States to near imperial status after the successful conclusion to the Spanish-American War, the nation's leaders decided that there was no valid reason their imperial ambitions should be confined to the Western Hemisphere. Warren Zimmerman states in his book "First Great Triumph: How Five Americans Made Their Country A World Power," Lieutenant Colonel Theodore Roosevelt rejoiced to his sister Corinne in 1898 that "We have scored the first great triumph in what will be a world movement."

Zimmerman even traced a similar sentiment back to the patently isolationist first President, George Washington, who wrote in 1786 "there will assuredly come a time when this country will have some weight in the scale of Empires." The founding fathers of American foreign policy, according to Zimmerman, were John Hay, Captain Alfred T. Mahan, Elihu Root, Henry Cabot Lodge and Theodore Roosevelt.

On December 21, 1899, after the conclusion of the Spanish-American War, Indiana Republican Senator Albert J. Beveridge recalled Winthrop's promise, as he stood reverently on the floor of the United States House of Representatives. He declared that: "God has made us the master organizers of the world to establish system where chaos reigns. He has given us the spirit of progress to overwhelm the forces of reaction throughout the earth. He has made us adepts in government that we may administer government among savage and senile people, as this world would relapse into barbarism and night. And of our entire race He has marked the American people as His chosen nation to finally lead in the regeneration of the world. This is the divine mission of America and it holds for us all the profit, all the glory all the happiness possible to man. We are trustees of the world' s progress, guardians of its righteous peace."

Zimmerman later stated how Teddy Roosevelt "really did believe" the United States "had a mission to spread the bounties of its civilization beyond its borders." Commenting on Americans in the last third of the nineteenth century, Zimmerman stated "It was a rare American whether of higher or lower education, who did not believe that his country had a special mission, sanctified by geography and race, to lead and dominate less civilized people." The bellicose Roosevelt stated that "the clamor of the peace faction has convinced me that this country needs a war." He also stated "only the warlike powers of a civilized people can give peace to the world." According to Zimmerman, Roosevelt had more on his plate than social justice did in Cuba. Cuba was the leading producer of sugar, which was "the oil of the 20th century." He states that the Cuban rebellion that began in 1895 was a "dangerous threat to American profits."

In the June 2003 issue of "Culture Wars Magazine," Marlene Maloney wrote that George W. Bush "morphed into another Teddy Roosevelt." During the campaign, candidate Bush, said, "our nation has been commissioned by history to be a model for the world. In the wake of September 11th, Bush added, in his State of the Union message on January 28, 2003. "We are called to defend the hopes of all mankind . . . We go forward with confidence because this call of history has come to the right country."

So there is little doubt that America has enjoyed a long and bountiful imperialist past. It has been part of the country's nature for one hundred and fifty years. British historian Niall Ferguson contends that America is an empire but one that "dare not speak its name." Americans insist they are only spreading democracy and "liberating" other nations from their tyrannical governments. According to columnist Joseph Sobran "when the war-making power belongs to the Executive branch, never mind what paper constitutions say: You have empire." It also has an element of what would commonly be called "racism," today.

American imperialism was a unique brand that bore little resemblance to the professional nation builders of Great Britain, sixteenth century Spain, Germany or France. Americans had neither knowledge nor love of foreign cultures. It was nearly impossible to recruit enough civil servants who could make colonial governments work, such as the British have done. It has been America's mercantile class who was most concerned with markets and trade. The American military had its role, such as the "Opening of Japan," to American commerce. While the American Navy, under Commodore Matthew Perry had effected this, it was the work of a trio of American merchants, such as Charles King, Aaron Palmer and Townsend Harris, who became the first American Ambassador to Japan who finalized this seminal event. But Japan was never thought to be anything more than a mere stepping-stone to China, which had countless millions of people. The merchants reasoned that if they could sell their products to the Chinese multitudes, there would be no limit to their profit.

This inevitably led to the Open Door Policy of Secretary of State John Hay, which ostensibly guaranteed free and equality of trade in the xenophobic coastal cities of Mainland China. The idea of "China Market Myth" had encouraged thousands of shippers, traders, and merchants to extend American wares to the Asian and Far Eastern shores. There was never any doubt that America's commercial dominance would be carried into Asia. Many Americans believe that commerce and technology would do as much as Christianity did to bring civilization and progress to the Pacific Region. According to Horsman, "the commercial endeavors of a superior people were confidentially expected to transform the world while bringing unprecedented power and prosperity to the United States." It would be American commercial penetration of the Open Door and American System that would bring civilization, progress, prosperity, and stability to the worlds. This would be the Novus Ordo of things, the New World Order according to George W. Bush. According to neoconservative Harry Jaffe, the United States is in pursuit of "an unrealized vision of American destiny as the Zion that would light up all the world."

It is primarily the same case today with Iraq and the rest of the Middle East. Americans do not have the required patience for long periods of occupation and nation building. As the calendar turns and days turn into months, it became apparent that the U.S. population and many of its fighting forces did not have the patience necessary for long-term success. It is business that drives the American engine of world conquest. As historian Carl Degler points out that American imperialism "differed from the classic European form in that it did not seek administrative control over markets and peoples, but principally access to markets." Islam is incompatible with all these notions of American Empire and it must go as a viable creed, different from the secular humanism of the West. The spiritual qualities, especially with their profound respect for all human life, even the weakest members of society have been squeezed, edited, legislated and coerced out of the social body politic.

Unfortunately this plays right into the power brokers' hands. While Christianity stands as an obstacle to the Cultural Revolution, inspired by Marxist modernism, Islam stands as a militant opposition to the traditional American imperialism and its rival ideology, the one-world order group. Islam, like Christianity, represents an archaic approach to modern problems that is radically out of step with historical progression. It is an obstacle that must be removed from the playing field to allow for the Manichean duality to play out.

According to columnist Sam Francis, America's victory in the Cold war completed the transition from republic to empire. Despite the protestations of George W. Bush to the contrary, Francis asserts that "no one who understands the nature of the New World Order and the new imperialism on which it is based thinks otherwise." He believes that imperialism has taken on a new look. Gone are the old-fashioned rituals of planting a flag on foreign shores. Public Relations led to the reprimand of an over-exuberant American soldier for his attempting to place the Stars and Stripes atop the public statue of fallen tyrant, Saddam Hussein in Baghdad. While gaudy displays were the order of the day in America, on foreign shores, the U. S. government realized their negative connotations. The U. S.'s crusade to export democracy, global capitalism, and the transnational pop-culture that binds them all together into a "unified system of hegemony" does not need flags borders or separate nation-states. Today imperialism requires only the military might and technology to obliterate anything or anyone who gets in the imperial path.

In a strange conflation of ideas, during the aftermath of the 9/11 attacks, Bush pledged to defeat the terrorists who attacked the World Trade Centers by "expanding and encouraging world trade." For Bush, free trade, no matter how detrimental to the American working man, has become an American pillar of faith. With economic aforethought, Bush saw the Iraq War as an opportunity for America to develop its own hegemony in the Middle East.

George W. Bush has mentally imbedded the bellicose philosophy of fellow Bonesman, Henry Stimson, Franklin Roosevelt's Secretary of War. This explains why he is so resigned and dedicated to finishing the job his father left in 1991. It is also imperative that the United States eliminate any obstacle to the formation of the "Novus Ordo" of things. The free flow of oil and the fundamentalist recalcitrance of so many of the Arab nations stand as a moveable obstacle in the path of conquest. American military must clear the path of Islamic Fundamentalism, so that these backward nations can reap the benefits of America's most prized traditions, that is, its democratic institutions and economic expertise.

Andrew Bacevich of Boston University and the author of "American Imperialism," marvels at George Bush's "fusion of breathtaking utopianism with barely disguised 'Machtpolitik.'" To him it reads as if it were "the product not of sober, ostensibly conservative Republicans but of an unlikely collaboration between Woodrow Wilson and the elder Field Marshall von Moltke." It summons what Harry Elmer Barnes called "permanent war for permanent peace." In his book Bacevich lists five components of America's foreign policy that make it an empire. He says, "Like it or not, America today is Rome." First, American leaders believe that the United States is the model society for the future. The nation's neoconservative leaders have vowed to remake the world in its image and likeness, which translates as democratic, capitalist, multi-ethnic and culturally diverse. This would be the end or in Bacevich's words, "the consummation of history," America's historical manifest destiny that is clearly not evident to the rest of the world.

America is the "indispensable nation." He says that the roots for this thinking should be attributed to Marxist-Leninism and Woodrow Wilson. It is the progressive, or what is sometimes called the "Whig Theory of History." According to this theory, History has an evolutionary inevitability about it that one government and its military wing constitute the vanguard of history and that the country should promote democratic revolutions all over the globe. Bush's messianism is the essence of Wilsonianism. Bush, according to Bacevich, sees himself as the instrument of god for world redemption. Bush disdains isolationism as much as any liberal. In a far stretch of the imagination, Bush opined "isolationism flew escort for the very bombers that attacked our men fifty years ago." Given Roosevelt mendacious plot to get America into the war, these words sound as comical as they are historically inaccurate. The second principle is "openness," defined by the author as "the removal of barriers to the movement of goods, capital, people and ideas." It was this very "openness" that allowed the Arab kamikazes to destroy over 3000 American lives. Bush's open immigration policy is an open invitation to another national disaster.

The third component is an insistence on American "global leadership, which Bacevich translates as a euphemism for "Imperial domination." The author believes the "Wolfowitz Doctrine," first enunciated during the waning days of the first Bush Administration serves as an "unofficial" American foreign policy ever since. It was the ever present, Paul Wolfowitz, who espoused the essentials of what has evolved into the Bush Doctrine. This policy unequivocally states: "the United States will not tolerate the emergence even of a regional power that aspires to leadership and challenges American domination in any of the major five regions, namely North America, South America, the Middle East, East Asia and Europe. In plain language the Bush Doctrine essentially means, "either you are with us or against us." In effect it makes any sort of dissenting discussion and even neutrality treasonous. This goes a long way in explaining David Frum's character assassinations of Buchanan, Sobran, Francis et al.

The fourth component is the maintenance of a global American military presence. In the July/August 2002 Issue of "Atlantic Monthly," Robert Kagan details a map that demonstrates the global presence of American troops. Finally, the last component of this global strategy is what Bacevich describes as "the militarization of U. S. foreign policy," or the deliberate use of military force as an instrument of policy. This is an updated version of Karl von Clausewitz's belief that "diplomacy is just war by other means." To President Bush, war is just an extension of diplomacy. The United

States promotes democracy, human rights and self-determination only when it is expedient to do so. Bacevich also contends that war is just one means used for global control. Money, trade, credit, propaganda, punitive sanctions, and international agencies under United States domination are other means.

According to an article by Benjamin Schwartz and Christopher Layne in the January 2002 issue of "Atlantic Monthly," American foreign policy has for more than one-half of a century, "sought to prevent the emergence of other great powers." It has been a strategy that has proved "burdensome, futile, and increasingly risky." The secret to maintaining American power throughout the globe rests on the world being in a periodic state of tension. There must be threats and fear of threats to justify America's dominant role around the globe. The authors allude to the supposition that most Americans would agree that a re-unified Korea would be in the country's best interests. Former National Security Adviser, Zbigniew Brzezinski says "No!" in his 1997 book, "The Grand Chessboard." A re-unified Korea would lead to an American pullback from East Asia. Japan might misconstrue this as a pullback of American interests and start to reassert its own influence in the area. Brzezinski warns that the global role the nation assigned itself after the 9/11 attacks is steeped in peril. The U. S. has set itself up as a global hegemon the whole world can hate. This can lead America down the bloody highway of empire and eventual internal collapse.

In the 1980's Saddam Hussein was America's ally. The U.S. supplied him, not only with military intelligence, but also with weapons and military equipment. It was U.S. intelligence that facilitated his use of mustard gas against the rebellious Kurds in Northern Iraq and the Iranians. In July of 1990, when Saddam accused the Kuwaitis of stealing oil from Iraq's huge Rumelia oil field by slant drilling and demanded that the country forgive some 30 billion in loans to Iraq, he appealed to Washington. When the U. S. Ambassador in Baghdad, April Glaspie, gave Saddam Hussein false assurances that the US would not intervene if he attacked Kuwait, he was lured into a power play on the chessboard of history that would eventually accelerate the move to establish American hegemony in the Middle East. According to Marlene Maloney in "Culture Wars Magazine," the U.S. then used a bogus photo, depicting thousands of Iraqi soldiers massing on the border ready to invade Saudi Arabia as an excuse for launching the first Gulf War. Unfortunately, the first President Bush did not complete the job. He stopped short of Baghdad and Saddam retained his tenuous hold on Iraq's military and economic power. The first Bush's failure probably doomed his presidency, as neocons were frustrated in their long-term drive to use Iraq as a beachhead for Middle East hegemony.

In light of this policy, the elephant in the room has to be Israel, over whom the United States has assumed a near benign protector status over since its origins in 1948. According to Buchanan, what the neoconservatives seek is to "conscript American blood to make the world safe for Israel. Neocons are modern jingoists, who want the peace of the sword imposed on Islam and American soldiers to die if necessary to impose it." The neocons seek American Empire, and the Sharonites seek hegemony over the Middle East. The two agenda integrate perfectly. Though the neocons falsely insist that their plans began with 9/11, the origins of their war plans go back at least to 1992. It was in this year that a startling document was leaked from the office of Paul Wolfowitz at the Pentagon. Barton Gellman of the "Washington Post" called it a "classified blueprint intended to help set the nation's direction for the next century." It called for a permanent U. S. military presence on all six continents to deter "all potential competitors from even aspiring to a larger regional or global strategy." This plan could insure that never again would there be an Adolph Hitler, Benito Mussolini, Joseph Stalin, Pol Pot or a Hideki Tojo to threaten world stability and commerce. Although it was denounced in 1992, the Wolfowitz Memo effectively, according to Buchanan, became the official American Foreign Policy in a 33-page National Security Strategy announced by George Bush on September 21, 2002. It effectively renounced and undid the previous fifty years of American strategy, such as containment and deterrence.

Wolfowitz has been a prime mover in American Foreign Policy for many years. Born in 1943, he grew up in an atmosphere of intense moral and intellectual seriousness. His father Jacob had emigrated from Poland as a ten-year old child. Wolfowitz inherited his father's keen intellect and his moral passion. He later taught at Columbia and Cornell Universities. Wolfowitz fell under the sway of Leo Strauss at the University of Chicago. Among the ideas Wolfowitz adopted included the belief that modern European liberalism had been a disaster, climaxed by the rise of dictators, such as Stalin, Hitler and Mussolini.

It is ironic that amid all the political posturing about "Weapons of Mass Destruction" and Nigerien "yellow cake," or soft plutonium, the plans for the invasion of Iraq date back well over ten years. According to Jay Bookman writing in the "Atlanta Journal-Constitution," for March 10, 2003 the report's repeated references to September 11th are misleading because this strategy predated the Arab attacks on 9/11. Its essence can be found in similar language in a report issued by the Project for the New American Century, a group of neoconservative interventionists outraged by the thought that the United States might be forfeiting its chance at global empire.

However, the 2000 report owes a large debt to a still earlier document, drafted in 1992 by Dick Cheney and Paul Wolfowitz in the Defense Department. That document also envisioned the United States as a colossus astride the world, imposing its will and keeping world peace through military and economic power. When the final draft was leaked to the press, it attracted so much negative publicity that the first President Bush hastily withdrew it.

But times changed with the advent of the second Bush Administration. "At no time in history has the international security order been as conducive to American interests and ideals," the report stated two years ago. "The challenge of this coming century is to preserve and enhance this American peace." Bookman believes that the report reads "like a blueprint for the current Bush defense policy."

The Project for the New American Century, a neocon "think tank," that included several future members of the President's War Cabinet appeared in 1997, including Cheney, Donald Rumsfeld and Paul Wolfowitz, and Richard Perle, the "Prince of Darkness."

Wolfowitz, a Jew whose sister is married to an Israeli, has a pipeline to many Israeli generals and diplomats. It is now run by William Kristol and funded by three foundations closely tied to Persian Gulf oil and the many defense industries. Not since John F. Kennedy's heralded "the Best and Brightest," has a presidential brain trust had this much effective power. The people who contributed to this report have influential positions within the Bush administration. Paul Wolfowitz is now Deputy Defense Director. John Bolton is Undersecretary of State. Stephen Cambone is head of the Pentagon's Office of Program, Analysis, and Evaluation. Devon Cross and Eliot Cohen are members of the Defense Policy Board, which advises Rumsfeld. I. Lewis Libby is Chief of Staff to Vice President Dick Cheney. Don Zakheim is comptroller for the Defense Department. Donald Kagan, professor of classical Greek history at Yale and an influential advocate of a more aggressive foreign policy, was the project's co-chairman.

George W. Bush's Administration is overrun with his "house intellectuals," who provide the justification for the movers and shakers of his regime, namely, Cheney, Rumsfeld and Wolfowitz. On the outside they have been buttressed by a newly emergent neoconservative press, led by Norman Podhoretz of "Commentary Magazine," and the "Weekly Standard's" William Kristol. Together they serve as the architects of an American strategy for world conquest. They envision the creation and enforcement of what they call a "Pax America," similar in nature to "Pax Romana," of antiquity. To this date the American people have not appreciated the ramifications of this imperial vision.

This strategy was all laid out in "Pax Americana," the National Security Strategy, which was released on September 20, 2002. Bush's neocon supporters welcomed this policy as "a long over-due codification of America's mission of global leadership," opined Gail Russell Chaddock in the September 23, 2002 issue of the "Christian Science Monitor." Pax Americana marked a significant departure from previous approaches, a change it attributes to the events surrounding 9/11. In addressing the terrorism threat, the President's report lays out a newly aggressive military and foreign policy that embraces pre-emptive attacks against perceived enemies. It speaks of American interests and ignores the idea of any unfavorable international opinion. The best defense is a good offense the documents boldly assert. The plan lays out a strategy for permanent American military and economic domination of every major region on the globe, unfettered by international treaty or concern. This will require a stark expansion of America's global military presence.

According to Bookman the President's real goal in attacking Iraq was "to mark the official emergence of the United States as a full-fledged global empire, seizing sole responsibility and authority as a "planetary policeman." The war would be the "culmination of a plan ten years or more in the making, carried out by those who believe the United States must seize the opportunity for global domination, even if it means becoming the American Imperialists that America's enemies always claimed they were. Rome did not stoop to containment or arms limitations. It just conquered most of the known world.

Bookman sees nothing but trouble down the road if the Bush administration continues on its current course. He believes the "lure of empire is ancient and powerful and over the millennia it has driven men to commit terrible crimes on its behalf." With the end of the Cold War and the virtual disappearance of the Soviet Union, a global empire was essentially laid at the feet of the United States. The conservative internationalists were chagrined that the nation did not cease the proverbial bull by the horns then. The trouble is that the average American is uncomfortable with the idea of living in the "New Rome."

Fortunately for the neoconservatives 9/11 happened like Pearl Harbor did. It provided the national horror that gave approval of fighting the terrorists, no matter where they may be. This begs the question: Did anyone in the Bush Administration, or any Israeli interests, know beforehand about the attacks or participate or inspire the attacks in any way? The fact that there had been the usual foul-ups, missed signals and Indian signs that something was going to happen, the evidence seems to say that something of this nature would inevitably happen given the lax security measures that became rule during the Clinton Administration. There was no need for someone to deliberately foment any national attack. The warnings in the wake of the 1993 attack on the World Trade Center and the revelations of Muslim plans to fly hijacked airliners into American building uncovered by "Operation Bojinko" in the Philippines in 1995 showed a decided lack of American security preparedness. When coupled with the Islamic fundamentalist hatred of America, the powers that be just let nature run its course. Now Israel had an ally who had sensed the same terror they did every day. According to author Michael Lind, several neoconservatives, including Catholic Bill Bennett, have declared "We are all Israelis now!"

The second Arab attack on the Twin Towers on September 11, 2001 was the effective catalyst the purveyors of world empire needed to launch their long-standing campaign to put the world in a "right frame of mind." On Sept. 20th, forty neoconservatives sent an open letter to the White House instructing President Bush on how the "War on Terror" must be conducted. Such living conservatives as Bill Bennett, Podhoretz, Kirkpatrick, Richard Perle, Bill Kristol and "Washington Post" columnist Charles Krauthammer, signed it. If Bush failed to attack Iraq, the signers warned it would "constitute an early and perhaps decisive surrender in the war on international terrorism." According to Pat Buchanan in his March 24, 2003 issue of "the American Conservative," the letter "was an ultimatum." A "cabal of intellectuals" were telling the Commander-in-Chief, nine days after an attack on America that if he did not follow their war plans, he would be charged with surrendering to terror."

The Israeli Lobby is not pulling Bush's strings as much as his Christian Zionists. According to Lind, "the faction of Jewish and non-Jewish neoconservatives within the Republican Party would have little or no influence on American foreign policy, if not for its tactical alliance with the voters whose zeal he needs to be reelected: white Southern Protestants." The strategy comes from Wolfowitz, but the political muscle comes from the Deep South. Michael Lind deftly explains all this in his book "Made in Texas: George W.

Bush and the Southern Takeover of American Politics." His book traces Bush's distinctive "Pax America" foreign policy to his Texas roots and its religion, "seventeenth century British Cromwellian Puritanism, as modified by nineteenth century British Darbyist Dispensationalism." The Dispensationalists believe the world is in the pre-millennium that Christ has yet to establish His thousand-year reign as written in the book of Revelation. According to these fundamentalists, the Messianic Kingdom relies on a chain of events involving Israel as a nation under assault during the final battle of Armageddon. This is the basis for their support of Israel that the world will be destroyed in Armageddon and the saved will be dispensed from death and be raptured with Jesus while the rest of the world, including most of the Jews, will be lost for all eternity. Michael Lind contends that Texas is the "epicenter" of this way of thinking and that Crawford, Texas, home to the Bush ranch, is right on the fault line. And also it is just eighteen miles away from Baylor University, the largest Baptist University in the world and the center of Protestant fundamentalism. Just seventy miles from Waco is the Dallas Theological Seminary, the seat of Dispensationalism.

The same idea was more eloquently presented in Barbara Tuchman's book, "Bible and Sword." She described in detail how the Calvinists "were a group led by God in the struggle against idolaters and tyrants." It was the "cry of Joshua's trumpet" that suited their circumstances "better than the plea to turn the other cheek." It was during the time of the Puritans that they began a movement for the return of the Jews to Palestine. Manasseh ben Israel forged an alliance with Oliver Cromwell that had this as its goal. It was not for the sake of the Jews "but for the sake of the promise made to them." According to Scripture, "the kingdom of Israel for all mankind would come when the people of Israel were restored to Zion." This movement began with the modern British Zionist movement in the late nineteenth century, culminating in the capturing of Palestine during World War I.

Lind also points out that there is a notable similarity between British nineteenth century imperialism and America's approach in the twenty-first century. The similarities are not coincidental. Modern American Zionism is a direct descendant of British

Zionism, which finds its roots in Calvinistic Puritanism. In England, where Judaism was proscribed, the Puritans took control of the traditionally Jewish commerce and financial institutions, as well as the military. According to Catholic apologist Hilaire Belloc "It is from Puritanism that we derive modern industrial capitalism, the centralization of wealth in a few hands, the dispossession of the masses and their exploitation by a small number of those who control the mean of production." This is what we call "Capitalism."

Lind believes that many neoconservatives are "products of the influential Jewish-American sector of the Trotskyists movement," which "morphed into anti-Communist liberalism between the 1950's and 1970's and finally into a kind of militaristic and imperial right with no precedents in American culture or political history." They greatly admire the Likud Party in Israel, especially its pre-emptive tactics in attacking the Iraqi Osirak nuclear reactor in 1981. They mix their Zionism with an old fashioned burst of "ideological enthusiasm" for democracy. They believe that God gave all of Palestine to the Jews. They are at the center of what Maloney calls a "metaphorical pentagon," comprised of the Israel Lobby, the Religious Right, plus conservative think tanks, funding foundations and the Rupert Murdoch/Kristol Media Empire. Bush's personal weaknesses made him ripe for a conversion to Southern fundamentalism and its fervent Christian Zionism.

Writing in the September 2002 issue of "Commentary Magazine," Norman Podhoretz laid out a plan for world suzerainty that has been in the works since 1992. In what may be termed a "Neoconservative Manifesto for World Domination," Podhoretz waxed even more regally that William Kristol of the "Weekly Standard." Podhoretz brazenly urged President Bush to "embrace a war of civilizations," as it was his "responsibility to fight World War IV," the Cold War, being the Third World War in his mind. It is a phrase that Podhoretz attributes to author Elliot Cohen. Podhoretz urged Bush to extend the world war to include Iran, Syria, Lebanon, Libya, North Korea, as well as our so-called allies like the Saudi Royal Family and Egypt's Hosni Mubarak. Bush must reject the "timorous counsels" of Secretary of State, Colin

Powell and "find the stomach to impose a new political culture on the defeated" Islamic world. Podhoretz seemed willing to spend billions and billions of dollars and countless thousands of American lives to achieve this utopian dream. It took Bush several months before he mustered up the courage for a preemptive strike on Iraq.

The key ingredient in his deep analysis of the "Bush Doctrine," was a fourth pillar that Podhoretz announced as "the assimilation of Israel's war against terrorism into our own." This, from Israel's standpoint, was the most important. An attack by the Palestinians or Hamas was now an attack on the United States and would be met with the same fierceness we showed toward Afghanistan and Iraq. The world was on notice. Mess with Israel and the united would be there swiftly with the full force of its military might and technology. In other words, American soldiers had been enlisted by their President to serve as "volunteers for the maintenance of Israeli suzerainty and local hegemony.

In his book, "Made in Texas," writer Michael Lind argues that "the geopolitical project of the Southern-dominated right and its allies among the mostly Jewish neoconservatives is to repudiate the post-1945 world order." The this "Old World Order" "corresponded to Southern conservative values, resembling the British-centered world system of the nineteenth century." It was a world with "a laissez-faire economy in which a unilateral American empire, having a special relationship with Israel and defining itself as a champion of 'Judeo-Christian' values, wages wars unrestrained by alliances, international organizations or international law."

Pat Buchanan sifted through the ideological morass to point out that the people who had the most to gain from this clash of civilization between the West and Islam were Israel, Sharon and the Likud Party. It is among the greatest unspoken truths of modern times that most neoconservatives have a singular favoritism for Israel even to the extent of favoring its interests over those of the United States. It is a given among Gentile American politicians that to criticize, ignore or oppose the interests of Israel can be a political death kneel. To run afoul of Israel's "American Amen corner," in the media Congress and its advocacy groups, such as the Jewish

Anti-Defamation League (ADL) to court political suicide. The first President Bush this fact of life, only too well.

U.S.-Israeli Relation is a contentious subject. Israel has demonstrated over the course of its history a penchant for dealing in stealth and misdirection with regards to the United States. The nadir of U.S.-Israeli Relations has to be the unprovoked assault on the USS Liberty off the Egyptian coast. On June 8, 1967, Israeli jet aircraft and torpedo boats subjected the men of the USS Liberty to a brutal assault that killed thirty-four United States Navy seamen and wounded another hundred and seventy-one sailors. The unprovoked attack, contrary to the "official" record, was not "accidental." It was preceded by more than six hours of intense low-level surveillance by Israeli photoreconnaissance aircraft, which buzzed the intelligence ship thirteen times, sometimes flying as low as two hundred feet directly overhead. The careful planned and high-performance jet aircraft, followed by slower and more maneuverable jets loaded with napalm, initiated a skillfully executed attack. The second stage was carried out by torpedo boats, which blasted a 40-foot hole in the ship's side. By actual count, there were eight hundred and twenty-one machine gun and rocket holes in the ship. The craft stubbornly remained afloat, and before the Israelis could find the murder of the entire fleet, rescue craft from the Sixth Fleet were finally en route. At this point Israel acknowledged its "mistake" and withdrew.

Details of the attacks were covered up for many years. Israel made the preposterous claim that the USS Liberty resembled an Egyptian ship and the cowardly president, Lyndon Johnson, jumped at the chance to bury the issue. The official version is that the USS Liberty was only reconnoitered three times and that the entire attack consisted of a five-minute attack and a single torpedo attack. Then Lieutenant James Ennes published the entire sordid tale in his book "Assault on the Liberty." First published by Random House, the book sold very few copies because its sales were deliberately undermined along the route from publisher to the public. Bookstores entered into a covert conspiracy, says Ennes, to thwart the public from reading about the events of June 9th. He bought the rights and published under his own label, gradually bringing the event to the surface, one reader at a time.

The "Liberty incident" is reminiscent of another American naval ship, the USS Indianapolis, whose Captain Charles Butler McVey III, who committed suicide in 1969, was court-martialed. The Liberty's Captain, William L. McGonagale was first investigated. After no dereliction of duty had been found, he was awarded the Congressional Medal of Honor at a near-private ceremony. The survivors of the USS Liberty were threatened with loss of rank pensions and even prison time, should they talk publicly about the attack. The truth lay in the fact that the USS Liberty was attacked on the eve of an Israeli pre-emptive strike into the Golan Heights during the Six-Day war. Israeli government, under Moshe Dayan, became fearful that the American intelligence ship could jeopardize the attack and thus determined that the ship should be blown off the face of the earth.

Though George Bush's quest for "Imperium sine fine," an "empire without end," is consistent with the American intellectual traditions of Manifest Destiny and Progressivism, it expects an evolutionary increase in the progress of the American political, economic and social enterprise. Unfortunately, the President runs the risk of over-extending the military's over-taxed resources, running up huge deficits and instilling popular unrest at home. The great historians of Roman antiquity, such as Livy, Tacitus and Seutonious grew to hate what the relentless quest for empire did to the Rome they loved.

Historian E. H. Carr once observed that "every approach in the past to a world society has been the product of the ascendancy of a single Power." It is up to this power to create the order that world government needs. A strong and vital America is the major obstacle they have to keep them from securing the Illuminati dream of a single world state. A naive George W. Bush could be playing right into their hands in his messianic crusade to extend the quasi-religious tenets of peace, brotherhood and friendship through the barrels of American guns. This is the nature of things and the roadmap along which it will mostly likely proceed. Too much of

America's foreign policy has been historically interwoven with such global behemoths, such as the World Trade Organization, the International Monetary Fund, the World Bank and soon, the International Court. America's previous policy of "gunboat diplomacy has been replaced with the more rapid advancing notion "humvee diplomacy." In the zero sum game of geopolitics, any loss suffered by the United States on the imperial front, will boost the other side and lead to the full loss of American sovereignty.

There will be no "Imperium sine fine," that is an empire without end. Given man's human nature and the inevitable limitation on national resources, any attempt to effect a global democracy over the weaker countries of the world is doomed to failure. The Romans tried and failed. The British failed and even the Nazis with their own imperial brand of "Land und Blut," failed. Bush's messianic obsession with empire and democracy is very dangerous. Under its imperial flag, Rome became more militarized and with that, more decadent. Bush was now laboring "under the banner of Heaven." The U. S. would have to expand so many of its resources that it would inevitably be too weakened to maintain its global hegemony. Since nature abhors a vacuum, I am certain international coalition, under the auspices of the U. N. will replace the former superpower. History tells us that such coalitions do not last long until petty differences start to undermine its global domain.

Epilogue

Quo Vadis?

"Nations don't die, they commit suicide." Arnold Toynbee

The Appian Way was one of the most important roads that connected Rome with its distant provinces. Roman Catholic tradition has it that it was on this road that Jesus appeared to St. Peter, who was fleeing the bloody persecutions of the Emperor Nero. Peter asked Jesus: "Domine, quo vadis?" or "Lord, where are you going?" The same question might be asked of this country. Where are America's policies taking the country? As in Peter's case, the United States has been fleeing from its traditional moral and Christian culture. The new Nero has been the cultural Marxists and the New World Order radicals who have knocked America off its moral course.

A similar query can be put to America's cultural institutions, such as its schools, religions, universities, motion pictures, media and the TV networks. Where are they going? What has happened to America's independent spirit? Could the United States be following the road of the great civilizations chronicled by historians Arnold Toynbee, Edward Gibbon, Will and Auriel Durant toward its destined date with extinction?

The New World Order being prepared for America will reduce the meaning of life to the many material and economic factors, such as the demands of production, market consumption, accumulation of riches and the demands of a ever-growing bureaucracy which will be required to regulate this leviathan.

Through its branch auxiliaries of the World Trade Organization, the World Bank and now a World Court, the U. N. has used its mighty powers to circumscribe the globe with its reach and the tentacles of its power. This will limit the spiritual and moral development of mankind and the vast majority of people will be treated as mere cogs in the wheel of progress, robotic numbers on a demographic sheet.

The first wall of defense is the moral order. Once that is weakened and collapsed, it is very difficult to withstand the onslaught of globalist weaponry. In this natural conspiracy, sex has been the linchpin of the Gramascian agenda to subvert American society. The Marxist assault on the culture through its women has been devastating to both men and women. At the nexus of the Marxist strategy has been the disruption of the good order of society. With grave social disorder, there can be no group resistance, no strong concerted opposition to their desire to enact the wave of the global future.

In her book "Treason," columnist Ann Coulter reminds the nation, "A large segment of American women "have traded faith in the Supreme Being for faith in gun control laws and day care centers." In his prescient book, "Slouching towards Gomorrah," Judge Robert Bork has written that a "nation's moral life is the foundation of its culture." In his book, "The Hope of the Wicked" Ted Flynn points out that part of this is by nature. He sees it more as a syndrome, analogous to Sobran's hive. Many of those in power are not even aware of the demonic roots of the liberal philosophy that generates their actions.

Homosexuality has been an important vehicle for effecting Gramsci's long-term goals. According to William Grigg in the July 28, 2003 issue of "The New American," The Lawrence vs. Texas Supreme Court decision "offers a critically important warning that the revolutionary Left has nearly completed its 'long march' through the institutions that began five decades ago." When gay marriage becomes a reality, the age of consent will be the next battleground.

Grigg believes, like E. Michael Jones, that "although the Lavender Revolution claims the mantle of liberation, it is actually a key element of this long-term drive to destroy individual rights by removing anything keeping the state from exercising total power." Writing in the Winter 1996 issue of the Marxist journal "Dissent," Michael Walzer provided several key illustrations of the Gramascian Revolution's progress. These included "the transformation of family life," including "rising divorce rates, changing sexual mores, new household arrangements—and the portrayal of all this in the media." According to Grigg, for over fifty years, Gramascian agents of change "in the legal system, academe, media, social sciences, and tax exempt foundations have pursued radical cultural changes.

Religion has always been an intricate part of the American culture, especially that of the Catholic Church. It has also been impacted by a Marxist assault on the nation's most important institutions. The Protestant churches and the Catholic Church have allowed their faiths to be watered down in hope that in "modernizing," they would attract more members and maintain those they already had. It has not worked. Empty pews have become commonplace on Sunday mornings. The long heritage of Western Civilization, from the Greeks, Romans, through Christianity has been pillaged and raped of its pristine beauty and spiritual presence. America now has a pagan culture of the flesh and not of the spirit. American churches no longer aspire to the heavens but sit squat and fat in a horizontal expansion that celebrates man and his material creations, instead of the Lord of history.

This begs the question: Is it possible to turn back the clock on this historic cultural movement? Can men and women ever return to the time when love and attraction, not power and competition characterized their natural relationship? When a nation slides into moral depravity, it is near impossible to resuscitate that culture. Cultures are not like the mythological Phoenix. They do not rise from their own ashes.

Like St. Peter, the country is at a cultural crossroads between the descendants of the Judeo-Christian code and the proponents of the Pagan Left. While the future looks bleak, there is always hope. Cultural warriors must bombard the newspapers with letters, phone calls and canceled subscriptions, demanding that the media show a greater respect for the traditions of this country. Most importantly, they must take a stand in their daily lives. How many have heard someone talk of being pro-choice and not speak up because they don't want to offend? People of good will have to take a stand and speak out in whatever way they can. Conservatives and honorable Democrats must demonstrate that legal abortion and assisted suicide attack the very foundations of our society. Americans must repudiate the pagan agenda of the Democratic Party, Planned Parenthood and the American Civil Liberties Union, the National Education Association and the United Nations who have wrongly led the nation's culture into a miasma of unbridled sexuality, suicide, sickness, disease, illness and death. A continued tolerance of evil can only herald the end of American civilization.

The Religious Right has to recapture the culture from the movies, radio, television, law, schools and universities. It has to cut off their money with a tax revolt, vote for candidates that will clean up the culture, and strengthen the few pillars of society left—the military, church and police so that they all survive the left's vicious assault. It must create a hospitable atmosphere for women in a crisis pregnancy and emphasize taking responsibility for one's own sexuality. Abstinence programs should be promoted because they respect traditional morality and they work. If not the idea of a natural conspiracy will triumph.

Jesus' answer to Peter's interrogatory was "I am going back to Rome to be crucified a second time." Peter recognized his cowardice and went back to Rome where he was imprisoned and later martyred. It is up to traditional Christians and others to fight the good fight, go back to Rome and not allow the enemies within to destroy and ruin the culture and the internal goodness that has been America. That is the only thing Americans can do.